P9-AGU-559

ROCKS IN MY BACKPACK

Tales of a Veteran Scouter

Tom Sholes

© Copyright 2007 Tom Sholes.
All rights reserved. No part of this publication may be reproduced,
stored in a retrieval system, or transmitted, in any form or by any means,
electronic, mechanical, photocopying, recording, or otherwise, without
the written prior permission of the author.

Note for Librarians: A cataloguing record for this book is available from
Library and Archives Canada at www.collectionscanada.ca/amicus/index-e.html

Current ISBN 978-1-60530331-4
Previous ISBN 1-4120-9112-8

Printed in the USA

This publication may be obtained or ordered through selected bookstores
or by logging onto www.RocksInMyPackpack.com.

DEDICATION

To my wife, Charlotte, who for nearly five decades, put up with my antics, yet was gracious enough to give me the time and space to don my campaign hat for so many years.

I also dedicate this book to the scores of adults and hundreds of Scouts, all of whom played such an important role in my life, helping to make it a truly fun and exciting ride.

WHAT READERS ARE SAYING

For my two cents, *Rocks in My Backpack* is the most entertaining book about Scouting I have ever read.
Paul Kautz, The Scoutmaster, BoyScoutTrails.com

I am enjoying the daylights out of your book. You are impressive and I congratulate you on playing such an integral part in the lives of so many young people.
Bob Johnson, former President of Mountain Medical Equipment

We loved seeing the pictures on your website. What great times you gave all these young people. It certainly gave them a life-long love of camping and adventure.
Jim and Andy Hart, Scout Parents

As a storyteller, Tom Sholes is a master. He takes readers from tears of laughter to tears of sadness in a matter of paragraphs. The descriptions are so vivid that I felt I was there.
Martha Warner, MA, Author and writing training consultant

I can't thank you enough for leading us on all the adventures that you did, for all the ghost stories in front of campfires, for cultivating in each of us a fervent respect and reverence for the beauty of wilderness, for the laughter and practical jokes and for the countless opportunities to learn and grow as a young man.
Grant Johnson, President, MedSystems Consulting, Inc. Eagle Scout

Excellent book. I thoroughly enjoyed the read. What an influence you had on so many kids.
Tom Kenning, Bank President and former Boy Scout

Have you made life interesting for my son! He laughed so hard he was crying. Truly amazing, as he has been so dormant. He wants me to read it again. Thank you so much for writing it.
Mother of a former Scout bed ridden with MS
(Note: She sent a case of *Rocks* to wounded troops at Walter Reed Army Hospital.)

ACKNOWLEDGEMENTS

Just as it requires a wealth of help to lead Scout units for 40 years, writing about it also demands strong backup. Let me acknowledge some of the key players in this endeavor.

This project, started some years back, fell into stagnancy until the author joined the Castle Rock (Colorado) Writer's Group. This covey of talented writers suffered through seemingly endless readings from my manuscript, but it was through their encouragement and motivation that *Rocks* was finally completed and published.

My two sons, Scott and Dave, both long-term members of my Colorado troop, provided constant encouragement and corrections. Most definitely, my wife, Charlotte, deserves credit for pushing me back into Scouting, although she often regretted it during 40 years of evening, weekend, and week-long absences.

As any writer knows, it is virtually impossible to effectively edit your own material. My good friend and professional editor, Patrice Rhoades-Baum, tightened up my verbiage and moved me "farther" rather than "further" along. She did a magnificent job highlighting paragraphs and noting, "Now, you can do better than that."

My granddaughter, Emily Moyer, a graduate of the Art Institute of Colorado, finalized the cover design. Patrice originated the idea of a website photo gallery, which was keyboarded into reality by my talented webmaster, Joey Buhrer. Special thanks goes to Cory McKee, marketing director of the Denver Area Council, BSA, for reviewing the entire manuscript.

Finally, let me extend heartfelt gratitude to the hundreds of Scouts and adult leaders who served as the cast of characters in this drama. Their names are scattered throughout the book as I share our memorable adventure, and are listed, in toto, in the Appendix. I shall never forget them.

Tom Sholes
Larkspur, Colorado

CONTENTS

Photo Credits

Front cover photo: Dick Theis
Troop 13 group photo: Bob Moen
Troop 117 group photos: Grissinger Studio, Littleton, CO
Wasechie Indian dancers: Lou Conti
Remaining photos by the author or by a variety of members of
Troop 117, Post 757, or staff
Back cover photo: Ginny Moyer

View an extensive gallery of Scout photos, arranged by chapter,
at www.RocksInMyBackpack.com.

FOREWORD

How do you get the most stoic, shy, hesitant kid on the block to plunge off the edge of a cliff attached only to a couple of seemingly way-too-thin ropes, camp out in a tipi, give up Monday Night Football for seven years, tackle his friends to the ground in rowdy games of British bulldog, take center stage as a member of a Native American dance troupe, drink right out of a Colorado mountain stream, strut his stuff in a faux tuxedo, publicly celebrate his achievements around the toilet bowl, wear his uniform backwards to an inspection by camp authorities, and do his best to crack the ribs of his older and wiser Scoutmaster in a spontaneous wrestling match? Simple. You sign him up as a member of Tom Sholes's Troop 117 BSA in Littleton, Colorado.

It didn't take me long to realize that I was in for quite a ride when I joined the troop in 1979. I had to leave my first Court of Honor halfway through because of a severe stomach ache, caused, I think now, by the realization that I'd been thrown into a fun-loving, high-energy group of guys—and how was a reserved, straight-laced boy like me going to find my place? As it turned out, I had no reason to worry. "Sholzie," as we began to call him as we got older (and bolder), made it clear there was room for all types of boys in his group, provided they were willing to let themselves have fun while becoming one of the top troops in the council. And probably the hardest working as well. Sholzie took great pride in running a high-quality program and made sure the boys knew there would be no free passes to advancement. If you advanced in Mr. Sholes's troop, you knew you had done something special and worthwhile. And if you weren't progressing, Mr. Sholes would nudge, prod, and encourage you, because he wanted you to succeed.

Some of my fondest memories of Scouting include bumping along back roads in the mountains of Colorado and Utah in the Sholes-family Carryall listening to Beatles tapes, sitting bundled up around a campfire listening to stories of caribou famines and flesh-eating owls, and seeing our master Scout coming along the trail with the glow of one who is truly in his element. Tom Sholes has had, for as long as I've known him, a zest for living fully, and that was readily apparent in the way he approached his role as Scoutmaster for nearly 40 years.

I am thrilled that Tom has taken the time to capture some of his thoughts and stories and share them in this book. It is the story of Scouting, Boy Scouts, and a Scoutmaster, but also of living life as an adventure and valuing our fellow travelers on the trail.

There's so much more to get to and, as Sholzie would say, "It's in the book." Enjoy the trip!

Mark Zentner, PhD
Counseling and Mental Health Center
University of Texas, Austin, Texas

INTRODUCTION

Four Decades of Scouting Escapades

My friend's head shook in disbelief. "You spent over three decades of Monday nights babysitting forty screaming Boy Scouts, then took on an Explorer Post for another ten years? *Why?*"

Okay. You can't blame rational people for being shockingly curious, especially if they know kids of Scouting age. Holing up weekly with such a congregation can numb one's senses, plus, as Mark Zentner mentioned, we always missed Monday Night Football. Yes, people have asked me, "Why?" Frankly, so have I!

There are some pluses to being a long-term Scoutmaster. For example, the pay is great. The Boy Scouts of America (BSA) doubles your salary every year! You also have a legitimate excuse "to dash out with the boys" at least one evening a week and usually one weekend a month. And how many other adults do you know who enjoy an expense-free week at camp every summer?

Being a Scoutmaster also enhances your popularity. Your mail normally doubles, and the quantity of phone calls received, mostly at supper time, warrants adding two phone lines. But then, many of those calls allow you to quickly solve earth-shaking problems, such as, "Mr. Sholes, the only socks I have that are clean are purple. Can I still come to the meeting?" Answer: "I don't care if you come in purple underwear, just get there on time, and let me eat my dinner!"

With tenure, a Scoutmaster's role automatically mushrooms, encompassing a latitude of specialties: teacher, organizer, boxing/wrestling referee (if not participant), father confessor, social worker, fund raiser, zoologist, biologist, anthropologist, archaeologist, survivalist, cook, bottle washer, garbage collector and transporter, adventurer, explorer, doctor, lawyer, and in my case even an Indian chief. Where else could one be challenged with such an abundance of self-growth opportunities?

I admit the first year was like crawling into a sleeping bag with a congregation of red ants. But like wisdom, Scoutmastering does improve with time. And in time, a good Scoutmaster may even come close to mastering Scouting. Face it, this zoo called *troop Scouting* is rewarding and *fun*. Kids at this age are so adventuresome, spontaneous, berserk, bizarre, absurd, and outrageous that anything can happen, and you can bet your campaign hat that, in time, it will.

I admit I had fun—so much fun that I've spun Scouting stories for years. Friends finally said, "Think of the number of other people you could torture with these tales if you wrote a book." So after years of creating ads, brochures, and boring manuals, interspersed with so many years of associating with exceptional kids and a wealth of adventure, why not have fun again with words and relive those adventures?

A neighbor dropped by one evening and asked what I planned to title the book. I thought for a moment and told him (for reasons you can probably guess), "Rocks in My Backpack." A voice bellowed out from the kitchen, "Why not 'Rocks in Your Head?'" My wife Charlotte was right; that could work, too!

Initially, I wasn't going to include stories from my early years growing up as a Scout, but thought, why not? Some great Scouting escapades unfolded in that era of small-town America when life wasn't so structured, crime wasn't as prevalent, and parents gave kids far more freedom. Fortunately, they didn't know how we were exploiting all that freedom!

Rocks is something of a memoir, at least a slice of it, because Scouting has been a substantial slice of my life. But revisiting so many decades can be perplexing. When reflecting back to the 1940s from a 21st-century perspective, doesn't one's memory muddle when sifting through so many years? And what about embellishment? Don't stories improve over the years to the point where they barely resemble the original event? And what about telling the whole truth and nothing but the truth? Well, on my honor I will do my best. We'll even hazard law suits and use real names—other than, of course, to protect the guilty!

Whether you've been a Boy Scout or a Scout Leader or plan to join those ranks, this book is for you. *Rocks in My Backpack* exposes a side of Scouting the BSA literature never addresses—and for good reason!

As a Scout and Scout leader, I have had a blast living Scouting. Here's hoping you have as much fun experiencing, vicariously, four decades of escapades and adventures.

Tom Sholes
Larkspur, Colorado

**Life is not a journey to the grave with the intention
of arriving safely in a pretty and well preserved
body, but rather to skid in broadside, thoroughly
used up, worn out, and loudly proclaiming:
WOW, WHAT A RIDE!!**

Anonymous.

1

GROWING UP AS A SCOUT WHERE THREE RIVERS MEET

Discovering Scouting in the Sleepy Town of La Crosse, Wisconsin

I loved Scouting in the shadows of the Colorado Rockies in my adult years, but this tale begins a thousand miles east in the upper Midwest along the banks of the muddy Mississippi. La Crosse, Wisconsin, was a sleepy, little river town where three rivers meet: the Mississippi, the Black, and the La Crosse. According to Indian legend, the meeting of three rivers is good medicine, protecting people from harsh and deadly storms.

The drums of the Winnebago Tribe sounded regularly around La Crosse, plus Indian nations such as the Chippewa, Sac, Fox, and Sioux drifted in and out of this lush river valley. This area was first explored by the French; later Lieutenant Zebulon Pike entered the valley early in the 1800s. Pike wrote, "Came up with (sic) prairie la crosse, so named from the ball game played on it by the Sioux. The prairie is very handsome. It is bordered by hills similar to those of prairie des chien" (60 miles down the river). Although he doubted that any man would ever set foot upon the Colorado peak that now bears his name, Old Zeb did summit one of the 600-foot bluffs several miles east of the Mississippi. Gazing across Prairie La Crosse, Pike lauded the natural beauty of the area, noting, "A man may only witness such a sight several times in his life."

La Crosse never mushroomed into a large city. During my Scouting years in the 1940s, the sign at the city limits read, "Pop. 49,707." Of course, that didn't count the June bugs that were so thick on the Mississippi River bridge that they used snow plows to push them off, and it certainly didn't include a census of the summertime mosquitoes. La Crosse has the dubious distinction of having a strain of encephalitis, carried by the eastern Treehole mosquito, named after the town!

There are tough winters and tough folks in the Badger State. Some talk funny. Either they have a Canadian twist to their "ou" diphthongs (house and about are dead giveaways) or there's a slight singsong inflection, a logical spin-off from the locals' Scandinavian heritage. Their favorite word is "Packers."

La Crosse was the kind of town in which every kid should have a chance to grow up—with the river on one side, bluffs on the other, and all the fun and nonsense that went on in between. Plus it was a great town in which to Scout, for Scouting in the '40s was on a roll. First, there was a war. Unlike today, kids loved to wear a military-type uniform. We wore uniforms to school and smiled proudly as girls ogled our badges. We marched in parades and ushered at ball games or patriotic events, always in uniform. We dove into paper or scrap metal drives to help the war effort and received recognition, such as the General Eisenhower Scrap Paper Medal. Scouts were looked upon as quality kids.

During those years, Scouting had little competition for a boy's time. There were organized sports and bands, but coaches and directors didn't demand the time and commitment they do today. Kids had time to Scout. Most parents realized the value of this program for a boy. In my early years as a Scout, I frequently told my dad I wanted to quit and just play ball. He always responded with the same answer: "Son, quit Scouts any time you want—as long as you have your Eagle!" I stormed off angry then; I thank him deeply now.

My entry into troop Scouting was heavily influenced by an injury my dad suffered when I was four years old. While constructing the new Eagles building on 5th and King Streets in La Crosse, he tumbled three floors to the basement, shattering his left leg and hip. He never fully healed and spent the rest of his life with a stiff left leg, two inches shorter than the right. A lover of the outdoors, he would no longer hike and climb among the bluffs and prairies. He knew he could never personally introduce his boy to the natural world he loved so much. Then he heard about Scouts. There was no doubt in his mind that his boy would become one.

One day, Dad arrived home with a used uniform he acquired from a friend—khaki shirt, khaki knickers, long khaki socks, a purple Scout neckerchief, and a well-worn campaign hat. I paraded in front of a long bedroom mirror waiting impatiently for my 12th birthday. Then I could join the Scouts of Troop 13 whom I saw regularly in uniform at Our Savior's Lutheran, an old, red-brick Norsky edifice we attended at 6th and Division Streets. The original Scoutmaster, Milan Skundburg, a humble, tall and slim gentleman, was at the helm but served more as a titular head. Troop 13's first Eagle Scout, Bert Withe, a robust man with a warm smile and a hearty laugh, directed the operation, which numbered at nearly 100 Scouts. It is here where our Scouting stories begin.

Embarrassed at the Starting Gate

It's hard to get excited about going to your first Scout meeting when you have to do it in knickers. I had two other pairs of brown, corduroy knickers, the kind that seemed to hum when I walked down the street. These were tight economic times, so my mother insisted I wear those "hummers" until they wore out, along with long socks and leather boots, the kind that nearly came up to your knees and had a cool knife pocket on the side. In those days, kids used a knife to whittle wood, not other kids, so you could carry a knife to school. But this costume caused me major embarrassment. A pretty blond girl whom I was stuck on walked behind me down Adams Street on the way to Hamilton Grade School singing, "There goes Tommy in his pantaloons." Now that hurt! I'd play football in them, slide into bases all summer with them, climb trees and fences, and roll in the dirt, but the darn corduroy would not destruct. Now I had to show up at my first Boy Scout meeting in Scout *knickers*!

My worst fears were realized. Between the baggy antique knickers, long socks, and campaign hat, I resembled a reincarnated Lord Baden-Powell, Chief Scout. The guys cracked up! Worst of all, the purple neckerchief was the trademark of a Catholic troop at St. Wenceslas school. Within the week, my Dad and I walked into Continental Clothiers, the local Boy Scout outlet, and I proudly returned home with long pants, a new shirt, an overseas-type hat and the red-and-black neckerchief of Troop 13.

Troop 13 met in the church basement, along with the Dorcas Society, Ladies Aid Society, the quilting guild, men's fellowship, Sunday school, and confirmation classes, fortunately not all at one time. On Monday night, the troop had sole proprietorship. Patrols huddled in individual corners of one large room, while the Senior Scouts retired to the kitchen where they frequently raided the refrigerator and occasionally uncorked a somewhat off-color story. Naturally, the rest of us waited for the day when we could become Senior Scouts!

It was here we first learned the Scout Oath and Law and the three-fingered salute. (Back then, it was a three-fingered, left-handed hand shake, interlocking the little fingers.) We learned over 30 uses for our red-and-black neckerchiefs—made from a solid square yard of material—ranging from a first-aid bandage to signal flags. We mastered use of maps and a compass, reading trail signs, sending signals via wig-wag (a flag-waving code) and Morse code, and identifying animal tracks and plants. On one outing, I suffered a temporary lapse of memory concerning a particularly noxious plant, to which I'll later confess.

There's a Strange Smell in the Kitchen

Wisconsin winters were cold, and in pre-television days, troops met frequently to show off their Scouting skills. In these rallies troops competed in events such as knot-tying, lashing, first-aid, signaling, creating fire by friction, and creating fire by flint and steel. Many troops were tough competitors. On the other hand, Troop 9 was no sweat. They met in a gymnasium, and all they did was play basketball. Throughout my entire Scout leadership career, I refused to hold troop meetings anywhere near basketball hoops. But most troops were sharp. To beat them each of us in Troop 13 had our specialty, and we honed it to perfection. My forte was creating fire by flint and steel.

Weeks before a meet, I would inundate my mother's kitchen with the fragrant bouquet of smoldering cotton cloth (mostly old sheets) baking in the oven until the strips were pitch black and so dry you could spit on them, and they'd ignite. I'd do the same with the natural materials I'd use for the "bird's nest," sealing it all in air-tight Ball jars. The edge on my flint was shaving sharp. Meanwhile, my dad searched junk yards until he found the ideal piece of hardened steel.

The big Council meet was held in the main gym at La Crosse State College. This antique gym featured an oval running track on the balcony. Corner shots were impossible, since the basketball would never clear the overhanging balcony, but it was a great place for a Scouting meet. It was a long-underwear Wisconsin night, yet the bleachers were jammed with parents and kids bundled in bulky sweaters and woolen jackets. Our first-aid and signaling teams did well, but our fire-by-friction guys should have used their bows for archery. A Catholic troop from the North Side was breathing down our troop's neck. Then came the call for flint and steel.

We were each provided a bucket of water and a metal plate, so we wouldn't leave tattletale brown spots on the gym floor. I carefully shaped my nest; opened my jar of dry, blackened muslin; and selected a choice piece, tucking it tightly against my bone-dry nest material. Other kids were banging away on their flint—practicing creating sparks, but I didn't want to dull my sharp edge. I knew it would spark. I saw my mother and dad waving encouragement from across the gym. A judge moved behind me with a stop watch. I kneeled and positioned my right hand, holding the steel bar directly above the nodule of flint. "Ready, set," and the starting whistle sounded.

A single, powerful stroke of metal striking against flint propelled several large sparks into my nest, imbedding them solidly in the muslin. I blew softly into the nest; it flamed. Three seconds flat! The Scoutmaster from the North Side Catholic troop charged across the floor shouting, "Check that nest! Check that nest!" I saw my dad jump up, with more fire in his eyes than in my nest. Jerking the nest from my hand before I could toss it into the water, the judge tapped out the flame, then placed it to his nose while staring me down like I had just robbed the State Bank at 4th and Main. He sniffed, the Scoutmaster sniffed, another judge sniffed. No lighter fluid, no gas, no gimmicks. Just an old Scouting trick called *being prepared*! We won the Meet. Troop 13 always did. And a proud Mom was less perturbed with the acrid smell lingering in her kitchen.

Troop 13 BSA, La Crosse WI – Memorial Day 1946

The Scout Circus Was a Zoo— and We Were the Monkeys

In competition, Troop 13 was never interested in second place. You would have seen that at Gateway Area Council's Silver Anniversary Scout Circus on the evening of June 15, 1946. Over 2,500 Scouts and leaders from 60 communities paraded, with colors flying, onto the football field at the fairgrounds to the cadence of an all-Scout marching band. Although most of the activities were demonstrations, they were contests to the participants, especially near the end of the program when troops would erect 24-foot-tall signal towers. Only a handful of other troops even considered building towers, while Troop 13 elected to construct four! We'd practiced lashing these edifices for over a month. The question was no longer *how* to put them up, we advanced to *how fast* we could put them up.

The sun had long set on the major La Crosse landmark, Granddad's Bluff, a mile east of the Scout Circus. The lights of the field spilled down on poles of varying sizes neatly stacked adjacent to each team of eight Scouts. Explaining the event, the Master of Ceremonies dwelled on the difficulty of erecting towers of this size. Was he laying the groundwork for an excuse should this event result in mass failure? Moments after the starting whistle sounded, the poor guy must have been relieved. Troop 13's teams hustled their poles into sections, with square and diagonal lashings flying. Support beams stood secured in less than two minutes. Raising the two sections at the proper distance from each other, our teams began the side lashing, with the upper lashers scampering up the towers with the agility of motivated gibbons. Troop 13 lashers quickly secured platform logs to the top, and before any other unit had their sections off the ground, signal flags were wigging and wagging on the crests of Troop 13's four towers. Here was a testimony to teamwork and desire—and of course, practice.

I Thought the Knickers Were Embarrassing...

Okay, I was a fire-building and log-lashing hotshot, but when it came to identifying flowers and plants, I faded to a botanical dunderhead. This inadequacy can lead to big-time adversity. During one of our many forays into the Mississippi River bluffs, Mother Nature rang my bell, causing a fast dash into a secluded section of woods. Wouldn't you know it. The little bundle of toilet paper, usually stuffed into my back pocket, was nowhere to be found. How embarrassing, not to mention inconvenient.

I simply reached around and grabbed the nearest leaves I could find. No problem. Boy Scouts improvise. A day or so later, I felt as though I was being rear-ended by a battalion of army ants. After a day of watching me squirm, Mom shot me off to our family physician. Doc McLoone, who brought me into this world some 13 years before, was a great doctor, but I never saw the man smile. When I dropped my drawers, and he took a peek, the old Doc cracked up. He laughed so hard he got me laughing, even though the state of my behind was not a laughing matter. "What Scout troop are you in?" He roared and guffawed some more. "I strongly suggest they enlighten you on the identification of poison oak!" He chuckled while handing me a prescription. I still don't know if I'd recognize that plant today, but you better believe a wad of TP is always firmly planted in my rear pocket.

Snakes and Greenbacks

Snakes in Wisconsin were seldom a concern. A few timber rattlers roamed the bluffs, yet we seldom saw one. Our favorite hiking haunt was a valley called Seven Springs. One late-summer morning we wandered single file into the bluffs along a cow path when one of the guys came within inches of stepping on a rattler. Its tail was singing as we surrounded it at a safe distance. Someone said, "Hey, there's a dollar bounty on these things." A dollar was a big deal in those days. It could get us all into a double feature at the Wisconsin Theater, plus a box of popcorn. So we dropped a rock on its head, made sure it was dead, sat down and gobbled our lunch, then stuffed the lifeless snake into a brown-paper bag.

The big, red-sandstone County Court House was a fair country hike from the bluffs, and we arrived there by mid-afternoon. County Clerk Esther Domke, a school mate of my dad's, was a businesslike lady with graying hair and huge horn-rimmed glasses. We all walked into the Courthouse, and I asked for her. Moments later, Esther stiffly marched out of her office. In her stodgy, cold, impersonal manner, she moved behind the big mahogany counter and asked, "Well, what can I do for you boys?" I said, "Miss Domke, we killed a rattlesnake and came to get our dollar." She rolled her eyes, and in a perky little voice informed us that she was sorry, but we had to have proof. With a perfunctory smile, she turned and began marching back toward her office. "Proof? We got that all right," I shouted. As she turned back, we dumped the dead rattler out of the sack and onto the countertop. The poor lady resembled a stop light, turning from red to yellow to green, With her mouth still hanging open, she spun and dashed into her office, pulled a dollar from her purse and threw it at us, yelling, "There, now get that damn thing out of here!" We grabbed the dollar and the snake and headed for the nearest ice cream shop, but not before carefully coiling the critter on the front steps of the Stoddard Hotel.

That wasn't the only snake that caused a little excitement that year. Summer camp was held at Camp Decorah north of La Crosse on the Black River. It was named after old One-eyed Decorah, a Winnebago Chief. That year, a blond Norsky kid named Robert, who had a snake collection in his basement, was unable to attend camp and informed everyone he would pay five dollars for a good-sized nonpoisonous snake, preferably a bull snake.

One afternoon after Jimmy Shannon and I finished a merit badge class at Camp Decorah, we decided to check out a row boat and explore a little island upstream on the river. This was one of those typical Wisconsin summer days: hot, sunny, and sticky with the air full of bugs. We pulled onto a beach on the island and secured the boat. Luckily we had on our army surplus jungle boots (a real rage during and after the war), because the island was genuinely swampy. Wandering about and swatting mosquitoes, we saw something slithering near a bush. "That's a bull snake," Jimmy yelled, "at least a three-footer, maybe more." We hustled to get the reptile cornered, then Jimmy, who had about as much fear as he had sense, grabbed the bugger by the back of the neck. Surprisingly, the old bull snake seemed sedate. Holding it close, Jimmy looked it in the eye, concluding it had a smile on its face. After all, we were rescuing it from a scorcher of a day.

But what could we put the snake in? We never thought to bring anything along. "How about my hat?" asked Jimmy. That hat was the talk of the camp. It was a multifunctional, cam-ouflage U.S. Army fatigue hat, several sizes too large, even for Jim's oversized head. Multifunctional? Let me tell you. Jimmy brought his dog to camp—without food. At the end of every meal, the guys would pass their scraps down to Jimmy. He'd check to see that no staff members were looking, then would scrape the scraps into his hat. Returning to our campsite, Jimmy would put the hat down in front of his scroungy mutt, and the dog would not only gulp down the food, but would lick the hat clean. Then Jimmy would simply slap the hat back on. So sticking our snake into that multifunctional hat and tying it off seemed completely logical.

The snake settled into the hat fairly easily. Luckily, it was only three feet long, otherwise it never would have fit. With a short length of twine I had in my pocket, we tied off the hat and happily returned to the boat, our heads spinning with visions of a five-dollar spending spree.

It was easy rowing back as we headed downstream. Jimmy was at the oars, and I was leaning over the bow cooling my hands in the water. Suddenly Jimmy screamed. I jerked back to see the snake rising out of the hat like a cobra oozing out of an East Indian basket. This snake wasn't smiling now; it was definitely disgruntled. The slippery reptile wiggled out of the hat and made a beeline for Jimmy, who dropped the oars and jumped on top of the seat yelling, "Do something!" The snake lifted itself up vertically, and I saw a blur of motion, followed by a gigantic splash—Jimmy had abandoned ship. I, too, was preparing to disembark when the snake eased itself over the gunwale and joined Jimmy for an afternoon swim—in fact, it was swimming right for him. I'm sure no other human has ever moved that fast in deep water wearing jungle boots! I jumped to the oars and quickly placed the boat between the rankled reptile and Jimmy, then pulled him back into the boat. I'll never forget the look in his eyes. He had seen death head on. And if that wasn't bad enough, our five bucks had slithered off into the depths of the Black River!

The Revenge of Army Surplus Peas

At times, getting caught in one predicament saved us from another disaster. Such was the case the summer I became the Patrol Leader of the Lion Patrol.

Troop 13 was back at the Frontier Unit at Camp Decorah, the only section where Scouts were housed in tents. The other troops spent their week away from home in the rainproof comfort of cabins. Determined to provide some real camping experience for four of the new kids in my patrol, my assistant and I checked out some food and two army surplus "mountain" tents (he and I would sleep under the stars). With packs on our backs, we six marched to a backcountry area a mile or two away along a stretch of the Black River. Over the hot coals of an open fire, we concocted a gourmet supper, topped off with hot, buttered cinnamon twists. As the shadows grew to darkness, my buddy and I uncorked a few of the grisly stories that had generated a goose bump or two for us when we were new Scouts. Then it was time for everyone to hit the sack.

The sky that night was spectacular, with shooting stars darting across the heavens every minute or so. I remember feeling sorry for the kids in the tents who were missing this great show. But after a busy day, you can only gaze at stars for so long before the eye lids droop and become glued shut. They were down so tightly we missed the massive cover of clouds that drifted in from the west, plus we never heard the wind that must have been driving these foreboding clouds.

The storm probably started with the usual pitter-patter of rain drops, but we missed that. I awoke startled, thinking I was sleeping under Niagara Falls. My buddy and I grabbed our now soggy blankets, each making a beeline for one of the tents. But upon unzipping the flaps, we each found two shivering kids sitting in inches of water. In another hour they may have drowned. These army mountain tents had air vents, little tunnel-like appendages near the upper front and rear. When the novices erected their tents, the vents were aimed upward. Instead of vents, they had become rain funnels! I don't remember much more of that night, but I sure remember the morning.

Wet, chilled to the bone, and embarrassed, we sloshed back into camp to witness a strange phenomenon. Outhouses were situated at strategic locations throughout the camp. Most were "two-holers" (the kind where you could do duets). Two holes or not, lines of guys, 10 or 12 deep, stood impatiently at each privy. Every guy undulated from side to side and up and down, resembling some strange African tribal ritual. Without warning, someone in the middle of the line would break ranks and storm into the woods. Minutes later he'd reappear through the brush while the others yelled, "Did you make it?" If he answered in the affirmative, a big cheer reverberated through the lines. We didn't see any guys respond in the negative.

"Hey, what gives?" I asked one of the camp staff members.

"Peas," he moaned with an unfortunate degree of personal

association. "Army surplus peas. We all had them for dinner last night, and now we know why the army got rid of them. If they had fed them to the damn Germans, the war might have been over a year earlier!"

Sure enough, staff members had tried to pawn those digestion diverters on us when we checked food out for our overnight. We refused them simply to lighten packs. After being an eye witness to that outhouse caper, I couldn't swallow another canned pea for at least a decade.

5 Scouts + 1 Haunted House = Trouble!

During the 1940s, mothers and dads seldom pulled taxi duty as they do today. You either walked or peddled your bike to your destination. But we wouldn't have had it any other way. Because that's when the fun began!

Troop 13 amassed scores of going-home-after-the-meeting stories: dismantling the chrome ring hood ornaments off new Buicks for bracelets, window peeping at the nursing school dorm... but the most memorable story involved a "haunted house."

The well-heeled folks populated a four- or five-block stretch on Cass Street dominated by large houses, mansions in some cases. One house near West Avenue stood vacant for years. Convincing reports from the kid network said it was haunted. This daunting three-story structure appeared dark and foreboding, even in daytime. A cement driveway, in dire need of repair, circled up to a covered entryway. Tangled vines dangled down the exterior walls, and tall elm and pine and scraggly bushes were recapturing the once majestic, landscaped yard. At night, this was the kind of place that tested one's courage. And naturally, courage always needed to be tested.

One foggy October evening, the troop meeting broke up early, giving us the extra time we needed to explore the outside of the mansion. Five of us made a beeline there, hiding our bikes in the bushes of the Cargill mansion next door. Only George had a flashlight. With the stealth of commandos, we eluded the glow of the corner street light, creeping cautiously onto the property from two sides. Someone tried the front door, but of course it was locked. Two others checked the back. A rusty lock on the nearly horizontal cellar doors was dangling open. Quietly pulling up these two flimsy panels, we staggered down six or eight cement steps where the actual doorway into the cellar stood. It's going to be locked, we thought. Heck, most of us hoped it was. But turning the knob, the old wooden portal squeaked open several inches. With a little push, the door spread wide enough to enter. No one wanted to be the first one to turn back, so we asked George to lead with his flashlight. Instead, George bravely passed his flashlight ahead. One by one we tiptoed into a dark, dingy, dusty cellar.

A dozen or so old glass canning jars and a handful of Red Wing crocks were partially hidden by cobwebs that decorated the warped wooden shelves. Several rodents scampered along a wall and darted into what must have been a coal bin. "Well, we've been in, now let's go home," muttered George. But a quick check with the dimming flashlight uncovered a stairway directly ahead of us. No, we decided silently, we're not leaving yet. Once on the wooden stairs, the aged boards creaked as if being disturbed from a long night's sleep. Within moments, we were standing in a large kitchen, its walls lined with spacious white cupboards. George again suggested that perhaps this was as far as we should go tonight. Promptly voted down, we moved single file through a swinging door into the dining room.

A massive table and chairs, all covered, sat in the center of the room bordered by a huge buffet and a dusty, lace-curtained bay window. Its shades were pulled several inches below the sills. Two partially opened sliding doors led into a huge entryway providing access to the parlor with furniture covered by dusty blankets or old white sheets. It looked exactly like haunted houses in the movies. And you couldn't tell if anybody—or anything—was lurking beneath those sheets.

Ron spun around thinking that he heard something in the parlor. We bunched together like threatened sheep. Giggling nervously, we dismissed the idea, while George, more forceful than before, suggested that perhaps this was as far as we should go tonight. After all, he had homework to do! He was starting to muster support, but Ron and I wanted to ascend the huge stairway that was partially illuminated from the corner street light— just to peek at what was upstairs. The other three informed us they would wait right there and advised us to make it quick; they had to get home.

Ron switched the flashlight back on as we stepped onto the second-floor landing. It was dim. Why hadn't George put new batteries in this thing? We could see a long corridor that led to three or four large wooden doors. While Ron flashed the light into one doorway I opened another and slowly entered a room facing the front of the house. I had taken only one or two steps inside when I saw him. He was sitting on the floor in the corner, wrapped in a blanket, his bearded face partially lit from the street light. I stood, frozen. My feet felt as if they were nailed to the floor. Long, black scraggly hair covered part of his face, his eyes were dark and deeply sunken, and his black beard was sprinkled with white. He didn't move. He didn't blink. I slid one foot backward muttering, "Let's get the heck out of here!"

Ron walked in and casually shined the flashlight into the room—within seconds he was ahead of me, stumbling down the stairs. "There's somebody up there!" he screamed. And the stampede was on.

Through the foyer, through the dining room, into the kitchen, down the cellar stairs, up the outside stairs—we never took time to shut a door. We dashed out through the driveway, stumbling over each other to find our bikes. In a flash we were on Cass Street, turning on 13th, and we didn't stop pumping those peddles for at least five blocks. Our hearts must have sounded like the cadence beat of the American Legion Drum Corps.

Each time I'm in La Crosse I find myself driving down Cass Street. The "haunted" mansion was razed, and a Lutheran nursing home now stands on that lot. Those nice, old Norwegian ladies will never know how much adrenalin was pumped at that location by five adventurous Scouts on a cold, foggy night long ago.

2

SCOUTING WITH AN AMERICAN INDIAN CONNECTION

My Introduction to Indian Dancing

The first time I heard real drums was the summer of 1940 when I rode past the little church of Reverend White Rabbit and gawked at the scores of bark-covered wigwams scattered across the Winnebago reservation near Black River Falls, Wisconsin. My dad and Bill Koch, a neighbor and Indian historian, were taking me to my first powwow. This scene fired my excitement. When we arrived, the bronze-faced dancers had already begun circling the dance arbor, a flimsy, open-air wooden structure built to shade the dancers and viewers from the intense summer sun. A hundred or so Winnebago in well-worn clothing stood watching on the periphery. Some wore shoes, some wore moccasins. Most of the women were adorned with multicolored shawls, drawn over the shoulders of cotton dresses dulled by too many washings.

In the center sat four chanters singing in unison, their shrill voices reaching up to high falsetto sounds. Their repetitious songs were incomprehensible to the non-Indian. They nearly seemed to be in a trance as they accompanied themselves with a steady rumble on one large hide-covered drum, punctuated with occasional sharp accent beats. The rhythmic clamor of hundreds of bells attached to the ankles of 50 or more beaded and feathered dancers blended with the voices and drum, creating a sound I had never heard before—a sound that soon crept inside of me, causing my thin little body to undulate up and down in rhythm with the songs.

I felt an arm ease around my back and saw a dark, wrinkled, and weather-worn hand rest on my shoulder. I turned to see a Winnebago woman, nearly as wide as she was tall, smiling at me. She leaned over and whispered, "I think it's time you learn to dance." Behind her, I spotted Bill and my dad nodding their approval and waving me on. No doubt they put her up to it, and my stomach began to churn with apprehension. She led me to the edge of the dance area, then leaned over and told me, "Some whites come here and dance, but none of them dance like an Indian. I'll teach you to dance good."

She started by showing me how to move my feet, then my body and arms, and moved all the way to my head, getting all of my steps and body parts moving simultaneously in harmony with the song. I soon forgot where I was, so engrossed with the good feeling emanating from the sounds and the movement. Several songs and a dozen circles around the arbor later, I turned to ask her how I was doing, but she wasn't there. She was on the side, smiling. It was only then that I felt conspicuous, blond and blue-eyed, no feathers—a plucked Norsky within the Winnebago nation!

This powwow was my first, small step into a lifetime filled with "feeling the beat." And several months later, I received a beautiful beaded Woodland apron from that lovely Winnebago lady.

We'll Be There with Bells On

Shortly after I joined Troop 13, Scoutmaster Bert Wethe decided that if Buck Burshears, a Scoutmaster in the little Colorado town of La Junta, could cause a stir in the Scouting world with a Boy Scout Indian Dance group, why couldn't we? Buck's Koshare Indian dancers were featured as the cover story in the May 1947 issue of *Boys' Life* (an issue still tucked away in my drawer with Buck's autograph on the cover). This story was our motivator. When several men on the troop committee showed concern that time spent on a dance group may impede the Scouting effort, Bert was quick to point out that the vast majority of "Buck's Brats," as Buck called his Scouts, attained the rank of Eagle Scout. The Indian program would enhance advancement rather than impede it. The troop only had one problem: no one knew how to teach Indian dancing.

I mentioned our dilemma to Bill Koch and, within a week, several Winnebago dancers showed up to share their skills with the troop. For costumes, we turned to Ben Hunt's *The Complete Book of Indian Crafts and Lore*, as our bible. (Ben was a colorful Wisconsin character and regular contributor to *Boys' Life*.) Bert rounded up bags of turkey feathers and fluffs and colored felt; our mothers' sewing machines and our own bead looms hummed. Meanwhile we studied and practiced a variety of simple dances. Before long, Troop 13 had a dance group, a long way from the Koshare's skill level, but it was a good start.

Our first performance was at a centennial pageant in Viroqua, Wisconsin. We stayed in tipis near the natural amphitheater where the program was presented and soon learned that Boy Scout Indian dancers not only attracted a crowd, but also attracted *girls*. The American Indian segment of the pageant was spectacular, featuring a gorgeous soprano standing in a beautifully beaded, white buckskin dress amid the pines high on a hill singing "The Indian Love Song." But dancing in full costume was hot, especially on a sticky Wisconsin summer evening. After our performance, we needed to cool off with a swim, but the public pool on the knoll behind us was closed due to the polio scare. Did that, or the tall fence around the pool, deter us? Of course not.

With no swimsuits along, our swim quickly turned into a skinny dip. After all, we always swam that way at the YMCA. Soon we heard giggles outside the fence. Obviously, we were still attracting girls. If that wasn't bad enough, one of our younger dancers dashed up to the fence to alert us that the cops were coming! Girls or no girls, we jumped out of the water, grabbed our costumes, and hustled over the fence—with nothing on but our war paint—and streaked in the darkness to our tipis. Moments later, we were seemingly sound asleep when several of the local gendarmes flashed their lights into the tipi, tossed several lost moccasins onto the floor and whispered, "Good night, redskins." After the performance the next evening, we limited ourselves to a legal shower.

That wasn't the only memorable swim with our dance group. Performing one evening in front of the grandstand at the La Crosse State College football field, we were especially proud to be dancing with the Black River Winnebagos. Colored spotlights enhanced the setting for dancing on an immense wooden stage. Below the front of the stage rested a huge water tank used for a log-rolling contest. Wanting to do our best in company with the Winnebagos, our hoop dancer, Jack, performed a flaming hoop dance. One of our hottest dancers, Jack was about halfway through his performance when we noticed he was hotter than usual; the loincloth covering his backside was on fire! We only had to tell him once (I guess he was already feeling an unbalanced warmth). But did he panic? Not Jack. Ever so cool, he made two more passes through the burning hoop, then calmly danced straight into the water tank. The Winnebagos were cracking up, and the audience, who must have thought it was part of the act, gave him a tremendous round of applause. Scouting does provide some astonishing moments.

An Initiation to Remember

Long before the Order of the Arrow, the nationwide Scout honor society, arrived in Western Wisconsin the *Braves of Decorah* served that function for the Gateway Area Council. Scouts elected to the Braves proudly wore black armbands with a white arrowhead insignia. Compared to the Order of the Arrow, the initiation ritual for the Braves of Decorah was far more glamorous and much more robust with some elements so harsh they probably wouldn't fly today. The austerity simply added to the mystique of the initiation. When completed, you knew you had been involved in something special.

Most Scouts were chosen only after they experienced at least three years at summer camp. Camp staff members made the selections, eliminating the chance of a popularity contest within the troops. No anxious Scout ever forgot the night he was tapped to become a Brave.

A late June moon at the half phase hung like a big white D in the eastern sky, peeking in and out of a few scattered clouds blowing in from the southwest. It was Friday, the final night in camp. Sparks from the traditional last campfire spiraled into the huge branches of pine trees surrounding a large bowl-like depression that served as the campfire site.

While counselors darted about leading the usual songs, jokes, and skits that comprise a Scout campfire, trepidation hovered over most of the campers, especially those of us who were hoping that this would be our year to become a Brave.

We were singing a robust ballad when suddenly, as if they erupted from the bowels of the earth, scores of "Indian braves" appeared from nowhere, completely surrounding the periphery of the bowl. The rousing song diminished to silence. Torches held high above their heads illuminated faces made indistinguishable by paint—red, black, yellow, and white—meticulously applied to their faces. Some were in buckskins, others were bare-chested or with breastplates, beaded necklaces, and colorful loincloths. Each stood frozen in place, glaring down on the assembly of campers whose eyes slowly scanned the circle of torches. I could feel my pulse pounding in my ears. No one moved or hardly breathed.

The silence was interrupted by the muffled, rhythmic beat of a drum echoing in the distance. Four braves approached from the east and descended, majestically into the bowl, followed by a solitary figure adorned in buckskin leggings and a beaded buckskin shirt. The feathers on his imposing, double-trailer headdress nearly touched the ground. He stood, straight and proud. His whole being seemed to reflect a keen sense of alertness. Approaching the fire, he stopped. The drum fell silent; a soft breeze sifting through the pine branches was the only discernable sound. He turned his head slowly from side to side, then nodded slightly.

On his signal, the four braves moved quickly through the hundreds of standing campers, stopping occasionally behind one, thrusting their hands harshly onto their shoulders. One smaller boy fell to his knees from the blow. Then it happened. I never saw the brave or heard him before his hands pounded down on my shoulders. He grabbed me by my shirt and dragged me to the fire, shoving me directly in front of the stone-faced chief. The flickering glow from the fire danced across his face, partially shadowed by the feathers of his bonnet. He said nothing, but looked me straight in the eye with a cold, emotionless stare that seemed to penetrate my soul. He rubbed a finger into a small cup he held in his hand and reached out, marking an X on my forehead. He finally spoke in a near-whisper, telling me that I must remain perfectly silent. I was led away into the darkness of the adjacent woods.

Soon I was joined by a dozen candidates, and we were herded into a tight circle. The chief approached us, accompanied by two torch-bearing braves. He warned us that a long, hard night remained, and our acceptance into the organization depended completely on our attitude, our behavior, and our willingness to obey their rules. He reminded us that speaking, under any circumstances, was not permitted. He turned and disappeared into the darkness.

The half dozen braves surrounding us suddenly yelled, "Run!" And run we did, from one end of the camp to the other, following a torch bearer and being "encouraged" by taunts and by the snap of willow boughs against our bare legs. Our feet pounded the soil of Camp Decorah for the better part of an hour. The night was warm and sticky, and soon my shirt was saturated in perspiration. Both eyes stung from the salty droplets running down my forehead. Finally they allowed us to stop at a sandy spot near the Black River where a young, but grossly overweight, Assistant Scoutmaster from another troop nearly collapsed. He kneeled down in the sand, his body pumping up and down like a bellows trying to suck in air. A broad-chested brave, half of his face painted black and the other half white, rushed up and stood nose to nose with a tall, thin lad standing on my left. "What's your name?" he stormed. "Raymond, sir," the boy answered. Raymond was immediately escorted away. He had forgotten, and he had spoken.

Six canoes came into sight, each with two paddlers and a torch bearer. We were too nervous to appreciate the beauty of the scene with the orange glow of the torches reflecting magnificently in the slowly flowing water. One by one each canoe pulled alongside the bank. We were escorted into the canoes and told to sit quietly in the center and hold tightly to the wooden gunwales. The only sound was the ripple of the paddles propelling the canoes into the center of the river as we moved downstream to an unknown destination.

We could soon detect the whine of cars crossing the Black River Bridge on Highway 53 echoing up the river valley. Shortly before reaching the bridge, the canoes crossed to the north side where we were yanked out, shoved into single file and told to *run*. A narrow footpath paralleled the highway and every several hundred yards a fresh team of escorts took over the tasks of leading, taunting, and snapping the dreaded willow boughs.

After a mile or so, where the highway swings westward to skirt the tall bluffs on the north, they stopped us and granted us a moment to catch our breath. The braves then sent us scrambling straight up the bluff toward a shadowed sandstone formation resembling a large sugar cube. It was known as Decorah Peak.

The climb at that fast rate was a breath grabber. Was this worth it? At this stage, no one was backing down. By torchlight, we were led to an opening at the base of the bluff that looked like an oversized laundry shoot. *"Climb!"* I was determined to get going before the big, tired Scout leader started up. The ascent is what climbers today call a *chimney*; pressing your back and fanny against one wall with your legs and hands against the other, you simply inch your way upward, in this case about 20 or 30 feet. How did they ever discover this place? We would soon find out.

My bare knees scraped against the sharp sandstone wall and were screaming at me by the time my head finally emerged at the top. The sight at the top immediately erased any pain. A small fire illuminated this mini-mesa, not much more than ten yards square. A small drum was sounding, and the chief and several braves were standing straight and quiet. I felt as though we had stepped out of a time machine and had been propelled backward over a hundred years. Maintaining silence, we waited until everyone emerged. The grunting and snorting emanating from the vertical tunnel eventually subsided when the chubby Scouter was successfully pulled through.

In a low baritone voice, the chief began unwinding a tale of the happenings on the historical site on which we stood. A century before, the farming Winnebago were attacked by a large Chippewa warring party. Greatly outnumbered, they, like us, hustled up the steep hill and shimmied through the same hole to find refuge on the peak. The attackers, realizing their adversaries had few supplies and little water, decided to simply sit it out. Within days the condition of Winnebago people was seriously deteriorating. One night, Chief Decorah jumped from an unguarded side of the peak, breaking both legs. He dragged himself to the river, found a canoe, and paddled down the Black River. Finding and alerting part of his band, they returned and drove off the attacking Chippewa.

And we thought we had it tough.

The initiation ceremony was very long, "Indian," and impressive. We sealed our vows by eating the meat of the fattened buffalo. We had ample time to contemplate our vows, because it took a long time to chew that piece of grizzled flesh. The trip back was simply a reverse of the trip in. Shimmy down the hole, dash down the bluff, run to the river to the tune of willow switches, and take a canoe ride back to the camp landing.

It was past midnight when we were sent to our tents to retrieve a single blanket, then blindfolded and escorted individually to various parts of the forest for "further contemplation and rest." Our rest was short lived. Within two hours, the heavens opened (déjà vu at Camp Decorah), and this time I sat with no protection from the downpour other than a single, wool army blanket. Contemplation was about all I had left, yet contemplation under those conditions was as logical as starting a fire by rubbing together two sticks under water. That night, the name of the game was *survival*!

I didn't expect those hard-core Braves to venture out in the driving rain and rescue a guy who was supposed to be suffering an ordeal, but hoping gave me something constructive to do. I learned in the morning, after I calculated my whereabouts and sloshed back into camp, that they weren't as cruel and cold hearted as I thought—they simply lacked smarts. The yahoos had found everyone else, but had forgotten where they had dumped me! They made up for their memory lapse with a sturdy breakfast of bread and water before sending us out for a day in the sun, shifting boulders the size of Mount Rushmore from point A to point B. Naturally, the braves decided some boulders needed to be moved back to their original spots.

Yet our initiation ended on a positive note. We were welcomed as full-fledged members of the Braves of Decorah (after we paid our dues), then sat down to a hearty meal featuring a big, thick, juicy steak, without surplus peas!

A footnote: Shortly after my ordeal, the Braves of Decorah became a chapter of the Order of the Arrow. The ritual changed, but this new OA chapter retained their original name. The old, black armband of the Braves must trigger a million memories for those who, on one special night during their Scouting years, successfully "climbed the rock" to meet the chief.

"Redskins" Raid Trempealeau

The year 1948 was the centennial anniversary for the great State of Wisconsin. Virtually every city, village, township, and hamlet scheduled centennial celebrations depicting, if not glamorizing, the 100-year history of the state. In 1848, our American Indian brothers were still major players in a territory sparsely settled by whites, and as Scouts, we felt they too should be remembered during a year that would primarily focus on pioneers. On that note, some enterprising Boy Scouts came up with a great idea.

We already knew the dances of the American Indian had magnetic appeal. With a simple mix of feathers, beads, and buckskins blended with the pulsating beat of the drum and the tinkle of bells, we concocted a winning recipe for drawing a crowd. The combination of the Braves of Decorah and Troop 13 harbored a tidy number of good dancers, many trained by Winnebago. But what about the real Indians? As a Winnebago friend had told me, "We dance for ourselves, we seldom dance to entertain others." The length and repetition of native dances were difficult for most white observers to understand or appreciate. That opened the door to interpretive dancing, the kind Boy Scouts do, with repertoires based on the more interesting segments of longer dances from a wide variety of tribes.

The chief of the Braves of Decorah organized the dancing group, choosing 15 Scouts who were good dancers and had worked hard to create colorful and authentic-looking costumes. Out of respect for our mentors, we gave the dance troupe a Winnebago name. We then mailed brochures to virtually every town in western Wisconsin, offering to dance during their centennial festivities. The response was terrific, and throughout the summer, we hopped, skipped, and jumped to our thunder drum nearly every weekend. And we got paid. We were now "professional Indian dancers!" Our summer tour went without a hitch, until we arrived in Trempealeau, Wisconsin.

Trempealeau was a slow-moving, little farm community bordering the mighty Mississippi River. State Highway 35 paralleled the east bank of the river to Prescott, Wisconsin, and ran through the center of town, flanked by stores and buildings, many from the late 1800s. Between the street and the river ran the Burlington Railroad.

Wisconsin might be cold in the winter, but the only chill in the air that August day we drove in to perform at Trempealeau's centennial celebration was our initial reception. We arrived early, knowing we were to participate in the Grand Parade. Hurriedly, we sought out the event manager, the gentleman who had responded to our brochure and hired us. The whole troupe waltzed into his store, and we introduced ourselves. His already-tilted toupee nearly completely dislodged as his lower jaw hit his chest. "I thought I was getting *real* Indians!" he shouted. "You're nothing but a bunch of snot-nosed kids." His face blossomed to a bright-red hue. He definitely was not reflecting the gaiety of the day. "You misrepresented yourselves!" By now he was shouting so loud that people were peeking in the store window. We explained that we had not misrepresented ourselves. In the brochure it said we were Scouts. "How in hell was I supposed to know you were *Boy* Scouts. I thought you were *Indian* scouts!"

By now, half of our gang had backed away to the door to facilitate a fast exit. Our "chief" apologized for the misunderstanding and said we would simply return home. "But you're on the damn program!" the manager bellowed, "and you're supposed to ride horses in the parade in an hour." Horses? We were supposed to ride horses? Only one guy in our troupe had horse experience; the closest the rest of us had come to riding a horse was on the merry-go-round at the La Crosse County Fair. But at this stage of the confrontation we thought it best to muster up the courage and do it. So we agreed to ride horses in the parade and give Trempealeau two great dance performances, one in the afternoon and one in the evening. We assured the manager that he had nothing to be concerned about, our performances would be exceptional. We sped off to change and go in search of our trusty mounts. Heck, we thought, this just might be fun.

We made quite an impression tinkling our bells past the whole parade in waiting, marching bands, Shriners in their funny red hats from the Twin Cities, 4-H floats, the Ladies Aid, and citizens who looked old enough to have founded the town, huddling and smiling in Cadillac convertibles. They were lined up, waiting to strut their stuff down Main Street. But where were the horses? They were back where any sensible person puts horses in a parade—at the tail end. And what a combination of horse flesh, everything from plow horses to thoroughbreds. "Are you the Indians?" one farmer asked with a tinge of skepticism in his voice. We assured him we were the Indians. Our hoop dancer asked where the saddles were. The farmer squinched his sun-wrinkled face. "Who in hell ever heard of an Indian using saddles?" He was right, of course, and we quickly chastised our ignorant accomplice while secretly wishing we'd have something to hold onto other than the horses' manes. "You boys all ride well enough?" asked another farmer swirling a toothpick back and forth across his lips. What red-blooded American Indian was going to admit that deficiency? "Shore 'nuff," we replied.

We should have had our first hint of impending doom when the lead band struck up and started drumming and tooting down the street. Apprehension swelled in the anxious eyes of the horses we were about to mount. Sirens blared from fire trucks that came in from three counties, and bearded geezers dressed like mountain men were popping off muskets.

The lead unit in the parade probably hadn't passed the reviewing stand in front of the hardware store when the word came, "Okay boys, mount up." About six guys streaked toward an old, gray nag that looked like it probably wouldn't live until the end of the parade. And how in the heck do you get on one of these things without stirrups? Several of us tried to dive upward onto our horses' backs, with little avail. The one guy who did it ended up facing the wrong direction. One wise dude tried a Roy Rogers mount from the rear and nearly became a permanent part of the tail section. Finally, one by one, those good ol' Wisconsin farmers helped hoist us aboard. "Good luck," one muttered. The tone of his voice didn't ring with confidence.

We were still minutes from departure, and the bristly horse hair was already irritating the sensitive Scandinavian skin of our bare legs. One farmer told us to press our legs tight to stay in position on the horse. Doing this felt like wrapping our tender thighs around a small porcupine. Several of us were already having allergic reactions ranging from itchy eyes to itchy stomachs. One guy actually began to break out in a rash. Dancers who brought feathered fanny bustles tied them to their backs, to their arms, to the reins, or held them in their spare hand, if they could spare a hand—this looked like a genuine two-hand operation to me. To top it off, several horses began misbehaving. The farmers yelled an avalanche of instructions. "Pull back on the reins." "Don't pull so hard on the reins." "Sit farther forward." "Sit farther back." "Let the horse know who's boss!" Heck, these horses already knew who was boss. Finally the dreaded moment arrived. "Okay boys. Head 'em out. And keep 'em under control!"

For the first block or two everything went smoothly. No one fell off, the horses were walking slowly—almost too slowly, but we had no intention of prodding them on. Tails were raising, and marbles were dropping. "I hope they don't make us clean the street," one of the guys remarked. "Shut up and look Indian!"

we retorted. We clip-clopped down the street to the applause of the crowd. One little girl pointed and yelled, "Look, Mom, real Indians!"

Hey, we thought, this isn't going to be too bad; in fact, it's really fun. But all good things come to an end.

I heard it faintly in the distance, a crescendo coming closer and closer: the Burlington Pioneer Zephyr, that epitome of streamlined passenger trains, speeding south from Minneapolis-St. Paul toward distant Chicago. This was one of the sharpest-looking trains of the time, and in a moment this silver bullet would be whizzing past, only a stone's throw away from Main Street—and we were right in the middle of Main Street. You could feel the horses' muscles tighten as they got jittery. Everything may have been all right until that darn fool engineer decided to send his greetings to the celebration by laying on his piercing, screaming whistle.

The first horse to bolt was near the back. As he reared up, one surprised little Indian slid right off its hind end and landed on his. A parade watcher dashed out to grab the reins, but it was too late. The race was on. Pulling the reins was absolutely no deterrent. Holding back these beasts was no option, and staying on was in doubt. In a flash, 15 horses, with 14 riders stampeded in a dead heat toward the power co-op float. Feathered lances and shields flew to the wind as riders quickly decided two hands grabbing manes were better than one. The pounding sound of hooves against the pavement alerted the Whitehall marching band just moments before the thundering herd would have made piccolos out of the tuba section. The American Legion veterans in their little blue overseas hats rushed for the curbs, having not faced such a determined charge since the Battle of the Bulge. The Lutheran ladies on the back of a flatbed truck looked in horror as the charging horde of "redskins" dashed past both sides of the truck. Color guards scattered with their flags and rifles. One elderly lady in the Cadillac convertible, smiled and waved as we galloped by, apparently thinking this was part of the parade, and an exciting part at that.

Up ahead, the parade was parting like the Red Sea as we stormed along, feathers flying, to finally take the honored position of leading the parade. Another half mile sped by before these hoofed hummers ran out of steam near the edge of town. As they changed gears from a full gallop to a trot, some riders, who had been on the brink of departing, decided this was the right time. Just when the beasts had nearly stopped, three police cars, with lights flashing and sirens blazing, added spice to the pursuit. If the horses hadn't been so winded, we could have continued the race down the main drag to Galesville, and that was long way down the road.

And who stepped out of one of the squad cars? Our red-faced, scowling, steaming, toupeed celebration chairman. It took some frantic explaining to convince him we didn't run that race intentionally. Fortunately, no one was hurt, little damage was done, and our dance performances that afternoon and evening were warmly received. Everyone came to get a close look at the phony Indians who had the gall to raid Trempealeau right in the middle of its Centennial Parade.

Goodbye to the '40s and My Scouting Youth

Yes, those were memorable times. We were kids of the Depression, but too young to remember the real hardships. Everyone talked about the Depression and that effected how we viewed life. We lived through the most devastating war in the history of mankind. Yet for kids, it was a time of fun and excitement; our war game consisted of rubber-band rifles and ash-bag grenades.

These years preceded most of the material goodies that are taken for granted today, such as television and microwave ovens. Heck, we didn't even have electric typewriters much less a computer. A chip had to do with either a piece of wood, sliver of ice, or buffalo. *Hardware* meant a hammer and nails, and there was no such word as *software*. No ballpoint pens, air conditioners, dishwashers (well there *were* dishwashers: us), and certainly no pizza, McDonald's, or KFC. You rode your bike, the bus, or a streetcar. Postcards were a penny, and you could actually buy something for a nickel or dime at the 5 and 10 cent store.

Best of all, it was a great time to Scout. I earned my Eagle Badge in December 1946 with about a dozen others from troops throughout the Council. We had all mastered much more in Scouts than we realized. One Tuesday morning at Lincoln Junior High, our teacher, Mr. Austin, suffered a grand mal seizure. Suddenly, he stopped talking. His head, then his whole body, began twitching before he crumpled to the floor with arms and legs thrashing violently. In seconds, six Troop 13 Scouts had his coat and tie loosened, a pencil in his mouth, furniture moved safely away, the class ushered out of the room, and the principal notified. We had learned the proper procedure for epilepsy at a Troop meeting the very night before!

I thought I'd nearly drown learning lifesaving in the sand-bottomed pool at Camp Decorah. If we failed to approach our instructor correctly, he'd grab you, drag you under, and hold you there until you thought your lungs would explode. Did it pay off? One warm, sunny spring afternoon a bunch of us were studying for high school finals down at a dredged beach on the Mississippi River. A classmate interrupted the peacefulness screaming, "Somebody's drowning!" Looking up we saw a hand break the surface in the swift current near a spot known to have a ten-foot drop-off. Two of us dashed into the murky waters aiming downstream to compensate for the current. Then we dove. In seconds we each felt the body of a small child, and brought the child to the surface. No, there were two children—two little girls still clutching each others' hands. We each took a little girl and swam to a sandbar. Both had taken on water, but within seconds we had them coughing up water and breathing. Bundling them in towels, we got them warm and calmed down. We took them by the hands and set out to locate their parents, who we found busy launching a boat two blocks upstream.

First-aid and lifesaving instructors had explained that some day we might save a life. Whoever thought the opportunity would arrive so quickly?

My final act as a Scout brought that decade of the Forties into focus. It was on Memorial Day, 1949, a week before high school graduation. A huge parade headed up King Street with one contingent moving south on West Avenue to the Catholic Cemetery, the other north to the massive Oak Grove Cemetery on La Crosse Street. Troop 13 marched that day, as it always did, but my responsibility that sunny morning was to recite by heart the Gettysburg Address at the ceremony to honor those who had died in the war. I had the words down cold, but I feared that the moment I moved to the podium and came eye to eye with a thousand faces I wouldn't remember if it was "four score and seven" or "twenty-seven and a half"!

The address went well. After the ceremonies, a lady in a veiled hat walked up to me and gently took my hand. Tears swelled in her eyes. "My son was a Scout like you," she said softly, "in fact you look a lot like him." She paused and glanced away for a moment, then turned back. With a pained smile etched on her face, she said, "He was killed in Germany two weeks before the war was over. Thank you for reminding me that the dead have not died in vain." She squeezed my hand tightly, turned, and walked away slowly through the trees, the flowers, and the stone monuments, disappearing in the direction of the Soldiers' Lot.

No, the war wasn't about rubber-band rifles and ash-bag grenades, was it?

3

STEPPING INTO BIGGER MOCCASINS: BECOMING A SCOUTMASTER

Now-Famous Words: "Try it, you might like it"

I left Scouting in the dust for college, a tour of duty in the Navy, more schooling, and marriage to my young wife Charlotte. After a sweet little daughter arrived, we bought our first house, a homey 725-square-footer on a quiet side street in the St. Paul, Minnesota, suburb of Roseville. Little did I know that Scouting was again only a door knock away.

Life was prancing along at a gentle pace: a good job, new home, wife and family, and friendly neighbors. I hadn't realized anything was missing until one evening when a knock sounded at my front door. A tall, thin, gentleman, well into his late forties, introduced himself. His name was Ralph Underhill. Knowing we were new to the neighborhood, he was making a friendly stop to invite us to the nearby Centennial Methodist Church. Running through the menu of goodies the church offered, he mentioned an active Scout troop. In fact, Ralph was the Troop Committee Chairman. Scout troop, wow! It was as though someone turned on the faucet. Memories flooded back. Soon we both ignored the purpose of his visit and spent the evening babbling and laughing over myriad Scouting stories.

The moon hadn't shifted into its next phase before Ralph was again at my door. His expression accented the wrinkles sneaking onto his face as he sighed, "We've got a big problem." Char came in from the kitchen and sat down. Ralph explained that the Scoutmaster at Troop 410 at Asbury Lutheran recently suffered a serious coronary and his only assistant had ulcers. They were ready to close down a troop of 25 boys. The committee at Centennial Methodist was considering adding them to the 25 Scouts they already housed. "This leaves the troop short of adult help," he explained. "I told the committee about you, and they would like you to consider becoming an Assistant Scoutmaster."

This was intriguing to me, but did I have the time? On top of that, I didn't even have a boy, much less one of Scouting age.

While wrestling with a decision, the kid side of my brain clicked in as I recalled the stern words of Judge Lincoln Neprud, the key speaker the night I received my Eagle Badge. "The best way to pay back your Scout leaders is to someday become one yourself." I was flipping back to the more pragmatic side, when Char looked at me and blurted her now-famous utterance: "Why don't you try it? You might like it." Over the next 40 years of weekly troop meetings, committee meetings, monthly outings, summer camps, and week-long pack trips, those words must have felt like an immoveable chicken bone lodged solidly in her throat.

Ralph sat hunched over with his elbows on his knees looking me straight in the eye. "Well?"

"Well," I finally said, scratching my head, "I suppose I could try it. Who knows, I might like it!"

A Novice Enters the Lion's Den

Troop 186 serviced a relatively new suburban area of small homes, young trees, and young families with fairly thin wallets. The real money in Roseville resided a little farther north. It was late April when I sauntered down Arona Street to my first Monday night meeting. The sun was lingering longer, allowing me to wrestle with my concerns in daylight. Would I have the same interest I had as a kid? I knew nothing about adult Scout leadership, so what kind of a leader would I make? Would I be accepted by the boys? More important, how easily would two troops merge? I envisioned one group propped against one wall and the other huddled against another like a sixth-grade mixer.

I wandered into the meeting room to the racket of 50 kids ricocheting off the floor, ceiling, and four walls. In the midst of total bedlam, Scoutmaster Lloyd Dewey (one of the most unruffled individuals I have ever encountered), sat shuffling through papers, while responding to scores of questions from dozens of kids. In a corner huddled in conversation stood four Assistant Scoutmasters. Hey, why do they need me? By the second week in July, I found out.

I spent the last three days of summer camp with the troop at Tomahawk Scout Reservation near Rice Lake, Wisconsin, a 2,600-acre bundle of fun operated by St. Paul's Indianhead Council. Nestled in a densely wooded forest area, the camp is bordered by a huge lake and, like all Wisconsin and Minnesota sites, came complete with wood ticks, garter and bull snakes, and a full complement of hungry mosquitoes.

Somewhere the troop acquired a humongous army squad tent, weighing a ton and resembling an olive-drab, single-pole tipi. It held eight cots comfortably or half of the troop on the floor in sleeping bags. At summer camp, I learned, the troop's junior leaders appropriated this edifice as their bastion. Younger kids entered only on the threat of annihilation. Upon arrival, I was informed that the Senior Scouts were honoring me by reserving a cot in there for me. At my young age, I was never sure whether the older kids regarded me as one of them or as an adult leader. I was afraid this invitation skewed their view of me in the wrong direction. But when I crawled into my sleeping bag that night and found it stuffed with pine cones, I was looking more like an adult leader. The next morning the Senior Patrol Leader hesitatingly asked me how I slept. With the never-ending chatter and laughter, I mentioned that sleeping in that canvas carnival was like going to bed in a nightclub. If that monstrosity has not completely decayed, to this day it is probably referred to as The Nightclub.

The real jolt hit the next day. Sitting at a picnic table near the center of our campsite, Lloyd nonchalantly announced that he and his family were leaving in a month for Africa as educational missionaries. Naturally I was curious which of the other assistants would take over the troop. After all, I was the newest, youngest, most naive, and least experienced. In his slow, deliberate manner, Lloyd drawled, "Well, it looks like you." I sat speechless. "You see," he continued, "when I told the other guys I was leaving, they not only turned it down, they resigned."

Resigned! Instantly I knew what ventricular fibrillation feels like.

"Lloyd!" I was probably shouting. "I've been an assistant for less than four months; that's my total leadership experience. You're asking me to take on 50 kids as their Scoutmaster, with no help?" The only time I felt so jelly-legged was on my first 60-foot rappel. Hadn't the irate wife of one of Lloyd's predecessor Scoutmasters stormed down and resigned for him? With three weekend campouts and a summer camp absence from home already under my belt, how was my wife going to handle this news?

I hadn't accepted this rapid advancement when Lloyd announced it to the kids before we broke camp for home. They seemed delighted. I was hooked. On the long ride home, my head gyrated with ideas: how to train leaders, better advancement methods (we didn't have an Eagle Scout yet), and more exciting campouts. Why not start an Indian Dance Group? More important, I needed to get help!

Well, I thought, I suppose I could try it. Who knows? I might like it!

Lloyd and his brave corps of assistants departed, and it took two meetings alone with 50 hyperactive orangutans to realize that being the sole leader wasn't going to fly. We had no program, no discipline, no junior leadership and a young, inexperienced Scoutmaster whom many of the Scouts considered to be one of the boys rather than an adult leader. Noise levels rivaled jet takeoffs. Dads pulled into the parking lot to drop off their boys while their cars were still moving! Their face said it all: "Thank God I don't have to stay!" Thirty minutes after my first meeting started, my voice disintegrated to gravel simply trying to maintain some semblance of order. Every ounce of energy was expended simply keeping this galloping herd from demolishing the church. Like magicians, they'd evaporate from the meeting room, invading every nook in that building. One keyboard wizard even tried a little boogie on the church organ! By the end of the first meeting, I was spent!

Following meeting number two, I fired off a letter to the parents stating that further troop meetings were on hold until I had three assistants and a full troop committee, which was a brassy move for a new, young Scoutmaster, but it worked. The phone rang with volunteers, and we never missed a meeting.

A Philosophical Clue from "Field Marshal" Franz

Slowly the combined troops began to gel. We had solid patrols, a program, and began training junior leaders. One of the new assistants was a dad named Fred Nixon. When it came to discipline, Fred was a mean machine, despite his small physical stature. The flighty 50 were slowly coming under control. But it took a one-night import from Hungary to completely cool their demeanor.

Franz, a war refugee, worked for me as a technical writer. His noontime stories were spellbinders. He had been a Scout and

Scout leader in Hungary before World War II, but when the Nazis overran his country, Franz was conscripted into the German Army and sent eastward to where few Germans wanted to venture: the Russian front. One bitter cold morning while advancing on what he thought was an evacuated Russian bunker, everything suddenly heated up, literally, when he caught the business end of a Russian flamethrower directly in the face. For two months he lay in a German hospital, his face bandaged except for a "breathing hole" and "eating hole," as he called them. The result was a badly scarred and distorted face. Fortunately, his war face didn't seem to bother Franz. In a way, it was his badge of courage. And it made an impression on the rowdy little Scouts of Troop 186.

Franz agreed to perform a uniform and proficiency inspection. I waited outside on the evening he arrived. Stepping out of his car, Franz looked like Field Marshall Rommel, smartly dressed in his old Hungarian Scout uniform with medals, even carrying a swagger stick. His dark-brown eyes shouted, "I mean business." Inside, Assistant Scoutmaster Fred lined up the troop by patrols and prepared them for inspection. But judging by the rumble vibrating out of the room, the Troop didn't seem to be taking this inspection seriously. I swung open the meeting-room door for Franz, and he strode in, stiff and erect. He looked briefly from side to side, slapping his swagger stick lightly against his leg. It was as though someone had just pulled the amplifier plug on the Grateful Dead. Mouths snapped shut, and eyes bulged. Fred called the troop to attention, and heels clicked. He gave a dress right and front command, and you could nearly hear eyeballs click. One little guy started hyperventilating so badly I thought I might have to put a bag over his head to maintain his CO_2 level. The ranks froze (except for mouthy little Ollie Frederick who took nothing seriously and had his mouth pressed tightly shut trying desperately to suppress a belly laugh).

Following a brief introduction, Franz moved to the first patrol leader and began bombarding him with questions in his harsh, baritone, Zsa Zsa Gabor accent. Methodically, he moved through the patrol, staring down each and every jittery lad and firing curt questions and comments. "How long have you bin a Scout? Vy are you only a Tendervoot? Do you veel your patrol leader does a goot job? Vy?" Shaky Scouts answered: "Yes, sir," "No, sir," "I think so, sir." They hadn't used that many "sirs" in their entire existence. By the end of the hour, even Ollie looked as though he had just survived a three-day algebra test.

Before departing that evening, Franz moved to the center of the room, removed his hat, and—framed with a melancholy, far-away expression—began describing his Scouting adventures in Hungary. He recounted how little they had, but how much they accomplished simply with the right attitude, spirit, and sense of true comradeship. He described the coming of the Germans and his dreadful war experiences. Then in hushed, somber tones, he told them how lucky they were to be born in America where they were free. But he reminded them that freedom comes with a price. And to be free, they must be responsible Scouts, responsible citizens.

His words became my motto throughout the rest of my Scouting years. Whether we were camping, backpacking, attending troop meetings, canoeing a river, or climbing a mountain, my operating framework became: *"The freedom you'll have depends on the level of responsibility you show."* In one hour, Franz brought a new level of discipline, spirit, and teamwork to Troop 186.

Left Behind in a Surprise Blizzard

Now that I lived in the densely populated Twin Cities, locating remote, yet accessible, camping spots was as easy as finding an ocean beach. Thanks to the Northern States Power Company, owners of a large tract of wooded land in western Wisconsin that they generously opened to Scouts, we didn't have to punch out too many miles to be able to practice our trade: pitching tents, cooking over open fires, and marauding the woods. This was all in the name of learning to survive gracefully in the wilderness, and in general, just having a blast away from the hustle of the city. Troop 186 spent one whole Saturday designing and lashing its very first signal tower, a 25 footer with a tilt resembling the Tower of Pisa. Obviously, they hadn't yet achieved my old troop's pioneering skills, but it stood, and they were proud. Best of all, they were now working as a team. Bobby Ramsey, Steve Dahlgren, Tom Rysgard, and Jimmy Nixon; the Donahaues, Johnsons, and Beutows; and little freckle-faced Bobby Worra— this was the core of what would become a great Scout troop. Incidentally, during this period, I finally had a boy of my own.

A late-October Saturday morning in camp started out clear and sunny, a perfect autumn day. By mid-afternoon, ominous clouds rolled across the St. Croix River, and temperatures took a nosedive. Snow piled up several inches an hour. Here we were, deep in the Power Company's forest land entertaining a bunch of young, inexperienced boys, most of whom were ill-equipped for Alaska-style adventure.

As usual, parents had dropped off kids and returned home, leaving us short of vehicles to pull off a full-scale evacuation. We decided to load as many boys as possible into the few cars we had brought, sans gear, and get them home. This left me and five older boys to ride out this early winter storm until morning or until someone could plow their way through snowed-in back roads to reach us. A vicious northwest wind bit into our faces and hands as we struggled to stash the excess sleeping bags and food into several small tents. We decided it was wiser for the six of us to keep our body heat centrally located in one large tent, rather than to separate into the smaller two-man tents.

The wind gusts were testing my ten-by-ten cabin tent, but with six pairs of cold and able hands, we stabilized it and snuggled inside. The wind whistled like sirens and, combined with the slapping of the canvas, we could hardly communicate. With six guys in the tent, exhaled breath vapor resembled Bay Area fog. By dark my thermometer hanging outside on a branch retreated to well below zero, and those were the days before we considered wind-chill factor!

The contents of our single five-gallon water container were shifting from liquid to solid when we elevated the container to tent-mate status. A fired-up Coleman stove tossed off an amazing amount of heat. And, to keep things simple, we stuck with a hot-water menu: soup, oatmeal, and hot chocolate (served in that order in the same cups). Everyone seemed full, in good spirits, and ready to warm up in the sack. But sleeping in this temperature proved challenging.

In those days in Minnesota, you purchased a sleeping bag that wouldn't bake you in the summer heat and humidity. In winter you were supposed to be smart enough to bed down in a cabin with a fireplace. But Scouting ingenuity came to the rescue. We discovered that two sets of bags would zip together and fit three guys each. This offered far better distribution of body heat, and the extra bag could go on top as a blanket. Adorned with wool hats and warm clothes, we snuggled in for a long winter's nap. It worked. We slept and stayed warm. And halfway through the night, we learned to roll over in unison.

By morning the storm subsided, but the degree of sag in the tent roof gave testimony to our situation. The nighttime snow inundated us. Someone stuck his head out to check the thermometer and said it looked like the mercury had drained out. Even wrapped in an extra sleeping bag, the water in the container was beginning to clink. It looked like a good day to snuggle deep into the bags. Chitchat shifted to the topic of our rescue. One pessimist muttered, "They'll never reach us in all this snow," while Ollie the optimist replied, "Hey, we might end up on TV!"

Less than an hour passed when a muffled hum in the distance grew louder, and then came a long blast of a horn. With everyone trying to exit the bags simultaneously, we looked like a scene from *The Three Stooges* movies. With snow flying, Fred Nixon led the charge with his service station snowplow, followed by a station wagon and pickup truck complete with thermos bottles of hot cocoa and coffee. We knocked down and packed up in short order and everyone was happy, other than the Optimist. "Didn't anyone even think to contact WCCO?"

An Old Lady, a Bloody Axe, and a Cold Dish of Revenge

Halloween was a fun time in Roseville, Minnesota, and an exciting time with the troop. Most of the troop would hit my house on Halloween night, then criticize me if I didn't dole out at least a half dozen candy bars to each kid. One Halloween I dug out an old Frankenstein mask I had used in high school to create a few "bumps in the night." I slipped on a black turtleneck sweater and hid behind a bush next to my front door. The twitter of several voices coming down the street sounded familiar: guys I would love to scare into oblivion. They approached my house quietly. When the door bell sounded, the Frankenstein monster slowly eased up from behind the bush emitting a low, vibrant, guttural snarl. But instead of finding a handful of guys from Troop 186, there stood a little five-year-old boy in a Mickey Mouse mask, frozen into a catatonic coma with the front of his trousers getting wetter by the second. The wiseacre Scouts, anticipating a Halloween prank, sent one of their unsuspecting little brothers to ring the bell and be on the receiving end of whatever Halloween "treat" I planned to dole out. But I got even during the troop's Halloween campout the following weekend.

An old, deserted farmhouse and dilapidated, weather-worn barn stood a half mile north of our favorite camping site on the Power Company's land. I lubricated their imaginations with a few haunted-house stories about the place to help enhance things yet to come. With the help of several older Scouts, this was the night to confirm our suspicions about that desolate old dwelling!

To make the visit more personal, we escorted only six boys

at a time to the house where my fabricated tragic incident occurred: the farmer's wife had been brutally axed to death by her husband, coincidentally about this time of year. This horror took place in the early 1900s. As legend had it (I recounted), her spirit returned to visit her old home from time to time. In fact, I affirmed, local legend suggests that her ghost was responsible for some bizarre murders of her husband's relatives who resided on nearby farms.

Lights were *verboten* on the long hike through the dark, shadowy forest. We spoke only in whispers. The haunting hoot of a distant owl rode on a chilly, light breeze, complementing the crackling sound of boots treading on a carpet of dry, autumn leaves. One little voice whispered, "I think I want to go back." He was soon dissuaded. We walked into the clearing where the small, boxlike house stood dark and lonely in the sporadic illumination of the moon, which was peeking in and out of layers of thick autumn clouds.

Squatting quietly in the darkness, we reconnoitered the house and the old barn. No lights, no sounds; it was empty. We found a cellar window was open so I slipped through the window and onto a small, wooden table and helped the others ease in before turning on my flashlight. It had been a fruit cellar at one time, dug under a small portion of the house with a dusty, wooden stairway standing at one end. Bobby Worra was in on this Halloween sham. With a finger pressed to his lips he said softly, "Listen." A faint rhythmic squeaking came from the floorboards directly above our heads. Ollie started to back out the window, but Bobby grabbed him, whispering that we were all in this thing together. Leading the way, Bobby headed slowly up the steps with the rest cramped tightly behind, not wanting to be left alone in the dark cellar.

We emerged into a small pantry next to the kitchen. The squeaking had subsided. Walking into the kitchen, we saw a large, wooden door with a faint glimmer of light showing underneath. Cracking open the door an inch or two, I saw a short, red candle glowing on the mantel of a stone fireplace on the opposite wall. Brave Bobby said, "Let me look," sticking his head into the room. "I don't see anybody. Come on in." We filed in cautiously. Old oak furniture stood at the edges of the room. A picture of the American flag hung on one wall. Two worn throw rugs covered a small portion of the wooden floor. We had just begun questioning how the candle could be lit when we heard squeaking in an adjacent room to our right. Flipping on my flashlight, I illuminated a human figure shifting back and forth in a rocking chair. She was dressed in long, black garb, and a knitted, black shawl covered her shaggy, gray hair. Her face and hands were chalk white. On her long, pointed nose rested a pair of pinch-type spectacles, magnifying her dark, foreboding eyes. The Scouts froze. I shifted the light downward to expose a rusty axe in her right hand with what appeared to be traces of blood. "Let's go!" I yelled in near panic, but as we turned, the kitchen door slammed shut. Bobby banged against it, but it wouldn't budge. Her rocking became more violent. "Try the front door!" I screamed. Locked. But a large latch slipped open easily, and we dashed out onto the porch just as Bobby yelled, "She's coming!"

As the gasping, heart-pounding covey of overwrought adventurers stampeded into the yard, Bobby yelled, "Head for the barn!" Unable to question the logic of any orders at this time, the scared little devils bolted 40 yards to the open barn door and stormed inside, waiting for Bobby and me to arrive. One boy turned, and there in the shadows hung a huge body, dangling lifeless from a rope. (Even I didn't know about this one! The older Scouts had rigged a harness and suspended Steve Dahlgren in a hanging scene so realistic that it gave me a jolt.) The barn emptied in a frenzied exit. Fearful that someone might dash out and vanish forever into the dense Wisconsin woods, we quickly corralled the covey in the yard, wished them Happy Halloween, and watched their expressions shift from fear to embarrassment at being duped. Still baffled they asked, "Okay, but who was that old woman?"

After agreeing not to expose this ruse to their buddies, they headed back to camp drained, but happy. Sound sleep was not the norm for the group that night.

They were still babbling about it come morning. "Who was that old lady, Sholzie?"

"Darned if I know," winking at Jack Hockelmeyer, who with his pointed nose was resting silently against a tree.

Some things about boys may have changed since I was a Scout, but certainly not the fun in having the "begangles" scared out of them.

4

THE BEAT GOES ON: CREATING A NEW TRIBE OF INDIAN DANCERS

The Birth of a Tribe

As in most large cities, St. Paul's gigantic Indianhead Council boasted hundreds of outstanding Scouting units. With the big Scout Show only months away, we needed to get innovative and do something to give our troop an identity, to make it stand out while helping these kids gain a sense of pride and accomplishment. What would be more colorful, flashy, and noisy—and stand out more—than an Indian dance troupe?

I found myself in a familiar dilemma. I'd been a Scout in a good troop but had never led one. I'd been an Indian dancer in a good group, but had never taught it. Realistically, it would take a year to field a dance group of kids. We had three months. The patrol leaders greeted the idea with scowling faces and hunched shoulders. My mistake, I mentioned it was going to take some real work; for that age group, *work* is a nasty four-letter word. Some of the boys actually seemed embarrassed by the thought of dressing and dancing like an Indian. So I reverted to old stories of the fun and adventure, dug up pictures of the famous Koshare Indian dancers, and with the core of support we had with the younger boys, I felt we pocketed enough interest to pull it off.

I hunted for books on Indian lore and dances and sent the kids in search of beads, buckskin, ribbon, and feathers. They became so focused I was concerned for the geese at Como Lake. The boys who wanted to dance would dance; others could help make a drum, spears, shields, and other props. Our upcoming deadline became a friend rather than a foe.

When it was time for the first dance practice, we still had no drum. We tipped over a plastic wastepaper basket, and we fished out a long-handled, wooden spoon from the church kitchen for the drumstick. This combination created the tonal quality of a ripe grapefruit, but it made noise.

Now, who wanted to drum? So many hands went up we could have formed a drum corps, yet not one of them could generate a steady dance beat. The guy with the spoon-banging that most closely resembled a drum beat won. I arranged the rest of the guys in a large circle and demonstrated a basic toe-heel step: up on one toe on the hard beat, drop the heel, and lift the other foot on the soft beat. Looking up, I couldn't believe what I saw. Before the beat even started, they were stomping around the floor, flopping their arms, and slapping their hands against their mouths with that phony Indian hoot. It looked like a convention of inebriated Minnesota loons. When the drumming actually started, this only exacerbated the situation. Some were down so low they were virtually duck-walking. One guy stretched up onto his toes with arms extended; all he needed was a tutu to star in *Swan Lake*. I considered asking for help from a Winnebago friend in Black River Falls, but realized this bunch could seriously damage the entire region's relations with Native Americans. How many weeks did we have before the Scout Show?

Costume construction was encouraging. Moms were sewing, and the Grey Owl Indian Supply in New York was making a mint from Troop 186 orders. The kids were going to look good, but the dancing... we had a problem. So I shifted to smaller dance classes to give more individualized attention, and that worked.

Rummaging through a St. Paul bookstore, I discovered a book describing hundreds of interpretive dances, most of which were far too complex to assimilate in the few remaining weeks. So I stuck with several simple, although rinky-dink, dances described in Ben Hunt's *The Complete Book of Indian Crafts and Lore*: a buffalo dance, the Apache Devil dance, an eagle dance, and a shield dance. Beyond that, we could fake a couple of pow-wow dances to fill any remaining time.

The Scout Show was held at the Hippodrome, a coliseum-type building at the Minnesota State Fair Grounds. The festivities began on Friday evening, and then troops camped at the fair-grounds overnight with the show continuing through Saturday. Each unit was assigned a booth to display their particular wares or talents, and we drew a ten-foot space on an outside corridor. This was hardly enough room for three dancers, much less 15. Our new drum was ready, the costumes looked great, and with a tinge of apprehension, the dancers were ready to perform. "But where should we dance?" they asked. I told them to dance in the aisles. Three warning beats of the drum sounded, and the tinkle of bells ushered in Troop 186's first dance performance.

The newly finished drum reverberated like thunder through the cavernous corridors of the Hippodrome, and all 15 dancers, complete with feather bustles, lances, and shields, commenced their performance with a buffalo dance before a handful of curious onlookers. The sound of the drum and tinkling bells drew people like flies to a watermelon; within moments, the dancers were surrounded by a crowd six deep. When the old buffalo finally dropped and died on cue, the response was not only applause but whistles and cheers. And they wanted more! I stood back with the pride you feel when you just learned you've just become a father. I watched as the boys huddled around the drummer, so pumped up, so excited. Within moments the Happy Warrior stomped out, only to be dropped by the evil magic of the Apache Devil. They barely stopped dancing from 6:00 until 10:00 p.m. And guess who showed up? The TV cameras from WCCO! Yes, Ollie, they finally made it.

After four hours with the roar of that thunder drum bashing against my ear drums, the vibrations rattling around in my head were about to split it right down the middle. Fred said he'd get the kids into the tents, and I drove home for aspirin and a little snooze. When I finally woke from my evening nap, it was nearly 2:00 in the morning. With the headache gone, I hopped in the car and headed south on Snelling Avenue, back to the fairgrounds to spend the rest of the night with the kids. Just as I was about to turn into the camporee site, my headlights flashed on a young boy wandering down the middle of four lanes. St. Paul's Snelling Avenue is no quiet, little country road. It's a dangerous thoroughfare. As I drove closer, I realized this boy was a Scout, because he had on his hat, shirt, and neckerchief—but that was it! Below his waist, he was bare-butt naked. Cars whizzed past him on both sides. I quickly pulled in behind him, jumped out of the car, and grabbed him by his arm. "What in blazes are you doing out here?" He said nothing. His eyes were a pair of glass marbles. This little guy was sound asleep!

I hustled him into the car and drove to the camporee headquarters tent but found no one. Fortunately, I spotted a layout map of troop locations tacked on a bulletin board. The troop number was on the boy's shirt, and within moments we stood in front of the largest tent in that section. Scoutmasters typically had the biggest tent. (I was an exception, since I vowed never again to sleep in the "Nightclub." It's hard to knock on a tent, and I wasn't even sure I had the right unit. I woke up this Scoutmaster, asked his troop number, and it matched my sleepwalker. I stuck my head in and asked if he was missing any kids. I could nearly see the disgusted look on his face in the dark. He informed me, in an exceptionally polite tone, that his Scouts were all sound asleep in their tents—just like he wanted to be. I agreed they were all sound asleep all right, but one had been cooling his heels (and a little more) on Snelling Avenue. That jerked his chain. In seconds, this big bruiser in jockey shorts came storming out of his tent with flashlight in hand. Shining the light in the lad's face he yelled, "Tony, what the heck are you doing out here this time of night in full uniform?"

"Sir," I said, "if you drop the beam of your flashlight, you'll find he's not quite in *full* uniform."

When his light dipped south of Tony's shirttail, he sighed, "Holy smoke! And you found him in the middle of Snelling like this?" I confirmed that and told him he was every bit as awake then as he is now—still fast asleep. He thanked me; gave me a limp, embarrassed hand shake; and led poor Tony back to his sleeping bag. If he was smart, he would have lashed one of Tony's legs to a tent stake.

Saturday was a big day for the dancers, with big crowds giving them big hands. Late in the afternoon, the Indianhead Council presented our guys with the Big Ribbon for Distinction and Excellence. The long hours of practice and creating costumes paid off, and Indian Dancing was now a trademark of Troop 186.

Water Wizards and Frosty Snakes

When the time for summer camp rolled around, nearly every 186er chomped at the bit to go. We always managed to scare up a couple of bucks for those who had a hard time affording the fee, so the whole troop could go. Our trademark tent, The Nightclub, would rise like a mystic monument surrounded by a host of green sidewall tents. Old Glory waved from the top of a stripped-white pine pole, and the troop flag, now adorned with a colorful array of battle ribbons, hung proudly in the entryway of our campsite.

Tomahawk Scout Reservation, with its magnificent waterfront, was the site of myriad swimming and canoeing contests. The Scouts of Troop 186 were a long way from being experts at everything, but when it came to water, most of these guys had gills. In canoes, they would zip across the lake as though they had a 50-horsepower Mercury on the stern. It didn't make any difference whether they were using paddles or their hands. Competitive? Add the word *contest* to an event, and they'd move so fast you'd think their lives were at stake. Whether the victory prize was a broken oar or the usual watermelon, no other troop had a chance. We consumed so many victory watermelons I used to worry that the kids would dampen sleeping bags. One year we even whipped the undefeated staff at their own game: softball. Afterward I thought we might have to find a new camp! If the swimming and canoeing victories hadn't turned this gang into a cement-solid troop, the softball victory clinched it. I saw it in the way they began to treat each other, the spring in their steps, the confidence in their eyes. We were going home with a troop on the move.

Water Wizards of Troop 186, Roseville, MN 1960

One of the fun traditions at Tomahawk was Indian dancing by Order of the Arrow staff members. And now they were playing to the critical eyes of Troop 186 dancers. We learned the Pueblo belt dance by watching these guys, but their specialty was the Hopi Snake Dance, in which dancers carry live snakes in their mouths. This is one of the most primitive of all Native American rituals, considered by most Anglos to be a weird, grotesque, and fascinating ceremony. Naturally, this was the night the kids waited for. They would walk by the snake cage at the nature lodge to gawk, and then shudder to think of one of those slimy critters writhing between their jaws.

Unbeknownst to the campers, the Order of the Arrow dance group only had one guy brave enough to put that slithering bull snake in his mouth. And two days prior to their evening performance this dancer was called home on an emergency. The whole camp was expecting a snake dance, yet the group couldn't muster up an eager mouth from the entire staff. Whether they drew straws or corralled an unwilling volunteer, we didn't know, but we were told the dance was on. We were about to witness one of the strangest performances in the annals of either real or interpretive Indian dancing.

It was a warm, mosquito-swatting evening. The sun had set, but a faint, orange glow still filtered through the mass of pine and deciduous trees west of the campfire area. Even a loon was tuning up—the Minnesota state bird. (Someone once suggested making the wood tick the state insect, so Minnesota could be the "Loon-a-Tick State.")

A torch-toting brave approached from the forest and stared harshly at the hundreds of Scouts and leaders sitting in a giant semicircle around the campfire. He plunged the torch into a pile of crisscrossed logs. Soon the flames surged up and out, creating a campfire bright enough to read by. After a score of rousing Scout songs and skits, a drum echoed from the trees, and a hush fell over the crowd. Hoots and screams pierced the silence and the troupe of painted warriors stormed in and began stomp-dancing, powwow style.

For the next half hour, the Order of the Arrow presented an accomplished mix of Plains and Southwestern Indian dances. The time finally arrived for the Hopi Snake Dance, and you could feel the excitement.

The drummers began vocalizing a high-pitched chant accompanied by a slow, methodic drum beat. They sang for nearly a minute, yet no dancers appeared. Finally two dancers, dressed in the skirt-like costume of the Hopi, short-stepped in. Each carried the feather fans of a *hugger*, those who stroke the snake's head and distract it. But there was no snake dancer. They made one pass around the dance area, and two more dancers appeared, moving slowly in the shadows. As they moved out of the shadows, the fading light of the fire illuminated another hugger and the snake dancer. But wait... what was that in his mouth? It looked like a snake, but it stuck nearly straight out from both sides of his mouth like a small broomstick! We sat mesmerized. It didn't wriggle. It hardly budged. The dancer looked more like an Indian flute player tooting on the center of the flute. He made a single pass around the group, while one of the huggers brushed the head of the snake with his feather fan. The snake dancer disappeared quickly into the shadows where we heard a distinctive hacking, like someone spitting out a chicken bone!

The story didn't break until morning. After the regular snake dancer left for home, the staff coerced one of the younger counselors-in-training to step up. The poor kid was probably afraid to refuse. But it was all he could do just to pick up a snake, much less tote it around between his pearly whites.

But let's give credit where credit's due. He may have been a gutless wonder, but he wasn't dumb. An hour before the dance, he sneaked into the camp kitchen and loaded this two-foot bull snake into the refrigerator. By dance time the poor, cold-blooded creature was stiff as a rain pipe. The purpose of this Hopi dance is to encourage rain. Under these circumstances, we're fortunate we didn't suffer a midsummer blizzard!

The Pain of Goodbye

At the onset, I didn't expect to last more than two meetings. Five years whistled by. The troop still numbered over 50, with a solid group of junior leaders. George Wright joined us as an Assistant Scoutmaster, and we had 11 guys just a wing flap or two from becoming Eagle Scouts. The dancers remained active and a signature for Troop 186.

Since we had so many older boys, we decided to develop an emergency service Explorer Post under the leadership of Fred Nixon. This seemed logical—they needed a challenge, and most were already first-aid hotshots eager to expand their knowledge of emergency care and assistance. It also spared the troop from conducting programs at two distinct levels, yet kept these guys nearby for junior leadership assistance. Well, what sounded like a great plan completely fell apart. Much to my personal disappointment, only two of those talented Life Scouts returned to the troop to complete their Eagle: Jimmy Nixon and Steve Dahlgren. That saddened me. Soon I would be leaving the troop, and I had hoped to see this honor bestowed on all the young men who so richly deserved it.

A job change and move placed me 30 miles away from the troop instead of one block. But even with the prospect of a long drive, making the decision to drop this unit was difficult. My decision was soon simplified when a pending move to Colorado became a reality in September 1963. I'd always wanted to live in Colorado. A post-Navy summer in Wyoming had injected me with a solid dose of "Rocky Mountain fever."

The details of that last meeting with Troop 186 escape me, although I remember that I wanted to fade out quietly without much hullabaloo and turn the reins over to George Wright, knowing the troop would be in good hands. I remember a few hugs and hand shakes, and then the long drive across the Twin

Cities with eyes partially clouded with tears. I always seemed to develop closer relationships with people, adults, and kids who share my strong feelings for nature and the outdoors. I would miss them and think of them often.

Also, I pondered the question, "What did I learn from this experience?" (My mind always plays this game.) The answers:

1. Charlotte was right; I liked it. This close association with kids had taught me more about life, people, and myself than I had ever experienced. I grew.

2. Never run a Troop of 50-plus kids alone—no way, no how!

3. Young Scoutmasters face special problems. They lack maturity, so older kids treat them as one of themselves. Soon the younger ones follow suit, and before long you've lost control. On the other hand, I watched hard-nosed, whistle-blowing, authoritarian Scoutmasters in action, which tended to result in a general negative demeanor in their kids. The secret was learning to walk that fine line between being one of the kids and being an adult leader. That way, you can mix it up with them, which they really like (after all, how many teachers or parents abandon that "Big me-Little you" management style?). Yet when you needed to shift into an adult leadership role, the kids can handle that and react positively. This fine line is not always easy to locate, but it certainly proved an ideal way to operate a troop.

4. Have more than enough activities to keep the kids busy from the time they walk through the door into a meeting until they head for home. If not, watch out.

5. Most kids come into Scouts to be entertained and to have fun, certainly not to learn. Heck, they spend all day in school learning. Teaching has to be sneaky, so they go home smarter but think they were entertained.

6. Develop an outdoor program that provides adventure, skills, and an appreciation (if not love) of nature.

7. Finally, help the troop develop an identity, so in a group of
    troops, it easily stands out. Identity and troop individualism
    develop cohesiveness and pride.

My focus would now shift westward to a new job, new friends,
and a new life. My son was now three, and I felt it was time to take
a break from Scouting until he was old enough to get involved.
But somehow, things never quite turn out as you plan.

5

GO WEST, YOUNG MAN: SCOUTING ADVENTURES IN THE ROCKIES

The Reluctant Transplants

The move to Denver proved tough on everyone. Family and friends were less than enthusiastic with our decision. In September 1963, I kissed family members goodbye and boarded a plane bound for an unfamiliar country over 1,000 miles from the region we had always known as home. My three kids looked confused as I waved while walking to the plane. Char remained puzzled as to why anyone in their right mind would leave Minnesota's 10,000 beautiful lakes to dwell in the dust and the dryness of the West.

Nearly three months passed before Char sold the house and the family could join me. On November 22, 1963, as I entered Denver's Stapleton Airport to head back and help pack up the house, I noticed scores of people huddled around radios and TVs—President Kennedy had been shot and killed in Dallas. With the subsequent, continuous news reports of the assassination, Lee Harvey Oswald's shooting, and the emotional toll of watching a president's funeral that week, it wasn't easy to find time to pack. After a Thanksgiving meal and final goodbyes with the family, the five of us finally made our way across the Plains and settled in a little brick house on Hickory Street in Littleton, Colorado.

A Troop with a "Little Problem"
Hoodwinks a New Scoutmaster

That winter a blond woman with a big, broad smile moseyed passed our house with her children on cross-country skis and met Char. Hope Bakken was a charmer, and soon she and Char became close friends. Come early summer when Char took the kids to Minnesota on vacation, Hope's husband, Jack called me. Hope had told him I had been a Scoutmaster, and Jack served as a Boy Scout Neighborhood Commissioner in the Littleton area. Jack approached me, confirmed that I had, indeed, been a Scoutmaster and told me about a troop in Littleton that was facing some problems. He wondered if I would join him next Monday evening and perhaps, "with my years of experience," we could detect the problem.

The following Monday Jack drove me to a small, red-brick Baptist church bordered by a park and a handful of tennis courts. The first thing I looked for was basketball courts, but there were none around. So my first potential-trouble theory evaporated. A door near the parking lot led to the basement stairs. Upon opening the door, I was reintroduced to a noise level with which I had become all too familiar. It didn't take a wizard to detect the problem. They had no Scoutmaster! Plus, these 30 kids were trying to start an Indian dance group. I'd been duped. Like a fly, I had been brought right up to fly paper. So when Char returned home, guess who inherited another Scout troop and a possible date in the divorce courts?

Troop 117 was not a new group. It traced its lineage to 1928, one of Littleton's first troops and operating under the number 112. Shortly after World War II, the troop disbanded for several years due to lack of leadership before returning with the new number. In its early history, Troop 112 had produced only one Eagle, Howard Higby, a true gentleman, who became a professional Scouter. Two boys in the current troop had completed their Eagle requirements.

On the following Monday, in the heat of summer, I was introduced to these boys as their new Scoutmaster, assisted by a former Scoutmaster, Irv Johnson. The reception tingled with the enthusiasm of the first wife meeting her ex-husband's new bride. These guys liked their old leader and were sad to see him depart. Their body language, especially that of the older boys, told me they were not ready to accept me. Being an unruly bunch, I suspect that my "responsibility is the price of freedom" philosophy had the elevation potential of a sand-filled balloon. The ringleader of their revolution was none other than the handsome, blond son of the preacher. What is it about preachers' kids anyway? Maybe they feel they already have a free bus token to the Great Beyond regardless of what little nincompoops they choose to be. Holding tight rein on the Baptist kids in the unit, he orchestrated ditching me on mountain hikes; maintained an aloof, abrasive demeanor at every meeting and troop function; and went out of his way to torpedo any activity I suggested.

I've heard that trying to convert a Baptist was a tough job, and this applied to Scoutmasters. Nothing seemed to work with this guy. Then, like divine intervention, his dad was transferred to a church out of town. With the revolutionary catalyst gone, the remaining Baptist kids slowly mellowed and fused with the troop with the help my Baptist Assistant Scoutmaster Irv Johnson, backed by an older Scout, Brad Kershaw, and his dad, Leon Kershaw. The transition seemed complete and, after six months, Troop 117 began to gel into a team.

The Massacre at Peaceful Valley:
New Indian Dancers Proudly Flash
their Feathers and Take the Title

During 1964 and 1965, 32 new boys headed down the basement steps, including the next Kershaw, the Knights, Trujillos, the Trevithick brothers, and a bespectacled kid named Hendricks, who moved in from Montana, so *Montana* became his new moniker. Ed Knight joined us as an assistant, while Mark Bayci and Brad Kershaw completed requirements for Life Scout. One night, a roly-poly we called Copey received his Tenderfoot Award along with another boy I'll never forget, Neil Mortenson. Mort would worm his way into my vehicle after a campout and, at a major intersection, would suspend his body halfway out the window screaming, "Help! Help! The mean hag's got me and won't let me go!" Meanwhile, this "hag" slithered down in the driver's seat, hoping he couldn't be identified.

Four great troops, the *Big Four*, as they were called, met within a half mile of us. These power units in Littleton included: Troop 444 under the able leadership of Stan Bush, which housed over 100 kids at the Presbyterian church (well beyond the comprehension of one who felt 50 was a madhouse); its sister troop, 344, which also met at the Presbyterian church; and Troops 114 and 314, which met at the Methodist church just two blocks north. As Troop 117 grew in size and stature, the term *Big Five* became common and complimentary.

After those Minnesota years, the thought of organizing another Indian dance group created acute abdominal cramps. But this troop already had a small core of kids who knew their right foot from their left, plus they weren't all blond. We actually had some dark-haired, brown-eyed, copper-skinned kids who looked the part. The Worley boys and Johnny Miller looked as though they could have come from the Pine Ridge Indian Reservation. Brad Kershaw made a great chief and along with Copey, Montana, Terry Collins, Dave Wright (a new Texas import), Steve Weir, and a handful of others, Troop 117 proudly walked away with the Award of Distinction and Excellence at Denver's annual Scout Show. With the award came a special invitation to perform at the dedication of the Denver Area Council's huge new Peaceful Valley Scout Ranch, 50 miles southeast of Denver.

This was a big affair. Colorado Governor John Love was scheduled to speak, along with a variety of other political and Scouting notables. Arriving early, we set up our tipi, slipped on our full regalia, and awaited instructions. The program commenced with a pageant depicting the story of this historical land beginning with the Plains Indians who inhabited the area, followed by early settlers, then ranchers. We were asked to perform several dances at the beginning of the show, then disappear behind a stone wall. On cue, our Indians were to charge out and attack a handful of settlers laboring in the fields.

Wasechie Dancers Dedicating Peaceful Valley Scout
Ranch, June 1966

A blazing June sun blanketed this treeless segment of the western prairie with no hope of a reprieve. Suit coats pealed off and tie knots slid away from necks. Bullets of sweat dribbled down our faces long before the first drum beat sounded. Yet the dancing went great; these guys knew how to tap moccasins. Scott, my six-year-old son, looking dapper in his red breechcloth, vest, and feather roach, had danced with us once or twice before. He may have been too young for Scouts, but Scotty already knew how to move his feet and body to the throb of the drum. In the first dance, Copey (who was built like a buffalo) did his dying buffalo dance with finesse. Next was a stomp powwow dance that showcased the troupe's exceptional dancing skill. It took a good eye to tell these pretenders from the real thing. We then vanished behind the wall and waited for our attack cue.

While hurriedly fingering the script, I heard the key words and instantly cut loose a notable war whoop while motioning the guys to charge. A dozen painted faces stormed the field with spears and tomahawks in the business position. The unsuspecting settlers in homespun shirts and sodbuster boots raised their hoes in a hopeless defense while their sunbonnet-topped ladies grabbed their skirts and ran screaming from the stage area. The slaughter, fortunately, was fast and painless. The attackers then hurried away into the brush and trees. A roar of laughter and applause broke the silence of the slaughter. Frightened and standing in the center of the bedlam was our six-year-old warrior, Scotty. Confused by the cue, he started his attack a tad bit late and failed to retreat with the other warriors.

The fun afternoon set the stage at a place Troop 117 would spend many memorable days in the next quarter century.

Our small, handheld drum was painted with the name *Tacumsunish* on it. No one knew the origin of the name or its meaning. We decided to develop a new group name by combining two Lakota words, *wasechu*, meaning *white man*, and *wacipi*, meaning a *dance* or *powwow*. The two didn't combine comfortably, and the result was *Wasechie*: the Wasechie Indian dancers, a name that stuck through the entire 30-year life of the group.

Shortly after the pageant, where our attack hit the front page of the *Denver Post*, a member of a white Indian lore dance group offered to give us a drum, suggesting that we show up with a pickup truck. This was a drum—measuring six feet in diameter and constructed from a bull buffalo hide. And did it sing! During an indoor performance with six drummers hammering this thunder maker, we cracked three windows in the Grant Junior High School gymnasium. I still maintain that the reason I wear hearing aids today is due to a couple of decades of being in short range of that bellowing bull hide.

During 1966 and 1967, we tinkled our bells in over 70 performances, took second place in Littleton's massive Western Welcome parade, and continued to dance away with the top ribbons at the Denver Area Council Scout Show. Indian dancing became our troop's point of pride and top revenue producer.

A Heart-Pumping, High-Altitude Swim

The next summer, we chose a week at Boy Scout Camp Tahosa nestled high in the Colorado Rockies, knowing it soon would close as a summer camp due to the new Peaceful Valley Scout Ranch. Virtually every kid who Scouted in Denver did time at Tahosa, which held a warm spot in their hearts. But that was the only warm thing about Camp Tahosa. A short distance south of Rocky Mountain National Park, Tahosa sported an impressive altitude. One Sunday following the medical check-in, we marched down for the usual swim check at Tumblesome Lake, a beautiful body of clear, mountain water that mirrored the fluffy clouds that always seemed to develop as noontime approached.

Any fool should know that when you're seeing Engelmann spruce, you're breathing thin air. But not this dunce with Upper Midwest roots who shortly before arrived from Minnesota, the land of 10,000 lakes, and every one of them feels like bath water in the summer. Guess who was the first to jump in, feet first, to swim laps? The moment I hit that mass of liquid ice cubes, my cardiac drum beat shuddered. Literally breathless, I struggled to walk on water—all the way back to shore. A staff member looked down from the dock smiling, "Well, that's one way to enter this lake, sir, but we normally recommend moving in a little at a time." Thanks, buddy!

It was a great week, blue skies in the morning, rain by 2:00 p.m., sun shining again by 3:00 in the afternoon, and clear, crisp nights. Welcome to Colorado. Lots of merit badges were earned, although most boys were smarter than their Scoutmaster and opted to swim at a warm pool in town.

It's a Long Way to "Temporary"

As canoeing is to Minnesota, backpacking is to Colorado. Come late summer, a tough, mountain backpacking trip seemed appropriate. I knew backpacking was the direction I would take this troop, but here I was again, moving into uncharted territory. I didn't know mountain country, and I didn't know anything about backpacking. Neither did these guys. Another episode of the blind leading the blind.

Our chosen route started south of 14,000-foot Mount Evans. The plan was to work up to Roosevelt Lakes, climb Mount Evans (weather permitting), and then wander down toward the mountain town of Evergreen where our rides would be waiting. I anticipated problems, but not so quickly. After only 30 minutes on a breath-grabbing, uphill trail, Copey, our buffalo-belly Tenderfoot, whose navel corniced magnificently over the belt of his backpack, decided deep down in his heart, if not his stomach, that this nonsense wasn't for him. Stopping in the middle of the trail, he announced he was turning around and going straight home. That was impossible; our transportation had departed. We coaxed, appealed, and appeased. That worked as well as wet matches. Finally his moaning, groaning, stopping, and stomping prompted a trailside summit between Copey, several of the junior leaders, and me. We finally convinced him that the first telephone booth we came to, he could call home and ask for a pick up. Isn't it amazing what will get you over the hump?

We gained elevation quickly and soon began trekking

through an area scorched by a recent fire. In amazement I watched as the kids' attitudes, noise level, and even their pace changed, reflecting the contrast with our earlier miles through multitudes of birds singing and playing in lush, green foliage and thick stands of lodgepole pine and Douglas fir. Here the ground was ash, and the trees stood like black, foreboding creatures against a sky now darkening with rain clouds. From both the forest and the intruders, there was only silence.

The afternoon rain was short lived, and by late afternoon we hiked into an area surrounded by huge boulders and blessed with a sassy, little stream cascading along one side. A slight slope drifted off to the east, but there was ample room on the flats to set up camp. Tents quickly rose, cooking fires ignited, and the bouquet of burgers, potatoes, and a mix of vegetables cooking in foil packets permeated the air. As the sun sank behind the 14,000-foot wall to our west and the first chill of evening drifted in, weary bodies began snuggling into their sleeping bags. It was early morning when I detected the first clue about one little guy who was to become a troop fixture. His name is Ross Kershaw, Brad's little brother.

I awoke to the orange glow of the early morning sun filtering through the thick stand of trees. Although it was summer, the morning air had a touch of autumn. The troop was still in deep, silent slumber, except in the direction of Copey's tent. Silent? That kid could snore. You'd swear he was bunking with a moose suffering sinus congestion. I snuggled back in for a quick, warm 40 winks, when Ross's buddy, Danny, reached in and shook me. Ross, it seems, was nowhere to be found. The two of them had slept under the stars, and both Ross and his sleeping bag had vanished.

Quickly pulling on some clothes and boots, I trailed Danny to the spot where they had bedded down on the edge of a gentle incline that dropped into a thick stand of shrubs. There was no sign of Ross. Perhaps he got cold and crawled into a tent. Checking who's-in-what-bag is always a challenge. You nearly

have to crawl halfway into each bag yourself to retrieve iden-
tifiable faces. But no luck. No Ross. I woke three or four older
guys, and we fanned out, checking behind every boulder and
bush in the vicinity. Then someone yelled from about 30 yards
down the hill. I stormed down the slope and found Ross in his
clothes, cuddled in a fetal position, sound asleep on the ground,
and partially covered with his bag. I shook Ross gently, and he
jerked to a sitting position, rubbing his glazed eyes. He had no
idea where he was—or even who he was—for at least 20 or 30
seconds. He had no comprehension of how he got there. Only
after we returned home did I learn that, like the Scoutmaster
in Minnesota, I too had a sleepwalker on my hands. And Ross
didn't have an ordinary case of nighttime wanderlust. This kid
was world class. I'd later learn that Ross not only meandered
about in the moon shadows but often spiced up his journeys
with "screamin' meanies," nightmares in which he'd physically
get into the action. His mother told me how, one night, she
found him standing like a support beam in the hall outside his
room, holding up the walls and howling that the house was
collapsing. I suspected this boy had all the ingredients for con-
cocting his share of bizarre happenings and that his nighttime
excursions would spice up future camping trips.

For the next two days we wandered through the bound-
ary area between the trees and tundra on the eastern slopes
of Mount Evans. On this, my first experience above timberline, I was choked from both the lack of oxygen and the raw
beauty. An ocean of miniature flowers pushed up in the rock-
laden meadows to overcome the harshness of the frozen earth
and relentless wind, offering a symphony of reds, yellows,
blues, and everything in between. The sharp-pitched chirps
of pikas and marmots, who have learned to dwell with relative comfort in such inhospitable environs, would warn of our
approach, breaking the monotonous drone of the constant
wind. Occasionally they would delight the kids by sneaking
out from cover, observe us from a distance, then dart back into

tiny tunnels between the rocks.

Weariness discouraged a climb to summit Mount Evans. The kids were tired and my feet ached in those stiff Minnesota boots; I wasn't about to shift into a "We gotta do it, boys" routine. Instead we dropped down into the protection of the Engelmann spruce in search of Roosevelt Lakes. Within an hour we found the lakes and a great camping spot, totally vacant.

Removing my boots to soak those aching feet was another memorable Colorado experience. As I tip-toed into the water, instead of expected relief, my feet felt like a million needles were pricking at them. Déjà vu Camp Tahosa. This was REAL COLD WATER. I couldn't take it for ten seconds. Along came barefoot Copey. "Hey Cope. Walk into this water. I bet you can't stand in it for a full minute." He bent down, gave it a quick feel, sneered, and boasted in his loud, resonant voice that he could *sit* in that pond neck deep for three minutes.

His boisterous braggadocio ignited an otherwise trail-weary troop. There was instant, camp-wide attention, and soon the ante was spiraling. Cope, with the oily finesse of a Brooklyn Bridge realtor, nickel and dimed everyone upward until the payback was well over seven bucks, a lot of moolah in the mid '60s. And all to the chorus of jabs and insults aimed at his level of, or more specifically, lack of smarts. Finally when he milked everyone for every cent he could snare, and the "We want action!" chant reached a fervor, Cope unceremoniously doffed everything but his underwear and, like a fearless hero approaching the gallows, marched straight into the pond.

By the time he reached belly high, *I* was feeling hypothermic. He turned around, faced his cheering, jeering compatriots, and promptly sat down, expressionless, on a rock with the water level rippling just below his chin. In seconds, the crowd fell virtually silent as the enormity of the feat settled in. This guy was sitting quietly in water with the temperature slightly above that of an iceberg. When the designated timer called out "One minute," Cope hadn't budged a muscle. Maybe he was already frozen stiff. "Are you all right, Cope?" I yelled, and he answered with a slight nod. In fact, he looked bored. "Two minutes," announced the timer. His tormentors' expression of financial confidence was dropping faster than Cope's body temperature. The countdown continued in seconds as we reached the two and one-half minute mark. As the ordeal entered the final moments, the troop, en masse, shifted to his side. "Ten, nine, eight..." they shouted in unison. "Five, four, three, two, one!" The cheer must have shaken the windows at the Summit House on Mount Evans. Did Cope jump right out of the water? Heck no. He sat for another 15 seconds, stood, and walked slowly and arrogantly from the pond straight to me. He threw his frigid, wet body around me and roared, "Where's my money?" While the guys were doling out their change, one disgruntled loser muttered, "You never would have done it without all that blubber!" Sticks and stones may break your bones, but Cope's pockets were full of quarters.

The journey to our pickup point the next day was all downhill once we reached a Jeep road marked "Temporary." The road might have been temporary, but the pride in all those faces after completing such a rugged mountain trip looked darn permanent to me.

6

TROOP 117 REACHES NEW HEIGHTS IN MISCHIEF AND MOUNTAINS

Monday Night Madness

On Tuesday mornings I shuddered to pick up the phone. A series of events had begun to try the patience of the good deacons of the Baptist church. One clown whistled through the church before leaving one Monday evening, elevating every thermostat needle in the building to maximum. By morning the boiler balanced on the verge of blowing. Then a budding felt-tip pen artist turned both the boys *and* girls' johns into his own personal Louvre. On one quiet summer evening, the exhaust pipe of a car in the parking lot mysteriously became jammed. The culprit thought the car belonged to an assistant Scoutmaster. No, the car belonged to the pastor! It was bad enough the pastor felt targeted, but guess how suave the reverend felt when the tow truck operator extracted a potato.

One Tuesday, the minister called and said he heard the police were summoned to the church during a troop meeting the night before. I did my best to explain: "You see, sir, it was really nothing. The boys were simply playing a game of British bulldog." Now if you know the game, you can guess what happened. But unfortunately, the good pastor had a void in his upbringing and was ignorant about this activity. You see, British bulldog gets physical and noisy. The whole troop lines up at one end of the yard with a single participant waiting in the center of the area. As the rest dash en masse to the other end, the boy in the center dives to tackle anyone he can. Those tackled and lifted off the ground must also remain in the center until the last runner is caught. A little old lady, new to the neighborhood, heard the commotion, looked out her living room window, then dashed to the phone reporting a gang war in the churchyard. Within minutes, four of Littleton's finest sped up in squad cars—lights flashing and sirens blaring, squealed into the parking lot, and flooded the yard with spotlights. All action ceased as three dozen confused Scouts in full uniform stood with baffled expressions shielding their eyes from the bright glare. I walked over and enjoyed a few chuckles with the local gendarmes.

While 40 kids pushed my limit, we kept enlisting some outstanding boys. Fortunately, I was always blessed with at least one or two excellent Assistant Scoutmasters. Developing boy leaders is the name of the game, so we placed a lot of responsibility on our older kids. Supposedly a good Scoutmaster sits in the corner in his rocking chair and lets the kids run the meeting. Admittedly that's a great goal, but I must confess that if I had a rocking chair, I simply would have collapsed into it after the meeting. There was too much activity to permit such luxury.

Yet during the late 1960s we developed some cracker-jack junior leaders. Brad Kershaw, who served so well in many leadership capacities with the troop and with the dancers, was nearing his 18th birthday, the deadline for completing the rank of Eagle Scout. Why Brad wasn't finishing his last few merit badges puzzled me. Then I learned how much time he spent conducting classes at home helping younger kids advance. At age 18, he became an Assistant Scoutmaster until the time he left for Vietnam.

Brad's brother Ross, Texas transfer Steve Weir, superb dancer

Johnny Miller, Dale Marshall, and, of course, Montana rounded out the guys who ran the operation. Montana, who probably couldn't see his hand in front of his face without his glasses, was a soft-spoken, intelligent natural when it came to leading. The troop felt the loss when his father was transferred to Oklahoma just before Montana completed his Eagle requirements. He finished the requirements in Oklahoma and returned to backpack the mountains with the troop as often as he could.

As a junior leader, Dale Marshall was one of the toughest boy disciplinarians I ever encountered. More than once I had to defuse him while he was suspending some grossly misbehaving kid a foot off the floor by his shirt, discussing, eyeball to eyeball, the right and wrong way to act. I admit it usually worked, but we thought it wise to convince Dale that fear was only one way to modify behavior. Dale's dad, Cliff, served as troop committee chairman for a handful of years as long as he didn't have to camp or backpack. A World War II veteran, he frequently reminded us that he had camped his way across France and Germany, and he would be damned if he'd ever spend another night in a tent! We assured Cliff that if he'd take care of the committee, we'd take care of the camping.

During this time, John Dillman, with two sons in the troop, joined us as an Assistant Scoutmaster, and we picked up a new kid simply by Indian dancing at his Cub pack. Don Fitzsimmons lived several miles east of the area in which we normally recruited, but he wanted to Indian dance in the worst way. This rather reserved little guy seldom missed a meeting or a dance practice, never missed an outing or summer camp, and loved the mountains. Well, he joined the right troop for mountain experiences.

Freezing on the Wall

A lad from Fitzy's Cub pack named Ron joined our troop. Ron set a troop record never to be equaled. Somewhere along the way

I learned a few climbing skills and a descent method called the *rappel*. To add a little excitement to outings, we purchased rope, harnesses, and a variety of carabineers and started rappelling. During every boy's first campout, he went down the wall—or at least tried. The kids loved this mountaineering skill, but more important, I saw real value to it. First, it was unnatural to lean back over a cliff, which you had to do to place your feet on the wall. For a beginner, that was the tough part. Letting the rope slide through your hand, then kicking off the wall and gliding downward was the payoff. Regardless of how frightened a boy was at the top, seldom did anyone reach the bottom without yelling up, "Hey, I want to do that again!"

What did these boys learn? Older Scouts set up the ropes, ensured the harness and 'biners were properly attached, and held the belay line, which would catch the rappelling boy if something went amiss. Therefore, this helped establish the proper relationship between the younger and the older Scouts. New boys learned to trust and depend on these Senior Scouts and the adults. For most boys, the first rappel was a frightening experience, so they learned they could accomplish something they never thought possible. Many went to the wall numerous times, only to walk away saying they couldn't do it. Yet, everyone finally made it, which brings us back to Ron. Twenty-two times he marched with determined steps toward the wall, got hooked up, and then tried his best to lean back. Twenty-two times he backed away; he just couldn't bring himself to lean back over that precipice. On his 23rd try, Ron made it. And here's where Troop 117 shined: the kids didn't criticize or make fun of a boy who was afraid to rappel. Instead they encouraged him until he finally succeeded. Success always feels good—to the individual boy and the entire troop. The rappel taught a lot more than a simple mountaineering skill.

18 Guys Top Out on Longs Peak

The lure of the Rocky Mountains was my primary enticement to venture into a new life in Colorado. Nearly every weekend during our family's first several years in the Denver area, we'd hop into the car and point it westward. The white mantle of snow on the peaks, the precipitous outcroppings of rocks, the cascading streams sparkling in the afternoon sunlight—everything about the mountains had a soothing, comforting, nearly medicinal effect. But the best way to see the Rockies was on foot. I'd already had a taste of backpacking—and sore feet as a result—with Troop 117's first foray into the mountains. Now, with spiffy new mountain boots, complete with Vibram soles and heavy, waterproof, leather tops from Hans-the-Bootmaker on Colfax Avenue, it was time to view the world from a new perspective: from the top.

It wasn't easy convincing Scouts who got bused to school and toted around by Mom to soccer and football practice and troop meetings to push their aching bodies up to an altitude of 13,000 or 14,000 feet. But one by one, they began to feel the magic of the mountains. On our first outings, we backpacked into a base camp and climbed a couple of mountains in the Indian Peaks area northwest of Denver. For our first ascents, we chose Mount Audubon and Apache Peak, with only a handful of takers. Dave Wright, Karl Koontz, and Paul Worley were the first Scouts to struggle through the snow fields and boulder-strewn meadows to top out and receive that special payback that comes only when viewing the world through the crisp, clear air on a summit. Arriving at that point in which the 360-degree spectacle opens up before you seldom resulted in whoops and cheers. I was never sure whether the boys' silence was precipitated by awe or whether their aching lungs simply lacked adequate wind to generate vocal excitement. For me, it was a combination, but I'm sure my mind was far too busy registering a vista of endless snow-covered peaks, their rugged beauty, and the immense power they emit. Except when a vicious, cold wind blew, our time on the summit seemed far too short.

From the summit of Mount Audubon, the distinctive flat top of Longs Peak, the 14,255-foot "king" of Rocky Mountain National Park, stood outlined on the northern horizon—proud, arrogant, and challenging. Before the summer faded, eight of us (five in short pants) unloaded from my Chevy Carryall at the trailhead and faced an 18-mile roundtrip hike with an elevation gain of 5,000 feet. In our ignorance, we were doomed before we took our first step. It was already 8:00 in the morning. You don't start climbing Longs Peak at 8:00 a.m. We later devised Rule Number 1: Hit the trail no later than 4:00 or 4:30 a.m. and stagger in semi-slumber with the aid of your headlight through stands of white aspen and lodgepole pine. By dawn, you cross Alpine Brook and veer around Jim's Grove, an oasis of limber pine that many climbers use as a base camp to shorten the day's climb by about six miles. The trail, now above timberline, circles around Mount Lady Washington to a junction of trails converging from other directions, then onto a series of switchbacks that lead you to an expanse of rocks known as the Boulder Field. Here the climb really begins, and your Mickey Mouse watch should read 7:30, not 11:15!

The wind picks up at the Boulder Field. I'm not sure if the wind originates in Wyoming or Rocky Mountain National Park, probably whichever is coldest. On our first summit attempt of Longs Peak, those who thought to bring long pants pulled off a quick change. Two who didn't were developing legs with a hue that closely matched the cloudless sky. (Later, we developed Rule Number 2: Dress warmly and in layers.) Before we ever circled Mount Lady Washington, the precarious East Face of Longs Peak, so steep and so high, still looked a long way off. I'm sure many newcomers think that's why they named it Longs Peak. From that point I noticed several of our expedition sitting more frequently, picking away at their fingernails. Hence, Rule Number 3: Keep moving and work your fingernails at home.

With as much encouragement as I could offer, short of providing piggyback rides, we arrived at Chasm View. Here the mountain drops away precipitously to Chasm Lake, an azure tarn sparkling in the morning sunlight 2,000 feet below the base of the East Face. With the wind pushing at our backs, no one dared to walk up to the edge and peek down. Instead, the boys slithered to the rim on the safety of their bellies and ogled the lake and the massive vertical wall leading down to it.

Our tardy morning departure was amplified when we noticed tiny moving dots already descending from the summit. The fluffy cumulus clouds that had dotted the sky now crowded together and became darker, and the summit was still an hour or two away. Logic overcame emotion. We opted for a brief lunch and a fast retreat. Like the book says, "He who climbs and turns away, lives to climb another day." But we'd be back, and next time, we promised ourselves, we would be standing on the top.

The following July, four of us topped out on two 14,000-foot mountains in one day. Dale Marshall, Steve Scott, John Dillman, and I scouted out Grays and Torreys Peaks as a possible first climb location for the troop. From the old Steven's Mine, we switchbacked our way to the top of 14,270-foot Grays Peak. These good-sized boys moved at a steady pace, but at about the 13,000-foot mark, Dale's head began throbbing with the effects of altitude. His head drifted back to normal once we reached the windy top and snuggled into the protection of a stone windbreak that former climbers were considerate enough to build. There we found the metal cylinder that the Colorado Mountain Club places on all fourteeners and proudly added our names to the list inside. I seldom ate much when climbing to those altitudes; such was not the case with youth. They inhale food anywhere! So with their bellies satiated, we struck out for Torreys Peak, just about a mile north, first dropping to a saddle 600 feet below before ascending. Within an hour we added our names to the list on Torreys Peak—our second fourteener of Colorado's 54. One month later, five of us stood again at Chasm Lake, eyeballing the route snaking up the east side of Longs Peak.

In those days, the usual trip to the top was up the north face using heavy, steel cables bolted to rocks in the steep sections to provide added safety. A slip and tumble at those pitches could result in a phenomenal nosedive of several thousand feet. In 1973, the Park Service removed the cables to eliminate man-made devices from wilderness areas.

With hearts and lungs pleading from the low oxygen at 14,000 feet, we emerged on top of the "king" and were surprised to find a large, spacious summit about the size of a football field. The view was spectacular. A half dozen other hikers reached the top and gawked at Storm Peak, Chiefs Head Peak, and McHenrys Peak, while several stood on the east side and looked down toward Estes Park and out onto the plains. I pointed a little left of Mount Lady Washington and, winking to one of the Scouts, said in a loud voice, "Look way out there. See it. That's the John Hancock building in Chicago." A middle-aged lady and her companion began squinting and, sure enough, within a minute they saw it too!

During the next several years, we began shaking bodies at nearby Camp Tahosa at 3:00 in the morning on the last day of summer camp. By 3:30 a.m., all Scouts who were First Class and above were heading north to the Longs Peak trailhead and the arduous 18-mile roundtrip climb to the summit. In our final climb, 18 Troop 117ers stood tall on the windy summit.

An SOS in the Park

In early summer 1969 we decided to explore the 25 mile Lost Creek loop trail starting and ending near the Goose Creek Campground in the Tarryall Mountains southwest of Denver. A covey of new boys and adults in the troop all seemed eager to test their backpacking skills with something more challenging than the usual weekend jaunt. A new, young Assistant Scoutmaster, Skip Oliver, signed on along with our troop committee chairman, Bob Scheller. So with Scheller, Oliver, and Sholes leading the adventure, the kids tagged this as the "SOS Pack Trip." Little did they know how prophetic this name would be.

Johnny Miller and several other older boys with driver's licenses dropped us at a location farther north near a Girl Scout Camp, then drove south to park the cars at our exit location near Goose Creek Campground. Both groups had about a 10-mile hike to our rendezvous point at Refrigerator Gulch. A gentle rain greeted our departure and Bob Scheller, who showed up in street shoes, hiked about a mile before those slick leather soles skidded on the wet grass. Down he went, seriously twisting an ankle. Within moments, the ankle exploded to the size of a grapefruit. Afraid to take off his shoe for fear we'd never get it back on, we bound his ankle to those beautiful brown Oxfords and examined our options, knowing we no longer had cars at our trailhead. We sent out our first SOS by dispatching a Senior Scout to contact several fishermen we had passed a half mile back. Fortunately, they were from Littleton and promised to take good care of our ailing chairman. On to Refrigerator Gulch and our rendezvous with our chauffeurs.

The gulch was well named. Situated in a small depression with a clear, gentle stream cutting through, it felt 15 to 20 degrees cooler than the surrounding area. This little gulch offered ample flat space for camping on both sides of the creek. A huge log resting on rocks provided a sturdy bridge. Tents popped up, and the kids cooked and consumed meals with ease. This hidden little campsite had all the attributes of providing a quiet, peaceful evening in the mountains.

The sun had disappeared behind the ridge to our west. I was sitting on one side of the creek having a heart-to-heart chat with a lad, let's call him Rocky (that wasn't his name, but it fits). Rocky was a 13-year-old, first-time offender who was sentenced by a local judge to a couple of years in Boy Scouts. He was a loner and considered himself nothing but tough. He discovered he wasn't quite as tough as he thought on those first ten miles of trail and was in dire need of a pep talk. In the middle of a sentence, one of the older boys tapped me on the shoulder and said, "Mr. Oliver needs to talk to you—right now." I gave Rocky a little hair ruffle and told him we'd chat later, then I tight-rope walked across the narrow bridge to Skip, who was straddling a log on the opposite side. Tossing my leg over, I mounted the log facing him and asked him what was up. He was holding his left thumb tightly with his right hand. He glanced up, looking like a kid who just got caught in his mother's purse, then pulled back his hand to expose blood oozing out of a deep gash on his thumb. I yelled for the first aid kit, but it was already in route. This cut was down to the bone.

"What the heck did you do?" I asked while tightening an absorbent bandage around the thumb. Sheepishly, he told me his hand axe glanced off a log with the business end striking his thumb. After the bleeding subsided, we bathed the cut with an antiseptic, a procedure he adored, closed it up tightly with butterfly strips that one of the boys cut from adhesive tape, secured the thumb to his hand to prevent movement, then considered our options. It was already dusk. To send him and one of the Senior Scouts ten miles back in the dark with a throbbing thumb was out of the question. That's probably what we would do come morning, although I hated to have a kid miss the trip. We gave Skip a few pain killers, and we hit the sack. Before I fell asleep, one cheerful little macaroon stuck his head into my tent and, sporting a sinisted smile, said, "Well, that takes care of Scheller and Oliver. I guess you're next, Sholzie. Sleep well." Here's wishing you red ants in your underwear too, Buster.

As nightime closed in, Refrigerator Gulch earned its name. In fact, it felt more like Freezer Gulch. More than a few of the lighter sleeping bags danced to the vibrations of shivers. Deep in this gulch, it seemed like forever before the sun finally donated a few warm morning rays. Before contemplating Skip's "evacuation," he popped out of his tent, insisted that his thumb didn't hurt anymore, and said he wouldn't go back under any circumstances. Our goal that day was McCurdy Park, which meant facing some tough miles ahead, including a hot, rock-laden stretch with contour lines on the map indicating a steep 1,000-foot-plus elevation gain. I informed Skip that Ross Kershaw had volunteered to go back with him and forewarned him that the heart-pumping climb with a heavy pack could cause that thumb to start seeping and loosen the butterflies. I might as well have cautioned the granite boulder sitting on the other side of the creek. He started on this trip, and he had every intention of completing it. That was classic Skip.

It was 9:30 a.m. before we marched everyone through breakfast and broke camp. The trail headed due west, winding uphill through an area of beautiful rocky crags. After several miles, we crossed Lost Creek and veered south. The temperature soared, trying to compensate for last night's deep freeze. Too bad Mother Nature can't adjust the temperature to your needs. We told the speedy seniors to hold up at a small pond just before the switchbacks for lunch. I was so concerned with Skip's thumb, I nearly forgot about Rocky. Waiting for the stragglers, I finally spotted the Rock. I think he was moving, but the pace approached that of a three-legged turtle. One of the older kids bringing up the rear was prodding him on and even from a distance the dialogue sounded somewhat heated. At the lunch spot, Rocky drifted off by himself and wouldn't eat. Worse yet, Skip's bandages were dark red.

With all that drainage, the butterflies were loose, so it was back to square one. It was sheer folly to attempt major repair with the steep switchbacks just ahead, so we simply performed preventive maintenance on the bandage and continued. Rocky had already departed behind some of the older guys, but less than a half mile up the switchbacks we found him lying in the center of the trail, whimpering that he could go no farther. Instead of putting him down, which I'm sure a lot of the boys would have thoroughly enjoyed, several Scouts squatted next to Rocky, told him how well he had been doing, how strong he really was for his age, and not to worry because he certainly would finish the whole hike. Several kids, some not as big as he, started taking items from his pack to help reduce the weight. This totally confused Rocky. Others were going to suffer more just to help him? Kids and adults alike offered words of encouragement to perk up his sagging spirits. Ever so slowly Rocky picked himself up from that steep, dusty trail, the dirt on his face muddied from his tears. He took a deep breath, cinched up his pack, then put one foot in front of the other for three more uphill miles.

McCurdy Park was everything we had heard. Spectacular rock structures, caves, overhangs to protect you from the weather, even a little shelter hut. Before dinner we slapped Skip back into "surgery." On the return trip the next day, we would climb only one minor pass and the rest should be downhill. I kept one eye on the Rock. It was his turn to cook dinner, which he did and did it well. He seemed less cantankerous. After supper I spotted him sitting alone on a boulder gazing at the lightning flashes in the distance. How badly I wanted to know what was cycling through his mind. I had high hopes that this three-day experience might turn this tough little turkey into a Boy Scout. He was carrying a batch of baggage, yet in this short period of time many of his needs were being fulfilled. First, Rocky needed to be challenged, and the length and difficulty of this trip was accomplishing that, if not nearly overwhelming him. Yet, it didn't overwhelm him. Second, Rocky lacked self esteem and self confidence. This would come when he finished the trip and felt accepted by the group, which had already happened. Third, Rocky needed—and had found—both friendship and a sense of belonging. Plus, he received a good lesson in sensitivity. Other kids were actually willing to take on added pain, so he could be more comfortable. And if he didn't learn anything else, he certainly learned that Boy Scouts are anything but sissies. He saw, firsthand, that they were tough and rugged. Before, he thought he was the only tough guy.

This trip introduced Rocky to an environment of beauty,

ruggedness, and vastness that I'm sure he never knew existed. That evening he sat alone, soaking it in and hopefully looking inside himself to begin a self-discovery process that would help him understand who he was and help him understand these other people who treated him with such warmth and kindness. During those few days, Rocky experienced living and interacting with people like never before. It may have been his first experience with guys who cared for one another, who looked after one another, who helped each other, and were kind and courteous to one another. Welcome to Boy Scouting, Rocky!

As the storm Rocky was watching approached, everyone was able to find adequate shelter without putting up a single tent. Some snuggled into the hut, others found ample space under rock overhangs. Ross Kershaw discovered a neat little cave and invited Skip to spend the night with him. Now anyone who knew Ross's nocturnal history, wouldn't sleep within 50 yards of the guy, but Skip was new to our troop. The cave Ross found was wide enough for two or more sleeping bags and about three feet high. Sure enough, midway though the night Ross's little demon insidiously crept into his head. As his blood-curdling scream reverberated off the cave walls, Skip jerked up from deep slumber and embedded his head into the jagged roof of the tiny cavern. Along with his throbbing thumb, we now pulled a 3:00 a.m. patch job on his noggin while he moaned, "Wow, what gives with that guy?" We call that *Kershaw Kappers*, Skipper!

To complete the loop trail, the next day we headed south and met our final trail at Hankins Pass. From there, it was a simple downhill journey eastward to Goose Creek Campground and to our cars. "S" and "O" had encountered their problems, while this "S" stayed relatively unscathed. But before the day was over, a handful of those who should have known better, got me—emotionally and physically.

Over the years, I never understood why the speedsters in a troop always hit the starting gate on the last day of the hike as though their very lives were in danger. All the way back, they maintained the pace of a trail horse moving back to the hay-laden corral, only to sit by locked cars for an hour or two and wait for the stragglers. I was up early that morning to start a fire and boil water for our traditional, last-day breakfast of cocoa, instant oatmeal, or anything else you could blend together with hot water. On this particular day, the cruisers were really in a hustle and with a hand wave headed out before I could recite my usual admonition, "Remember, if you come to an unmarked fork, wait up." They knew about another trail teeing in from the west less than a half mile from our camp. What they didn't know was that one mile farther down the path the correct trail veered off to the east for a short distance before turning south to Hankins Pass. Instead of veering east, the cruisers took the straight trail, which also met the Hankins Pass trail several miles farther west of the pass. They followed it downhill, all right, but the dunderheads headed west. If they hadn't run into a lonely rancher on horseback looking for lost cattle, they may have maintained that speedway pace until they hit Moab, Utah.

When I reached the first fork, I wondered why they hadn't waited. But my pack seemed unusually heavy, and my hips and shoulders were drawing a good share of my attention. Anyway, I thought, they wouldn't be so stupid as to head the wrong way. We wandered through beautiful ponds and crags. Footprints on the trail provided some mental relief. I expected them to be waiting at Hankins Pass, but apparently they were out to break a speed record. We gulped down lunch, and then continued the last several miles to the cars. Man, that pack seemed heavy. When we came around the last bend and caught our first view of the cars, I couldn't believe all the vacancy signs. No kids, no packs, nowhere! Ringing wet with perspiration and with legs that felt like rubber bands, the thought of doubling back and going up Hankins Pass to look for those clowns nearly brought tears to my eyes. Skip was in no shape to go along, so I volunteered one of the kids who still seemed alive and well to join me.

We puffed our way back to the top of the pass and headed

down the other side when we spotted a single file of downtrodden bodies dragging themselves up the trail. They resembled the German withdrawal from the Battle of Stalingrad. I enjoyed every bit of their misery. They didn't stop and didn't look up as they walked past us. But someone muttered, "We made a wrong turn."

The SOS trip became legendary for accidents, challenges, and personal growth. Oh yes, when I got home, I discovered two large rocks in the bottom of my backpack.

Troop 117, Littleton, CO, 1969

Some Troop 117 boys with whom I started began to move on to college or jobs. It was always hard for me to see kids with whom I had shared so many experiences depart. But all I had to do was turn around. There stormed another galloping herd clamoring down the stairs; full of vim, vigor, and noise; and adding new contributions to the Monday-night madness.

7

A WAR, A TEST, AND BACKCOUNTRY FUN AND TURMOIL

Winning the Local "Vietnam" Battle

During the late 1960s and early '70s, one major event created a stunning effect on the Boy Scout movement: Vietnam. The patriotic spirit and the desire to be in uniform, march in parades, be involved in paper and scrap-metal drives—hallmarks of World War II (our country's last "popular" war)—took a dramatic, 180-degree spin as antipathy toward the Vietnam conflict accelerated. I remember chuckling at a cartoon showing a group of Scouts in full uniform marching through the woods with patrol flags flying; nearby, three barefoot kids in overalls were fishing in a pond. One kid pointing over his shoulder grunts, "Here comes the establishment."

Whether you supported the war, were out toting a picket alongside the protestors, or were ignorant of the My Lai massacre, the Mekong Delta, or Ho Chi Minh, you were instantly earmarked as part of the war-pushing "Establishment" if you were associated with Boy Scouting. This was only natural. After all, we wore khaki uniforms, had ranks, carried flags, saluted, lined up in formations, and were regarded by many as a junior army. Some people even suspected the .22 ammunition used at our summer camp rifle range was supplied by the government. Face it, even though Lord Baden-Powell never intended the Boy Scouts to be a paramilitary group, it looks military. During Nam, this image of Scouting—especially among potential members and their parents—was exacerbated. The result: Scouting's membership numbers began to resemble the 1928 stock market.

On the contrary, throughout the whole Vietnam era, Troop 117 not only held its numbers, it increased in size. In fact, in my 40 years of troop/post leadership, this was the only time a Council Executive ever invited me to lunch. His motivation? He wanted to know what we were doing right. Somewhat to his distress, I told him we had slacked off on uniform demands. Blue jeans were in and those silly looking khaki trousers with the red-rimmed pockets were out. I defended my position using none other than the good Lord Baden-Powell himself. I quoted him: "You never fish with the food you like, you fish with the food the fish like." Well, these fish liked jeans, so jeans were in on a compromise deal: Troop 117 Scouts would still wear their shirts and troop neckerchiefs. Plus, Monday nights became more creative; we increased the number of high-adventure, challenging activities. But the real frosting on our troop's cake may have been the meetings and outings we shared with Girl Scouts. Talk about neutralizing the Vietnam effect! But we'll get to that later.

Ross Kershaw, now an Eagle, had survived enough of his nighttime antics to serve with distinction as the Senior Patrol Leader and then as our Junior Assistant Scoutmaster. Brother Brad became an Assistant Scoutmaster, along with John Dillman, Art Trevithick, and Skip Oliver, while dad Leon Kershaw still chaired the committee. Advancement was healthy and the quality of the boys in this troop soared thanks to a notorious game of 120 questions.

The Egregious Troop 117 First Class Test

I hesitate to admit before God and everybody that at times I broke a rule or two set forth by the BSA. Heaven forbid! I'd rather take the approach Aunt Eller used in the Broadway musical *Oklahoma* when she said, "We ain't goin' to break any rules here, we'll just bend 'em a little." Such was the case with the First Class Test.

Far too many Scouts waddled in for the traditional Scoutmaster's Conferences prior to advancing in rank with skills and knowledge levels that appeared severely anemic. Turning them down proved hard on them and me. Junior leaders were too easily passing kids on lower-rank advancement requirements. A cheap Tenderfoot leads to a cheap First Class Scout, which could result in a cheap Life Scout and eventually a cheap Eagle. If there is one thing I can't handle to this day, it's a cheap Eagle Scout. I felt it was important to maintain a high level of "kid quality," and the place to nip this easy advancement in the bud was when a boy went up for First Class Scout. First Class is a plateau rank in Scouting; in Troop 117, a boy who achieved that rank could hold a leadership position.

My decision to develop a written test was delicate. The BSA does not permit a unit to modify Scouting requirements for a rank. But performing a little mental end run on that issue, I surmised that the BSA should be interested in quality advancement and this test was simply a quality-control device. My biggest concern was how the kids would take it. A written test? This rang too much like school. Maybe I could give it a different name: *Quiz? Assessment? Evaluation? Analysis? Critique? Benchmark?* No, they'd smell right through that. I decided to call it a *test* and see what would happen.

Flipping through the pages of the *Boy Scout Handbook* and *Boy Scout Field Book*, I dove headstrong into this project. I recently had completed courses on adult education, and test methodology was fresh in my mind. Taking the key elements from Tenderfoot, Second Class, and First Class requirements, I mixed them up with a variety of test-question formats—multiple guess, matching columns, fill in the blanks, and demonstrations—every conceivable method that would be both thorough and interesting. I accented factors relative to first aid and general safety. Then I considered activities in which the troop frequently participated, such as wilderness backpacking and survival, climbing and rappelling, and later white-water canoeing, adding a handful of commonsense questions relative to each of those activities. In a fit of viciousness, I tossed in one question I was certain no one would answer correctly: How to tie a Prusik knot. You have to be an old mountaineer to know that one! It was the predecessor of the Jumar ascender. Initially, of course, none of the Scouts answered correctly, and they were convinced there was no such animal. So we showed them, and the gimmick worked—they learned something new without even realizing they were learning. On the next campout, boys strung ropes into tree branches and using the knot, were clambering up the lines like a community of rhesus monkeys.

The test did what it was intended to do: protect the quality of the rank. Plus, the test became a troop tradition. "Wait until you hit the First Class Test, buddy!" It was perceived as a challenge and, of course, these boys lived for challenges. The passing score was 75%. If a boy failed, the next time he needed to achieve five percentage points higher. Seldom did a boy give answers to another. "I had to suffer through it without help, and so do you!" More important, a failed test indicated to the leaders where a kid was weak, so we could provide some rapid, remedial assistance.

To analyze the test beyond our immediate parochial domain, I sought out a handful of Eagle Scouts from other good troops in the neighborhood. Out of five Eagles who consented to suffer through the test, the best score was in the low sixties. When the Patrol Leader's Council for Troop 117 heard this, they quickly decided that when a boy transferred into our troop at a rank of First Class or above, it was only fair that this boy should take the test—and pass. Only once did this decision create a problem. Let's call this lad Jeffrey.

Jeffrey was a 17 year old whose father was a big, bad, bird Colonel who had just transferred to Colorado from a post in the Far East. Jeff had spent his Scouting years in military troops overseas and had completed all the requirements for the rank of Eagle. His dad simply wanted the troop to confer this honor on him. Before doing that, I wanted to see evidence of the boy's leadership capabilities, so I moved him into a Patrol Leader spot shortly before our usual spring trip to the Utah canyons. His dad informed me that Jeff had received excellent training, was a forceful leader, and was an outstanding backpacker. I placed Jeff in charge of three younger Scouts who would be part of his eating group for the trip. Before we left, I sat down with Jeff to give him the First Class Test. He disappeared shortly afterward. Then I found his test dumped in a wastepaper basket with nothing on it other than his name.

Several weeks later we drove to Bluff, Utah, and spent the night at the Sand Island campground before heading to the mouth of Fish Canyon. Early in the evening, one of the younger boys in Jeffrey's group came moping up to me on the verge of tears, telling me he couldn't carry everything Jeff had given him. Jeff was nowhere to be found. Opening the lad's pack, I pulled out five pairs of jeans, a clean pair for every day. Cleanliness may be next to godliness but not on a pack trip. A lightweight pack is. The boy should have known this, but his mom didn't and she's the one who packed his bag. And Jeff never checked it. I then looked at the food Jeff had given him to carry. Seven heavy cans, including a large can of pineapple juice! Jeff's image as an "outstanding" backpacking expert was fading faster than that big orange ball in the west. When I finally found Jeff and sat him down for a little chat, I might as well have been talking to the red sandstone bluffs behind him. Was I detecting that this boy didn't want to be here? In fact, did he want to be in Scouts?

The next day Jeff grumbled the entire seven miles to our camping spot along Fish Creek near the entrance of McCloyd Canyon. When we stopped en route to climb up a canyon and explore 1,000-year-old Anasazi ruins, he was unimpressed. Several times he simply stayed with his pack and read a magazine he had carried in. His antisocial behavior didn't improve once we reached camp. He discovered a small cave and moved into it alone and stayed there, other than to come down and warm up a can of beans for his unlucky eating group. Attempts by both junior and adult leaders to converse with Jeff to try to resolve his problem were about as successful as his meals. Jeff's surly attitude continued throughout the trip.

After this trip, I learned that Jeff's father had contacted the Denver Area Council and had asked why his son was being forced to take a test that was not in the Scouting requirements. Someone at the Council had told him the test was simply part of Sholes's Scoutmaster Conference, and a conference was definitely part of Scouting requirements. So the Colonel had begrudgingly instructed his boy to take the test, while he began to make plans for Jeff's Eagle Scout Court of Honor. Jeff sat down and agonized through most of the 120 questions but refused to do any of the rope work demonstrations. While he waited, I quickly reviewed and scored his test. The lad failed miserably. I told Jeff we had a lot of work to do, but I was sure that in a month of two we would have him up to speed—if that's what he wanted. He shrugged his shoulders, said little, and left for home.

Early the next Monday evening, the Colonel and a noticeably uncomfortable son entered the meeting, ready to discuss plans for the Eagle Court. You could just about hear the feathers on the Colonel's birds ruffling when I informed him, as Jeff was well aware, that there wasn't going to be an Eagle Court anytime soon. His body became rigid and slowly straightened, showing me every inch of height he could muster, like a bear trying to impress you before the attack. His jaw tightened while his wide, brown eyes narrowed to slits. This guy was transforming himself into a living, breathing facsimile of George Patton with the malingerer at the hospital. He proceeded to unleash a verbal barrage accented with an array of colorful words that would embarrass a sailor. I let him run out of steam, then simply asked him, "Colonel, I assume that people under your command must achieve and maintain certain levels of proficiency to gain advancement in rank, is that not correct?" He slowly acknowledged this statement with a degree of suspicion. I handed him his boy's test, suggesting that he review the 20 first-aid questions starting on page seven. In moments, his board-straight stature began wilting—not one first-aid question was answered correctly. He pulled a chair from a table, sat down, and with a hand resting against his head, thumbed through the test page by page. When he finished, he slowly turned over the test and set it on the table. A big, red "32%" stared him in the face. Rubbing his two huge hands together for a second, he took a deep breath, then said hesitatingly, "It's a good test." He stood for a moment, staring at the floor as though he was trying to say something. Without a word, he turned, motioned his boy to the door, and they both left without a word. I never saw either one of them again. That test did its job in protecting the quality of the Eagle; I hope that, in the long run, that experience did something positive for both the Colonel and his son.

Wintry Camp Tahosa: Toilet Seats and Bathing Beauties

If the lake at Camp Tahosa could tickle your innards in the summer, the temperatures at that altitude in midwinter would cause a Siberian to seek shelter. Yet two experiences up there among the Douglas fir and Engelmann spruce had a decided effect on me and on the Boy Scouts of Troop 117.

One Friday afternoon, we headed to the camp's chilly heights to participate in a District Klondike Derby. In this derby, Scouts mush through the snow pulling a wooden patrol sledge they designed and constructed. Some sledges were rather simple, others unusually ornate. All firmly attached to a pair of worn-out downhill skis. Throughout the day the boys participate in a wild array of contests, including pioneering problems, fire building, first aid, cooking and eating an egg without utensils, snowshoe races, archery, axe tossing—anything goes at a Klondoree. One thing you could count on at Camp Tahosa: you knew there would be snow for your sledge. That night, there was plenty of snow everywhere, other than in an open meadow where most troops busily pitched their tents.

While our troop decided where to settle in, several of my junior leaders asked me why I thought that meadow was free of snow while the snow in the woods was nearly three feet deep. I gave them my favorite reply, "What do you think?" One squinched his face a little, looked around, then said, "Wind?"

"Right, Charley Brown, and that meadow will be the coldest spot in this camp tonight."

A few of the younger boys, already tired and cold, coughed out feeble protests, but everyone responded positively to moving out of the meadow and into the deep snow, particularly after the Senior Patrol Leader explained his rationale. With shovels and snow flying, Troop 117 Scouts dug spaces for their tents. By the time the wind started howling, everyone was comfortably snuggled into their shelters, surrounded by three-foot-high insulation. Only the colorful roofs of a dozen tents extended above the snow.

I was almost asleep when I heard wild laughter outside. One guy blabbing in an obnoxious, arrogant voice shouted, "Hey, look at this stupid troop. They're all sleeping in collapsed tents!" More laughter. Like groundhogs in the spring, heads popped out of the tents, and what did they see? About ten guys with Order of the Arrow sashes, the "super campers" nonetheless, making a final check on the wellbeing of the troops. Where were they camped? You guessed it—in the meadow. And who, pray tell, did we have to help move into the mess hall at 2:00

a.m., suffering from borderline hypothermia and frostbite? That act of ignorance had such a long-lasting effect that more than a decade passed before any member of Troop 117 would accept a nomination into the Order of the Arrow. A lesson to be learned there, OAers.

Being ridiculed for having some backcountry sense was bad enough, but an occurrence at the next day's snow sculpture event triggered the troop. Snow sculpting was a new event for this gang, but you wouldn't have known it. Their artistic achievements were magnificent (in their usual off-center brand of creativity). One patrol chose to carve the cool, white stuff into a full-size toilet—seat down, lid up. From a distance, you'd have thought the camp just installed indoor plumbing outside. It looked that real. Not to be outdone in the bathroom scene, a second patrol begat a lovely young maiden enjoying her bath in a standard-size tub. I'm sure some Scouters would consider both subjects a little risqué, but I viewed these simply as expressions of teenage boys, and I seldom saw reason to slap a damper on their creativity unless they got downright raunchy. To me, a nude is not lewd, especially when made out of snow.

The judging occurred late in the afternoon after the other events concluded. I wandered about and viewed the variety of snow-carved competitors and honestly felt that those two "works of art" would be hands-down winners of the major ribbons. Waltzing back into the sculpture park just as the judges completed their evaluation, one of the judges turned to me and said, "Great toilet, but we had to disqualify it." I asked why, and he replied that the entire structure had to be made with snow. When I told him it was, he suggested I look inside. Yep, that wasn't exactly snow in there. And the bathing beauty didn't win either. Some slinky surgeon sneaked in and performed a double mastectomy on the bather! Right or wrong, both acts of mutilation were promptly blamed on the Order of the Arrow guys, and the ribbons adorned someone else's flagpole.

The memory of another winter journey to Camp Tahosa in

that era still lives in infamy—the night I consented to build a snow cave with Kevin, my secretary's young son and his best buddy. The snow lacked the height we preferred, but the snow mound seemed wide and deep enough, so we went to work. Shortly after supper, Tahosa's wind resumed. That motivated our entry into our miniature snow cave, and we quickly blocked the entrance with a pack. The roof was so low it required an acrobatic entrance into my brand-new, nice-warm, Eddie Bauer, rectangular, goose-down sleeping bag. In fact, the cave was so low that when I rolled over on my side, my shoulder scraped the "ceiling" and sprinkles of tiny white flakes drifted down my neck.

When a Coleman lantern outside was finally extinguished and its glimmer through the doorway cracks flickered away, the whiteness of the cave quickly decayed to a dull gray. It was then that I felt as though someone had locked me in a trunk. Claustrophobia. I'd heard lots of people talk about it, but I never had experienced it and never thought I would. This was crazy! The walls closed in. The oxygen was obviously depleted. I was being both crushed and smothered. I hung on the verge of ripping out of my bag and plunging outside, into the snow. Finally, my better sense took over. I told myself, "Hey, this is stupid. The walls aren't caving in, you can breathe. Just close your eyes and go to sleep." I admit I had to play games with my head awhile, but I finally fell sound asleep, until about 2:00 in the morning, when I heard the distinctive tones of someone whimpering. Pulling my head out of the bag, I sat up, forgetting where I was. Now I had snow in my ears, down my neck, and inside my bag. That brought me around, and I realized the blubbering was coming from Kevin.

"Hey, guy. What's the problem?"

"My bag is wet, and I'm really cold." Now the whimpers accelerated into full-blown sobs. I reached into his bag and could have rung water from his shirt.

"Didn't you put your ground cloth under your bag?" He

thought he did, but at this stage investigating the etiology of the problem was pointless. He was soaked and violently shivering. We needed a fast solution.

After a 15-minute wrestling match with him, his bag, my bag, the ceiling, his pack, and my pack, we finally adorned his vibrating body with dry clothes, and I pulled him into that brand-new, nice-warm, Eddie Bauer, rectangular, goose-down sleeping bag. It was like hauling in a 90-pound block of ice. Wow! This was like being chained to a glacier.

As soon as he purloined the vast majority of my remaining body heat, the turkey was back in Never Never Land, sawing logs. Meanwhile, I was cold, and here it came again: the nagging sensation, tense muscles, and pulsating throb in the nape of my neck. The walls, the ceiling, the floor, the world—this time they really were closing in. It felt like the hair-raising, final minute of an old Buck Rogers serial. I wanted out. To fit this half-frozen knucklehead into the bag, I had to lie permanently on one hip, pushing hard against the side of the bag without one spare centimeter of wiggle room. Then one leg started to cramp. Geeze, I had to move. I had to get out. Soon my panic reached life-or-death proportions. I hurried back to mind games, knowing that if I dashed outside in these temperatures, I'd be in Kevin's shape in no time. Then the other side of my brain took charge saying, "Yeah, you might freeze to death, but people say that's quite peaceful." Suffocating. What could be worse? The games must have worked, because I remember coming to when someone yelled in, "Hey, it's morning. Is anyone alive in there?" I had to think for a moment to be sure. It was the most horrifying night of my 37-year existence. Little did I know that another horrifying night a couple of miles north in Rocky Mountain National Park awaited me the following summer.

A host of fun weekend trips and a great summer camp highlighted that year. Then on August 1, I nearly ended my Scouting career. In fact, I nearly ended any career—high on a lonely snowfield in Rocky Mountain National Park. I had recently changed jobs and a friend from my old Honeywell writing group had been laid off, which was frightening for him at age 55. The morning he received his pink slip he called me, sounding deeply disturbed. I suggested that he, his son, and I climb McHenrys Peak on Saturday to take his mind off his problem for a day. I succeeded in doing that! On the way back down, I slipped on a snowfield, lost my ice axe during a self-arrest, and plummeted 50-feet over a wall and onto the rocks below. His son descended alone for help and by 10:00 p.m., we saw lights of a rescue team moving up. Although I was pretty busted up and suffered through a cold, excruciatingly painful night at 12,000 feet altitude, I was alive. Thanks to the Park's crack rescue unit, including a daring helicopter landing, I was delivered safely to a local physician. I had landed on my right scapula—that big, tough bone on the back of your shoulder. On an x-ray, my scapula resembled a rock-smashed windshield. I came away with a few dents in the head and busted ribs, but with the able assistance of my chief therapist, 10-year-old son Scott and his football, we played that shoulder back into shape in a matter of weeks. I'm happy it's a story I lived to tell, because within the next year, that little therapist became an official member of Troop 117. And how could he go wrong being assigned to Andy O.'s patrol?

Andy: A Never-Ending Source of Amusement

If there was any kid who should have come with a warning label, it was Andy O. His round, freckled face capped with messy, brown hair dangling down his forehead was a dead giveaway; his eyes leaped with mischief. Yet, regardless of what he did, he was the kind of kid with whom you couldn't stay angry. While chewing him out, he'd look at you with those big, innocent cow eyes, then this huge, contagious grin would worm its way onto his mouth. Before long, I'd have to turn away or, in some instances, hurry away to privately gag ,my mouth in a fit of laughter. Andy was unique.

To this day, I have no idea what went on at his patrol meetings. I'll probably never know, and maybe it's best that I don't. But I do know this. When Andy had a patrol meeting, kids seldom missed it. Whatever he planned, it was creative. Everything Andy did was creative. For example, the troop bought each patrol a wooden army foot locker to stow their gear. The lockers were theirs to decorate as they saw fit. Andy called a patrol meeting, put strips of cardboard down on his basement floor, and poured different colors of paint onto the cardboard. Then in single file, he marched his patrol barefoot through the paint, then onto all sides of the patrol box until it was completely covered with variegated tootsie tracks. On campouts, when his patrol mixed instant pudding for dessert, Andy saw no sense in dirtying more dishes, so he'd get creative. He'd simply leave all the pudding in its preparation container and pull his patrol into a tight circle around the container. On a given signal, eight spoons would dive in and chocolate pudding would fly. Between the slurps and slops, the clatter of the spoons attacking each other and banging against the aluminum pan sounded like a Musketeers saber battle. Had the pudding been red, the scene would have *looked* like a saber battle.

One summer evening, I finally got even with Big A. Andy, who lived a block away from me, had hitched a ride to the troop meeting and was probably too sluggish to walk or call someone to pick him up. Rather than ask for a ride home, he—in his creative way—opened the hood of my Volkswagen bug, crawled inside the tiny trunk and had a buddy shut the lid. His intention was to knock on the hood when I pulled into my driveway, then jump out with a wiseacre, "Thanks for the ride, Sholzie."

As I walked out from the church and locked the basement door, one of the kids whispered, "Andy's in your trunk." I smiled, nodded, got in and started the car, put it in reverse, popped the clutch, zoomed backward, hit the brakes, did a couple of donuts around the parking lot, and dashed out onto the street, flying over the curb. We headed for a small, undeveloped park a block away that featured a twisting dirt road that would eas-ily qualify for four-wheel-drive status. Its bumps were especially exciting at about 30 miles per hour. After bounding a block or two through the park, my trunk companion and I were still a mile from home, so I enhanced the journey with a few abrupt starts and stops, a couple more curb launches, fast right-angle turns, and finally pulled up in front of Andy's house. I popped open the hood, then sat and waited. Slowly, this hulk extracted himself from his dinky dungeon. His hair was ruffled far worse than I'd ever seen it before. His eyes looked glassy, and his nor-mal motor mouth dangled and quivered as he looked up at me and growled, "Okay. Who told ya?"

Just because Andy hitched rides home doesn't mean that this guy was sluggish. Before he left Scouting, Andy's folks moved up to a mountain community 30 or 40 miles from Littleton. That summer, Andy rode his bicycle all the way down and into town for meetings. In fact, on one journey down the mountain, he was pulled over for speeding! There was only one Andy O.

The Long, Red Line

In the early 1970s Troop 117 exploded. Fortunately we had the boy leadership to handle the size. Kids like Fitzy, Marshall, Shorthill, and Theis were backed up by the Johnson, Parson, and Moore brothers, Coddington, and a little kid named Greg Schroer. I met Greg while teaching a class in family backpack-ing for the local recreation district. He never missed a session and, while most participants were families, Greg always came alone. It was easy to see that this kid lived to be outdoors and had developed a special rapport with nature at an early age. All it took was an invitation, and this lad jumped at the bit to join Scouts.

My recruiting gimmick worked too well. I uncovered the boy leaders in the fifth and sixth grades at the local schools, then made a special effort to motivate them and their parents to investigate the advantages of Scouting. Once they joined, they pulled others from their classes like the Pied Piper. Along with these popular boys came some active dads. We already had pinned a half dozen Eagles, and another dozen were in the nest. In addition, outdoor talents were becoming exceptional, and the troop was going berserk over backpacking. Of course, I had written this attractive point into my recruiting script, but it also caused a problem. Good backpacking gear is expensive, and many of these families weren't rolling in greenbacks.

Without good boots and a comfortable pack, backpacking could rival a day in the Spanish Inquisition. Although cobblers in the group were scarce, nearly every family had someone who could sew. Why not save everyone's money and design and sew our own backpacks? But we needed high-quality packs—complete with strong, light-weight frames. This was an immense undertaking, and the unfolding of this project is a story of Boy Scout ingenuity.

We needed a design that was practical for use and that could be sewn using home sewing machines. Once we had a good design, we could make a pattern. Kids, Scouters, and committee members all marched out, armed with pads, pencils, and tape measures, to attack the backpack departments of virtually every mountaineering store in the south Denver area. Finally, we achieved the perfect design: a two-compartment pack with outer pockets on each side, a large front pocket, plus a map pocket on the cover.

Led by committeeman, engineer, and chief "seamstress" Dick Theis, machines began to hum. We chose a bright-red, coated nylon, reasoning that "if they're wearing red, we might find 'em." Dick discovered a special, lightweight, conduit material in Missouri for frames; found the frame hardware; and solved the nightmare of bending thin-wall conduit using a special space-age bending tool we acquired from our high-tech neighbor Martin Marietta. Dick sewed the initial backpack, showing it off at a Court of Honor. At the time, you would have paid $70 for this backpack. The complete kit of material, hardware, and frame would cost a boy only $12. With Dick's detailed sewing instructions, this was going to be a piece of cake.

I'm a fairly gentle guy who seldom shouts, pounds on tables, or throws things at people, and I wasn't totally ignorant of the operation of a sewing machine. But as I sat evenings on my back patio for one week that summer, I swear (and I certainly did) that I articulated for my neighbors virtually every colorful expression known to a bo's'n mate. And I wasn't alone. Parents and leaders of Troop 117 endured arm-to-arm combat that week. The material was tough, achieving the exact sewing tension was critical or the special thread would bunch up. Attaching pockets nearly required standing on your head, and sewing that damn divider between compartments elevated blood pressure levels throughout the city of Littleton. Trying to sew through that entanglement of material, I nearly came out of it with my index finger permanently attached to my middle finger. Piece of cake? I probably spent the 50 bucks I saved on Excedrin! While struggling to sew my backpack, the thought hung over me that I had to sew another one for my kid. Never again will I belittle the professional or avocational seamstress. All in all, 25 to 30 packs eventually were created. Granted, some seams were a lot straighter than others, but after being in the trenches myself, I couldn't help but feel an inner glow watching that army of bright-red backpacks bouncing up a mountain trail.

Troop 117, Littleton, CO, 1976

Bring on "Bertha"

Equipping this crew was one challenge. Transporting them to the hills was another, especially on long trips with 30 to 40 people. Bill Shorthill's dad, Ralph, managed the hundreds of school buses operated by Denver Public Schools and came up with the answer: ask the First Baptist Church to share the cost of a bus. Ralph would find a good bus at a good price. The church wasn't interested, so Troop 117 bought a bus. The BSA doesn't recommend that troops get themselves into such financial investments, particularly considering all the insurance and maintenance costs involved. In retrospect I may have to agree. But the fun we had in that 52-passenger orange jalopy more than compensated for the headaches it created. Just seeing the expression of a Jeep driver when he came face to face with a school bus on a four-wheel-drive road was worth the price of admission.

That bus went everywhere. It was probably the first school

bus to successfully traverse 12,000-foot Independence Pass. That ascent burned more oil than gas. At times the bus handled like a wounded B25 bomber, and the decibel level inside almost resembled one.

With the bus usurping the need for parent transportation, we could now expand our horizons and move out to the far reaches of beautiful Colorado. The first big test of "Bertha Bus" would be an excursion over the Continental Divide to Aspen.

Arriving safely at the trailhead, we slipped Bertha, with all 52 seats, snugly into a slot in the parking area surrounded by light-skinned aspen trees. After shouldering our new array of homemade packs, we hit the long trail winding up alongside Snowmass Creek toward Hagerman Peak. From the parking area the peak's snow-mantled summit rose high above the dense forest. It looked so close that Andy O. remarked, "This hike looks like a snap. We should be there in no time." It takes awhile to learn that big mountains have an amazing way of distorting distance.

No other hikers followed us up the trail. It stands to reason that if the Boy Scouts sign on the bus didn't deter some solitude-seeking backcountry adventurers, a snake-dance line of 20 bright-red packs carried by a troop of cantankerous canaries would send them shifting rapidly to Plan B—if not onward to the next watershed or the next state.

Snowmass Creek in early June was roaring. After several touchy crossings, the trail ascended a V-shaped valley bordered primarily by fir trees and oceans of wild flowers—multi-tinted Indian paintbrush; bluish, purple larkspur and monkshood; those intriguing little pink elephants; and, of course, Colorado's state flower, the blue columbine with its five white center spurs back-dropped against five blue pointers. The bouncing red packs added to the splash of colors, all clipping along at an impressive pace. Well, impressive for them, but a tad bit agonizing for the four adults trailing behind. The recovery time for kids is amazing. They could drop, exhausted, on a rock and within minutes be refreshed, reenergized, and zooming ahead at full throttle. I wonder where we adults misplaced that ability?

The sun hung in the mid-afternoon sky when we trudged up the final steep segment, arriving at the sizeable, snow-free flats bordering the lake. What a sight: Hagerman Peak looked like it had emerged several thousand feet straight up from the bowels of the lake. Its near-perfect reflection rested motionless on the smooth surface of the azure-blue water, some spots still caked with ice.

The peace and quiet of the moment was short lived as tents popped up, accompanied by the usual camp-making clamor. Fortunately, there was only one other tent in sight at the lake, and it was obvious that this couple was overjoyed with the invasion of a Scout troop. The young man worked the ski season at Snowmass Resort and spent the long, cold winter convincing this cute, young thing that she should take a restful, romantic pack trip with him come June. Can you imagine the word on this poor guy's lips when 25 Scouts and leaders came bellowing into his sacred Shangri-La? As dawn broke, long before the first barrage of babbling teenage drivel polluted the tranquil morning air, the couple executed—with commando stealth—a strategic withdrawal to some unknown staging area far more conducive to peace and serenity.

Shortly after breakfast, the canaries came alive. Brian Parsons, on a hastily constructed raft, was Huck Finning around Snowmass Lake in jeans and a brown, broad-brimmed hat. Soon he was plowing in to bust up the remaining ice cover, priding himself on being the "first operational ice breaker" ever on Snowmass Lake. Had he taken a dip, we'd have been pounding ice cubes out of his ears for the next two days. To the west, Coddington, Amen, and a score of others with winging arms and arched backs were executing a charming penguinesque descent down a 100-foot snow-packed hill. Ahh, the ingenuity kids can muster when you rescue them from the magnetic pull of the one-eyed monster.

For three days they roamed, explored, climbed, laughed, and sang crazy songs. From the meal-time aroma, it became evident that their cooking skills had vastly improved. Before this trip, I had hesitated to accept any offer to eat with them. Of course, each evening, everyone would gather around to watch Andy O. run his pudding derby. During those three days, no other party arrived. We discovered later that "the word" had filtered downhill.

On departure day, the troopers moved out early to march down to the bus, which would deliver us to a trailhead leading to the base of picture-perfect Maroon Bells. Tents dropped and packs were loaded with unusual speed and efficiency. A few lads wandered up to the lake, standing silently with their heads moving slowly upward for a final look at Hagerman Peak. I love it when kids begin to notice, if not appreciate, the natural beauty surrounding them in these special settings.

With packs hoisted, the evacuation began in a rush. Yes, the trail-horse syndrome again. Normally, I made it a point to bring up the rear for fear of losing stragglers. But with the older kids, there's seldom a need for that. The real reason to play caboose, of course, was the solitude. I could finally hear the birds or stop to admire a wildflower without fear of being trampled. But I had to pay for that solitude with an a cappella chorus of verbal abuse for being the last one to the bus. But this particular day, I got even. About a mile from the parking lot, three attractive pseudo cowgirls emerged from a side trail. Their western hats had far more material than the remainder of their costumes. I stopped and chatted and asked them if they'd seen any kids, and they hadn't. Then the light bulb went on. I asked one if she'd mind snapping my picture with the other two. When we showed the trip slides at the fall Court of Honor, the final picture was old drag-along with his arms around two bikini-clad cowgirls captioned, "Why the Scoutmaster is Always Last."

I didn't know it at the time, but we were only months away from being inundated with a covey of pretty young things.

8

A GENDER SHIFT: TROOP 117 GAINS A NEW PERSPECTIVE

Camping with Girls?

One early autumn I received a call from a Littleton Senior Girl Scout leader whose group was facing "aging" problems. These young damsels were bored with their normal routine and yearned for some high adventure. Marilyn explained how hard it was to keep older girls in the Scouting program. She feared that once their interest waned, they'd be gone. "I understand your guys backpack and mountain climb, go snow caving, and the like," she remarked. Hesitating for a moment, she asked, "Is there any way your boys could teach my girls how to do those things?"

I thought, "Wow, wait until the young studs hear this."

I called a special junior leader meeting the next Monday. I must have looked like the proverbial cat who swallowed the canary, because they all had that "Okay, Sholzie, what's up?" expression. "Have I got a deal for you..." I explained that about 15 senior-high-school and junior-high-school Girl Scouts would like to learn outdoor skills: backpacking, climbing, rappelling, cross-country skiing, etc., and they would like the guys in Troop 117 to teach them. I leaned back and waited for their chests to puff, snide little smiles to slip across their egotistical faces, and snappy little sparkles to spring into their eyes. Instead, they folded their arms across their chests, and they glanced at each other with an expression bordering on nausea. The overall excitement-happiness level rivaled waking up in the morning and discovering that, during the night, you and your sleeping bag rolled onto a fresh present from a cow. One finally muttered, "Naw, we don't want to do that." What, I thought, has happened to the red blood in American boys? They tried to explain.

"Girls? They could never do the stuff we do. Heck, they'll just slow us down. If things get a little tough, we'll have to wait for them while they sit and whimper. And we'll end up carrying their stuff, you know, bobby pins, lipstick, and all the other junk they drag around."

I sat stunned. What an arrogant bunch of little chauvinists. Finally I said, "Hey, we promise to help other people at all times, right? We promise to be friendly, courteous, and kind, right? Well, I think you need to be friendly, courteous, and kind enough to at least meet with the girl leaders and find out exactly what they need." Embarrassing them with a little Oath and Law worked—at least to the point these midget misogynists finally, but begrudgingly, consented to a meeting while expressing inconsequential hope of accomplishing anything.

I called Marilyn, and she seemed far less concerned with my problem than I was. Obviously, the lady wasn't born yesterday; when the meeting night arrived, she sent forth into battle nothing less than her "first team." These girls were bright, cute, and not intimidated. Although my guys definitely took notice, both groups remained so ridiculously stiff and businesslike that the meeting looked like a pre-war powwow between the Hatfields and McCoys. Could it be that neither the boys nor the girls had a clue regarding how to relate to each other under these circumstances? The kids looked at each other, smiled, but said virtually nothing. The adults kept some semblance of dialogue moving. Finally the group agreed the boys would conduct a couple of training sessions on winter camping and, if everything went well, we might try a joint winter outing.

The boy leaders selected three topics for the first session: sleeping bags, clothing for winter camping, and a discussion on snowshoes versus cross-country skis. Various guys were assigned to each topic. When the big night arrived, the instructors seemed well prepared both in topics and materials. I had the boys line up chairs several rows deep in a big semicircle around the presentation area, asking them to leave chairs for some girls in between where they sat, hoping it wouldn't end up looking like a sixth-grade mixer with all the boys sitting on one side and all the girls on the other. Shortly, the outside door to the basement opened, followed by a few moments of giggling, twittering, and arguments about who should be first down the stairs. Marilyn finally led her charges down the stairs. But where had all their confidence gone? From their expressions and body language, these gals seemed to be infiltrating the bear's den of Boy Scouts with the same level of poise and assurance as invading the men's restroom At the base of the stairs, they huddled together for protection like corralled sheep. Our greeting fell flat. When we invited them to take seats among the boys, they eyeballed the situation and promptly plopped themselves firmly on the floor. I began to think we had bitten off more than they could chew.

The presentations on winter clothes and sleeping bags went smoothly, yet the overall atmosphere retained the warmth of a Russian mausoleum. Audience participation was virtually nil. "Are there any questions?" was consistently met by hunched shoulders or expressionless faces and dead silence. A recess for refreshments did absolutely nothing to break the ice. Then we arrived at the topic of snowshoes versus skis.

Troop 117, at that stage, preferred snowshoes. More boys had access to them and, although there were several downhill skiers among the group, few boys owned cross-country skis. Naturally, the presentation was skewed toward snowshoes. I noticed a firm-faced brunette named Jan twitching as she listened with agitated intensity. Finally, she stood, and in a strong, determined voice exclaimed, "I disagree with nearly everything you have said!" Rick Theis, who was giving the presentation, stood dumbfounded. Jan began a tirade on how boring snowshoes were and how hard you had to work both coming and going in the mountains; whereas on skis, you had the pleasure of zooming down the trails and having fun. She proceeded to expound on different skis, boots, poles, and bindings. Obviously, this young lady knew her subject, which was a shock to the young chauvinists who couldn't comprehend that a female-type girl could possibly have acquired this level of knowledge, plus express herself so succinctly on, of all things, outdoor equipment. In the wake of a room full of stunned guys, the girls waltzed out that evening sporting the head tilt and posture of confident victors.

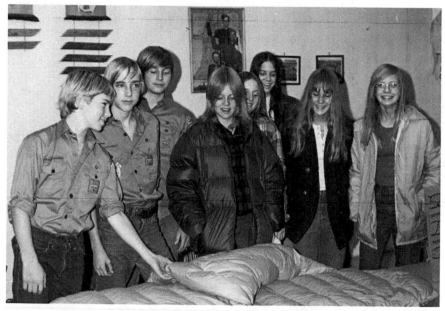
Introducing Girl Scouts to Outdoor Gear

At the next GS/BS meeting, we decided to stress outdoor cooking and present the topic in a way that forced the two genders to communicate. The solution: divide the group into eating groups of two boys and two girls, provide them with a stove, assign a dish to cook, and let them go at it. Did it work? The boys fired up the stoves, the girls did the cooking, and hardly a word was spoken between them. Strike two.

How did they finally break through this teenage communication barrier? It was as simple as British bulldog.

Jan was anything but an amateur regarding cross-country skis. Her dad, Ray, owned and operated a little sporting goods store on Littleton Boulevard called The Outdoorsman. To get this group moving and to help prove his daughter's point, Ray generously offered to supply each Scout with cross-country skis for an evening get-together at a local park. We waited until we had a good snowstorm, then pitted the boys and girls against each other in a mile-long, cross-country ski race. Since many of the kids had never set foot on cross-country skis, this was an exercise in uncoordinated folly. Bodies were strewn in every direction. Some guys crossed their skis on their initial step and fell on their face at the starting line. Some jabbed at others with ski poles when they wouldn't let them pass on the track. Somehow, several became spliced together like pretzels. You couldn't tell whose boots belonged in which skis.

They had a blast. Fortunately, Troop 117 had a couple of guys who could move out on skis, so the boys weren't totally embarrassed by a bunch of girls who seemed to know how to maneuver those slats. With the competition and the incessant joshing, intergroup relations were beginning to thaw, even on a bitter, cold night. Following hot dogs and hot chocolate, some of the girls asked about the game the boys loved so much called British bulldog. They wanted to know how to play it. Remember, this is a physical contest, not one you'd commonly consider a coed activity. But with a couple of feet of snow on the ground and everyone bundled up like Inuits, why not!

As usual, one of the moose-shaped guys was chosen to be "it," and the two genders of Scouts lined up at one end of the snow-covered field. On the signal, this first charge in the dark would have passed for a midwinter buffalo stampede. The snow was so deep, it looked like a running race in a swimming pool.

Naturally, the moose's first victim was a girl, whom he easily corralled and hoisted into the air. The game proceeded until the last Scout was mass tackled and ceremoniously hoisted. Three games later, snowballs were flying, faces were getting washed with the white stuff, and there was little doubt among the adults that the get-acquainted problem had just thawed on a freezing night. On the ride home, one guy with a scratch above his eye commented, "You know, those girls are a lot tougher than I thought!"

It was time to ascertain if this female ruggedness was for real or simply an illusion. The test: a winter backpacking trip. The site: a cross-country ski trail near the east portal of the famous Moffat Tunnel, the 11-mile hole in the rock that, in 1928, ushered the first train under the Continental Divide. The trail wasn't difficult. It headed southwest and ascended gradually to a series of interesting old cabins and barns, which could provide wind shelter if necessary. Plus, the trail ran adjacent to South Boulder Creek, a continuous supply of fresh water. (In those days we didn't know anything about giardia, so we always drank out of the creeks. Thankfully, no one succumbed to what we now call "beaver fever." Maybe a little knowledge is a dangerous thing.)

About 25 kids, mostly the older contingent of both groups, piled their skis, red backpacks, and a few pairs of snowshoes into the big, orange bus. We headed up to Rollinsville, parking near the tunnel. We were blessed with the typical deep-blue Colorado sky, but clouds had begun to thicken over the mountains to the west. The beautiful weather, combined with the fact that this was the first Scouting trip in which I had both a son and daughter along, brought on a true Rocky Mountain high. The Harvey girls and the Johnson boys, Brian LaGrone, Greg Marshall, Brian Parsons, and big Greg Jones, and, of course our resident ski expert, Jan Miller, all glided along with ease. Even with packs filled with lots of warm, winter gear, this group was moving out. Only those with snowshoes were dragging behind, much to Jan's delight!

With an eye to the gathering clouds, the newly communicating coed campers decided to secure their sleeping facilities before fun and games. Some chose to bunk out in the breezy barn, others in dug-in tents and homemade shelters, while Greg Schroer and Scott Ferguson whittled out a snug snow cave. The girls liked that idea so much that if drifts were more prevalent, over half of them would have burrowed into the snow for the night. A little hillside adjacent to the camping area was ideal as a beginner downhill slope, and farther up the trail the steepness and sharp turns gave more accomplished skiers an afternoon of fun and thrills. This was shaping into a successful outing.

Late Saturday afternoon I heard some screaming followed by a whole chorus of female belly laughs coming from a steep hill that led down to the creek. Apparently, one of the junior-high girls was making yellow snow when the drift under her feet gave out—she executed a ten-foot slide on her bare behind. I didn't know what had happened, and I was even more confused when she shrugged up the hill, wandered over to me with a serious expression, and asked if I had brought along a "bun warmer!" More giggles. No doubt the manners and behavioral patterns of junior-high girls rivaled, if not surpassed, those of their male colleagues. I realized it would not be wise to let my guard down. In comparison, the senior-high ladies were nearly matronly, a stable bunch, straight laced, and mature. They, too, needed to stay alert. Weeks after the trip, we learned that the junior-high hussies tricked them into believing that the Boy Scouts had created a contest to see who could capture the best photo of a Girl Scout going to the john (with Girls Scouts I guess it's called the *suzie*). I wondered why the Seniors always headed to the woods en masse. Regardless, they all weathered a cold night and a breezy and cloud-filled Sunday morning, and they ate like Nebraska thrashers. Best of all, the genders were finally becoming buddies. Developing true respect for each other was not far behind.

That spring, I called the Denver Area Council Headquarters

and asked our district executive if we could take some guests to Peaceful Valley Scout Ranch for a weekend campout. He didn't see a problem with this and wondered how many people we would take. I told him about 20 Girl Scouts. Dead silence. He asked me to hold for a minute, and I heard a lively discussion in the background. I waited and waited, enjoying the confusion I was creating and dying to know what the answer would be. Nearly five minutes passed before he returned to the phone and nonchalantly told me, "That'll be fine, Tom." He didn't even flinch when I asked him to reserve one large cabin.

It was now time for the ladies to truly prove their worth... on the wall. That first day at camp, we gathered up our ropes and 'biners and headed to our favorite rock wall, about a mile north of the cabin. It was a vertical 30-footer that dropped into a narrow gulch. The girls had talked a lot about rappelling, but were they up to the challenge? As always, we anchored the rappelling rope to a large ponderosa pine, and one of our larger guys took charge of the belay line. A handful of boys volunteered to rappel first to show how to properly hook up the "diaper" (the harness) to the carabineers, the descent position, and how to get on the wall and descend it. It looked simple enough until that beginner moved back to the wall, then had to face the scary sensation of leaning back into space to safely step onto the wall. Boy, girl, man, or woman—I've seen few things that grab a person's attention like the first step onto a vertical wall. And the girls didn't disappoint us. Their knees shook at about the same frequency as those of the boys, but down they went, exhibiting that same big smile at the bottom and yelling, "Hey, can I do that again?" When the girls went off the wall, the young chauvinists finally regarded them as equals.

The ladies didn't accompany us on our long backpack trip that summer, but come mid-autumn, we invited them to join us on a weekend trip into Wild Basin in Rocky Mountain National Park. Autumn in Colorado is a special time and this had all the earmarks of a spectacular fall weekend. Not a single cloud obliterated the deep blueness of the sky, one of the advantages of low-humidity Colorado. The park is especially enticing after the tourists leave, and Wild Basin, located in the southeast segment of the park, offers some of the region's finest hiking.

A full busload piled into the orange monster, and we headed up to the park. We turned off State Highway 7 at the sign indicating the Wild Basin Ranger Station to register our trip. The dirt road winds from Copeland Lake through a gate and past some private residences, passing over a short span bridging North St. Vrain Creek before turning sharply to the right and heading to the parking area near the ranger station. To our surprise, the station was closed, so we tried the outside phone, which provided a direct connection to the park headquarters located near the town of Estes Park. The phone was dead. We had no burning desire to pilot that bus all the way to Estes Park for a permit, so we fudged a bit—we tacked a note on the station door stating our route and E.T.A., then backpacked up toward Ouzel Falls on the Thunder Lake trail. The trail moved uphill gradually, but the packs seemed heavy, weighted down with the winter gear necessary (to be on the safe side) when invading the Rockies in autumn. With the dense concentration of trees and hills blocking our view to the west, our first clue of a major weather change occurred when the treetops began gently swaying. Before long, they were oscillating vigorously and were soon joined by a thick umbrella of nasty-looking clouds. The sudden drop in temperature prompted a stop for added insulation—wool hats, sweaters, and mittens—and when the clouds began hurling snow downward, it was time to find a place to make camp.

Horizontal real estate was at a premium along that trail, and soon Mary Lou, the Girl Scout leader with us, became increasingly anxious. Finally we located an area capable of handling our dozen tents, and we hustled to make camp. The white stuff was rapidly accumulating, transforming the autumn forest into a winter wonderland in less than an hour. Everyone seemed in good spirits. Tents were up and cooking stoves were humming when Mary Lou pulled me aside and said, "I'm missing a girl." After a quick check, I discovered that I was missing a boy. In moments, I uncovered a little two-man pup tent snuggled behind a large rock.

"Hey," I yelled, "Who's in this tent?"

"Kenny," was the answer.

"Who's with you?"

There was a long pause, then, "Veronica."

"Oh, what are you two doing?"

"Cooking."

"What's cooking?"

Two heads finally popped out—I assume to assure me that everything was on the up and up—but I suggested they do their cooking outside so they wouldn't burn down the tent.

The snow kept falling. Unbeknownst to us, a park ranger had discovered the bus, but not the note tacked to the station door. Realizing that a major storm was heading in, he took the troop's number off the plaque on the bus and contacted the minister of the First Baptist Church in Littleton. The good reverend admitted that he knew little of the goings on with Scout Troop 117 and suggested the ranger contact the Scoutmaster's wife. Char assured the ranger that this gang was prepared for bad weather and, to her bewilderment, seemed to relish camping in it. From the ranger's perspective, that information eliminated a need for a nighttime search, which certainly must have appeared far less alluring than snuggling up to a roaring fireplace that stormy night.

Back in the hills, the sagging roof of my tent revealed there was more than a little snow descending on us. When I peeked out at dawn, snow was piled up two feet and still coming down. I didn't mention my key concern to anyone: How would we navigate the school bus out of that road? School buses were notoriously bad in snow. In Denver, a few inches of snow usually caused school to be cancelled. Right now, though, we had to get kids packed up and out of the woods. As usual, they responded like the troopers they were: dressing in their wool clothes and gaiters, dropping tents, and packing packs. Training does pay off. Soon we were fed and on our way, frequently changing the lead person responsible for breaking trail through the deep snow. If the kids were concerned, they didn't show it. These were prepared, outdoors people having a blast in the mountains in the snow.

Fortunately, we had parked the bus aiming straight toward the road. Bertha would have never survived a U-turn in that much snow. Using the one shovel we kept in the bus, plus an array of cooking pots, the kids scooped out an initial path to get us moving, but the length of our trip was in serious doubt. We needed weight over the rear wheels, so anyone who was the least bit shaped like a rhino sat over the tires, while other heavy weights moved toward the rear. Crawling into the cockpit, I fired up the boiler (that outrageous machine would always start), then barked the final order: "Okay. Sit down, shut up, and hold on!"

The bus zoomed out as though it was on dry pavement, yet the plume of snow left in our wake told the true story. We were in deep powder, but we were really moving. Holding onto the steering wheel was like wrestling with a maverick calf. Although the road was narrow and buried in snow, it was easy to discern due to the line of trees on either side. Man, I thought, if we can maintain this speed, we might just make it. Suddenly, a lone figure appeared in the middle of the road—some crazy guy on cross-country skis. Worse than that, it was a National Park Ranger! I didn't want to make this guy a hood ornament, yet I had to keep old Bertha making tracks. Laying on the horn, I waved him out of the way. He stopped in amazement, then performed a snappy, sidestep dance into the trees just as the bus sped by, dusting him with a powdery fog. Checking the rear-view mirror, I watched him execute a step turn, and then chug after us for all he was worth. Could this be the first time a vehicle would be ticketed by an official on cross-country skis? But no way was he going to catch us.

We approached the 90-degree turn leading up a small incline that crossed the bridge over the St. Vrain Creek. I knew this could be trouble. I slowed Bertha to a crawl to make the turn, and then slowly accelerated to gain momentum to ascend the bridge. I didn't want to gear down too far, yet I needed more power. We were nearly at the bridge, but slowing down fast. I felt the front wheels hit the bridge, but now we were just inching forward. The kids were jerking back and forth trying anything to gain momentum for the final yard or two.

I knew how Mighty Casey felt the day his big bat moved nothing but air. Bertha was stalled on an incline with the rear tires nearly reaching the bridge. I backed up the bus for another try, but it started sliding off the road. We were had. The kids piled out of the bus, everyone offering solutions, none of which would work. We were stuck. And who rounded the turn? None other than the jolly ranger. Immediately I started contemplating the comforts of federal prison and reviewing our crimes: entering a National Park without paying, backpacking with dozens of kids without a permit, and attempting to run over a ranger.

Luckily, the guy was easygoing, especially after he heard about our attempt to make contact. He even shouldered the blame, saying that the gate to the road was supposed to be locked. He radioed for a mountain tow truck and was complimenting the troop on their winter clothing when one of the guys happened to call me by name.

"Sholes... Sholes," he whispered to himself, with that searching-for-something look in his eye. Then he turned, squinted one eye, and stared intensely at me for several seconds. "Hey, you're not the same Sholes we choppered off of McHenrys Peak a couple of years ago?"

I looked him straight in the eye and said, "I'm the guy. The National Park Service pays me to come up every couple of years and create an emergency to see how efficient you guys really are."

He shook his head. With a sly smile, he said, "Mr. Sholes, I hope they pay you well. You sure do one hell of a job."

Incidentally, the humongous, pull-anything-out-of-a-jam, mountain tow truck became mired in the snow, and guess who had to dig it out? The tow-truck operator soaked us for $120 to pull our bus free. We didn't charge the guy a cent.

9

LOST CREEK WILDERNESS: OUR FAVORITE HAUNT

The Sneaky Creek and the Body

A friend clued me into a unique tract in Pike National Forest called the Lost Creek Wilderness Area. Only an hour from home, the region comprises 15,000 acres of rugged backcountry highlighted by spectacular rocky crags and a mysterious creek. Lost Creek meanders through the center of the area, snaking in and out of granite slides. It disappears nearly a dozen times underground, sometimes for a mile or so, into caverns and ice caves before emerging into Goose Creek. In the late 1800s the thirsty Denver Water Board decided to exploit this water source to the tune of over $300,000 by damming up the tricky little creek and creating a subterranean reservoir. A work crew constructed several log cabins and a barn and dug a huge vertical shaft. Unpredictable underground wanderings of the creek proved too elusive. They abandoned the project, leaving a well-preserved ghost town.

The troop's first backpack journey to the so-called Shaft House was a pleasant surprise. The four and a half mile trail was wide with a gradual incline. We encountered a few steep "grunts" along the way, yet the view of the aspen and pine clinging to the red-hued granite across the little valley eroded any serious pain. After about three miles we spotted the rusting remnants of an old, black Model T Ford partially camouflaged by undergrowth near the bottom of a dry creek bed in a spot that appeared to have been a bridge crossing. Arriving at the cabins accelerated everyone's excitement. "It's a ghost town!" they yelled, dropping their packs and dashing from building to building. The dovetailed log dwellings nearly looked new. In fact, one contained most of the original furniture, including a wind-up Victrola complete with a collection of 78 records still in the cabinet. But no needles. (We returned within a month with a bag full of needles, enjoying our lunch to the scratchy tunes of the 1920s.)

Near the cabin, a gravesite had been carefully covered with hand-sized stones. A faded, wooden cross inscribed with the name *Palmer* stood near the head of the grave. The next week at work, I mentioned this during lunch, and an engineer listening at the other end of the table spoke up. "Let me tell you about that," he said. "My dad and Palmer were friends. Palmer was an eccentric, old hermit who moved into that first cabin some years after the Water Board left." He went on to tell how his father would venture out to visit Palmer and fish with him. Every two weeks or so, Palmer would drive an old Model T into Littleton for supplies. When a bridge collapsed across a gully on the road, he'd park the car and hike the rest of the way to the cabin.

One week, Palmer didn't come into town. In fact, he failed to show up for several weeks, so this fellow's father hiked into Lost Creek to see if anything was wrong. He yelled a greeting as he neared the cabin, but there was no reply. The response to his knock on the cabin door was silence, so he lifted the latch and strolled inside. He was struck by a pungent odor. Hurrying, he climbed the steep, wooden stairway between the kitchen and the small living room, and there, lying face-down on the bed, was Palmer, severely bloated and obviously dead for quite some time. The next day, his father escorted the county sheriff to the cabin. The sheriff found no trace of foul play and determined

that Palmer succumbed to a heart attack. In true Western fashion, they rolled Palmer up in the mattress on which he had died,
lowered him out the window with a rope, and buried him about
20 feet from the cabin. The Palmer story would be the basis for
a variety of Troop 117 Halloween adventures for years to come,
rest his soul!

If You Pack it in, Then Pack it Out

To this day, few things elevate my outdoor ire more than empty
pop cans, beer bottles, cigarette butts, candy wrappers, shot-
gun shells, and anything plastic. I never figured out why people
can tote all those goodies into the wilderness when they are
full and heavy, but once they've consumed the contents, all
their strength mysteriously evaporates, and they can't carry the
darn things out. There's probably a little Edward Abbey in me,
although that old desert curmudgeon used to toss beer cans out
the car window, figuring that "they" already screwed up the terrain simply by putting a road there. I became especially disgruntled as our beloved Shaft House cabins transformed over the
years into a massive garbage dump, along with what appeared to
be the intentional destruction of the buildings.

Granted, the folks who worked there in the early part of the
century were no John Muirs when it came to caring for the land.
They left their calling card on a hill a quarter mile southeast
of the cabins in a midden of tin cans, pots, pans, and broken
machinery. At least they somewhat hid their mess. The squatters
who moved into the cabins during the late 1960s and early '70s
seemed to pay lip service to cherishing the Earth, the Air, and
the Water yet left our favorite haunt in a state of ruin. Windows
were broken, furniture gone or destroyed, the log barn demol-
ished for firewood, and tin cans so thick you could hardly walk
within ten feet of either cabin. We loved this spot in the valley so much that we backpacked in there at least twice a year.
Finally, the rubbish heap grew to the point that I couldn't enjoy

the place anymore. One Saturday morning I enlisted a small army of Scouts, and we marched in with backpack frames and gunny sacks and set up the first (and probably only) Lost Creek environmental recycling center.

Even though the lads hiked to their favorite spot knowing they could not stay overnight and with the noble purpose of cleaning the place, this army began to edge toward mutiny once they viewed that mountain of trash from the perspective of compacting, packing, and toting it five miles out—all in the same day. But after a little "good turn" and "protect the environment" pontificating, the project got underway. This was an operation to behold. With their usual creative flair, the troop set up a can-crushing operation that I envisioned evolving into a hand-crushing operation. One guy would set a can on a flat rock and pull back, just as another kid would release the crusher rock. A third kid would move the flattened container into a gunny sack, while the first kid was reloading the rock. Of course, a main object in this operation became *speed*: which team could crush the most cans (or hands) in a given period of time. Fortunately, only the tip of one finger fell victim to the process, and this was an easy repair job.

By mid-afternoon the gunny sack brigade was packed, all sacks lashed to the pack frames, and the army headed downhill with the good feeling of doing a good turn for an old friend.

"Keep Your Heads Low, Boys— the Man-Eating Owl Haunts These Parts"

One late September we hiked to the Shaft House for a weekend outing. The aspen trees high on the mountain across the valley were shifting into their yellow autumn dress. In some years, they unleashed a reddish hue, much to my delight and perhaps to the few kids who were mature enough to appreciate autumn tree foliage. Plus, we were blessed with solitude, since the majority of the summer intruders were now staying at home dreaming of ski slopes, especially if an early snow blanketed the tops of the front range of the Rockies.

This was to be a lazy weekend with no major plans for Scout advancement. It had been only a month and a half since Troop 117 had exited summer camp with nearly a record number of merit badges. This was time to relax, hike around, enjoy the scenery, do a little climbing, cook a couple of tasty meals, and talk a little about troop plans for the coming year.

While the boys were busy setting up camp, I wandered with several older guys up the trail from the cabins to the spot where the actual shaft had been dug. Wisely, the deep, vertical hole was now filled in with large boulders, leaving a mere depression in the earth. The only noticeable artifacts remaining from that engineering fiasco were a large, bulky winch, whose rusty appearance evidenced its eventual demise in the hands of Mother Nature, and a sizeable boiler, already in early stages of decay. Beyond the site were several cozy campsites nestled in a crag-enclosed amphitheater before the trail runs deadhead into a wall of stone that appears to be the end of the trail. Not so. If you stop there, you miss one of the finest scenes in the entire valley.

By veering left along the wall, you arrive at a ten-foot vertical drop-off. Years ago an old metal ladder aided that descent; today you either jump or shimmy down an unstable log "modernized" by several questionable crosspieces nailed to the top. Once down, you find yourself in a grotto-like enclosure surrounded on all sides by granite walls. Narrow passageways branch off between huge boulders, some dead-ending after a short distance, others leading to a maze of options that some first-timers hesitate to explore. A short walk on a select path leads out of the rocky enclosure up to several giant boulders. Jump onto one and walk gently to the edge. Wow! You instantly know the meaning of the "big picture." The valley springs alive. In the late afternoon sunlight, the reds, pinks, and grays of the rocks; the various autumn hues of foliage; and the deep-blue sky accented by cotton-puff clouds blend like the instruments of a symphony into a memorable visual composition. It is the essence of rugged wilderness. And within this magnificent panorama, your eyes finally focus on the creek itself, sparkling in the sunlight, then vanishing as though by sorcery into deep caverns formed by the crags. It was from this vantage point that I saw my one and only mountain lion in the wilderness, sprawled out on a rock far below me. Before I could dig my binoculars out of my day pack, his keen sensing mechanisms alerted him to an aroma he probably perceived as danger. He slithered off the rock into obscurity.

Returning from this favorite overlook, I stumbled upon a dead short-eared owl. I stopped and stared at it for a second. My hiking companions were ahead of me. I quickly picked up the dead owl and thrust it into an inside pocket in my mountain parka while simultaneously contemplating its usefulness. Using the creature's feathers would be great for one of the Indian dance costumes, but possession of owl feathers, like eagle feathers, was illegal. Finding a dead owl is a rare gift; we had to use it for something special. Then it hit me. This troop, like most Scout groups, demanded stories in the evening. I had evolved into a talented storyteller, specializing in scary tales I made up on the spot. But that was hard work. I had to be thinking and plotting two minutes ahead of where I was talking. I often wish I had written down the good ones. That would have saved me a lot of mental labor with new generations of Scouts. By now, Old Ben Sweeney, who gave splitting headaches with a double-bladed axe, was getting a little stale, as was Saskatoon Dan, who dated to the year of the caribou famine. This owl had the makings of a great tale. I chose Jerry Moore to be my co-conspirator and began devising the plan.

That weekend we elected to camp at a secluded location down by the creek rather than up on the flats near the old cabins. The area was surrounded by large boulders and offered more foliage than the flats. There were ample tent sites for the group, but the sites were scattered since open land near the creek was at a premium. Jerry and I reserved a spot for the evening gathering just up from the creek where two boulders provided the right amount of isolation for a campfire.

After dinner and dishes, the sun was still hanging high enough to permit another hour of exploring, and there was a lot to explore in this area. I once found the fabled ice caves of Lost Creek. Thank goodness they were difficult to locate, because they were dangerous. I crawled into one. It was pitch black, but I could hear the creek roaring somewhere in the darkness far below. As I inched forward, I moved onto ice that had a slight slope to it, and I began to slide downward and into the endless bowels of the caverns. In panic, I threw my arms to the sides. Luckily, a wall immediately to my right offered a series of noble handholds that allowed me, in my trembling state, to inch myself back toward the entrance and exit with a pursed-lipped sigh of relief. I never revealed the location of the ice caves to the kids but warned them that they were a potential death trap.

The sun slowly vanished, a match was put to tinder under the firewood and then we tortured a song or two before moving into the meat of the evening. I loved the camp songs. They reminded me of my old troop as a kid. We had been a singing group. But as time wore on, singing, at least at the troop level, lost its "coolness." Too bad, because campfire songs are a fun, memorable part of Scouting. When the sky turned jet black, I began unwinding the tale of the man-eating owl.

The dancing flames of the campfire tossed flickering light on the adjacent rocks and trees while a slight, insidious breeze brushed through the tree tops and undergrowth. My stories always had a local twist. Old Ben Sweeney's cabin, the site of many gruesome slaughters, had scores of locations throughout the state of Colorado, depending on where we camped at the time of the telling. Naturally, tonight, the man-eating owl was known to dwell in the mysterious craggy caverns of Lost Creek.

"When the owl was just a fledgling, a little hooter so to speak, its mother was killed for fun by a thoughtless, heartless hunter. Tiny and sitting camouflaged on a branch of a tall ponderosa, the little owl witnessed the butchery of his beloved mom and since that time developed a perilous posture of misanthropy. In light of such trauma, this feathered fledging developed a deep hatred for people, especially 'men people.'"

As I described a variety of reported, local encounters with this man-eating owl, a distinct hoot filtered in from a distance. Everyone fell silent. It was as though human ears actually turned, like a mule's, in the direction of the distressing sound. I ignored the hoot and continued describing the viciousness of the owl's attacks: how it would sweep down in silent flight toward its human prey, smash into the victim's head, and flail furiously while digging its talons deep into his skull. As usual, I was getting my kicks watching the expressions. That was always a clear indication of the success ratio of a story. This one had all the earmarks of a high scorer. In the firelight I could see that their eyeballs had grown to the eye/head ratio of an owl's. I especially was getting a bang out of ol' Drew Baird, a Texas transfer, who—like all true Texans—was 90% mouth. And when the next hoot sounded, the bulge of his eyes matched the circumference of his gaping mouth.

"Was that an owl, I heard?" I asked. There was no answer. You couldn't hear a breath. This group was nothing but ears and eyes. There it was again, "whoo, whoo, whoo" in rapid succession and close to the campfire. I was beginning to tell them that hearing the hoot must be an unusual coincidence, when a shrill, blood-curdling scream erupted from one of the tents. Everyone sprang to their feet, spinning anxiously toward the noise. The shrieking continued, now accompanied by wild thrashing in the underbrush. Jerry Moore dashed out of the darkness, screaming for help. The dim light of the campfire illuminated a huge owl clinging to the top of his bare head, wings beating furiously, and talons penetrating his forehead. Jerry threw himself on the ground, retching in "pain" while I yelled, "find me a stick—

anything." There was no one left to help; it was as though the whole troop had vaporized. The earth must have opened up and sucked them in. Troop 117 had vanished *in toto*.

One by one, trembling boys filtered back to the campfire, then discovered the ruse. "Hey, that really was a good one, Sholzie," they admitted, even though they weren't sure if they had witnessed fact or fiction. Drew Baird took absolutely no chance. It required a troop-wide search-and-rescue mission of over an hour to find the tenacious Texan and to convince him the air raid was over and it was safe to return to camp. Somehow, I don't think ol' Drew slept too soundly that night. But the Academy Award for that year belonged to Jerry Moore. He nearly had me believing the attack of the man-eating owl.

Troop 117 Meets the Ghost of Old Palmer

The true story of old Palmer dying in the cabin and being buried in his mattress is intriguing enough, but spicing up the story around Halloween could make the old hermit downright exciting. The idea to go to Lost Creek for a Halloween haunting came out of a Patrol Leaders' meeting—they wanted to generate something really scary. I told them about the Halloween adventures we had concocted in Minnesota in the old farm house, and that's all they needed. The Palmer cabin! The plan was underway.

Most of the Leadership Corps feigned sports activities the weekend of the first Halloween caper. In reality, they drove to the trailhead several hours early and parked their cars in a remote location. They hiked in and pitched camp in a secluded area a half mile farther north from where we normally camped, on the flats a couple hundred yards south of the cabins. The troop arrived before noon, and we kept the guys jumping with advancement activities and rappelling, so they wouldn't wander into that clandestine camp on the hill.

Darkness filters in fast by late October. The early evening routine was to eat and clean up before dark, then get a campfire going. After a round of campfire chatter and marshmallow smores, one of the "in" guys turned to me and said, "Hey, Sholzie, how about telling us about that old hermit who died up here."

"You mean old Palmer?"

"Yeah."

I began unwinding the tale and contorting the truth nearly to the breaking point. "Rumor has it that ol' Palmer might actually have been murdered, and the Sheriff knew it but did nothing. Many think the Sheriff himself might have been involved. Some say that Palmer had money stashed up here. That could have been the motive. Anyway, lots of folks have reported strange things happening around here and feel pretty strongly that Palmer's spirit still hangs around his place, especially in October, when all this happened. Some think he's looking for revenge, but all this seems pretty far out to me—although I have heard some bizarre sounds around those cabins at night." I had achieved their undivided attention.

My suggestion to stroll up to the cabin in the dark to see if we could detect anything strange was met with mixed reviews. A few brave hearts were ready to go, but the majority vocalized feeble excuses to stay near the nice, warm fire. We eventually goaded them into a brief "investigative journey" with the older "in" guys successfully belittling the manhood of anyone who persisted to remain behind.

It's a short walk from the flats to the cabins. The troop was, of course, clued in that anytime you're dealing with the spirit world all lights must be out. To enforce that, the only flashlight permitted was a dim one I carried. (For some unexplained reason, spirit beings detest lights!) In total darkness, we snaked single-file across the flats, down and up across a dry creek bed, and finally the group, crowded together like caterpillar segments, stood silently outside the cabin in which Palmer died. I suggested that we walk quietly around to the north side of the cabin and examine the grave. I shined my dim light back and forth across the grave. The wooden cross that once stood propped by rocks and was crudely carved with *Palmer* was now gone; only a slight depression remained, covered with hand-size granite rocks and freshly fallen leaves. From this vantage point, we could look up at the window from which his body was lowered. We reflected for a moment on the lonely life of a hermit, living alone with no electricity, no modern facilities. It was easy to see how simple it would be for someone who had a grudge or sinister purpose to commit murder. Requesting that everyone remain quiet and orderly, I whispered that we would now enter the cabin and move up to the room where he died. Few seemed enthusiastic about doing this, yet not a soul voiced an objection. No doubt, standing alone outside that dark, shadowy cabin was not a cherished option, either.

The front door opened easily, although its hinges groaned a squeaky chant from years of rusting. The anterior room was small. A black hearth in the stone fireplace on the opposite wall testified to decades of hard use. A rough-hewn wooden bench sat in front of the hearth; another rested against a wall. Using my light to let everyone see the room, I motioned them to sit and asked them to be especially quiet and listen. The only sound at that moment was a breeze rustling the tree branches. Speaking softly, I recapped the story, just to enhance the atmosphere, before opening the door to the back of the house and peeking into the adjoining kitchen. The dismantled remains of a woodburning stove stood in one corner along with two broken wooden chairs painted a now-faded, ugly green. Several floorboards had apparently been sacrificed for heat, leaving gaping holes near the entry to the kitchen. To the right of the kitchen door, a steep, narrow stairway led to the one bedroom that composed the entire upstairs: the room where Palmer had died.

I cautioned them on the steepness of the stairs and suggested they follow me up slowly in single file, holding onto the wall to the right. The stairway creaked like an old man who had worked too long and too hard and was unhappy with this extra burden.

Finally the last little guy, who must have promised himself to remain in a good position for a fast exit, topped out and entered the bedroom. Here, the floor was still intact with no threat of breaking through. A few bits of garbage lay scattered, but the room, walls, and windows were in reasonably good shape. The furniture had long since vanished with the exception of two bare, spring mattresses piled on top of one another in the far corner of the room. This would be the last object that the dim beam of the flashlight would illuminate.

I'd hardly told of the discovery of the bloated body on the bed when several of the kids standing in the front suddenly pushed backwards into the group, saying they heard a sound, like bedsprings squeaking. "Aw," I replied, "it's probably only the wind," then continued nonchalantly with the story.

"There it goes again!" someone half shouted while trying to whisper. "There's something in that corner, Sholzie, I'm not kidding." A couple of the kids already backed onto the stairway when I pointed the light in the direction of the sound. There, on the top of the two rusty bedsprings, rested a well-worn brown blanket. But more disturbing than that, it seemed as though there was something underneath the blanket! The faint illumination lingered on the scene for only a moment when it became evident that the "something" was moving. By now, that wasn't the only thing moving. When a low, painful groan erupted from beneath the blanket, flashlights appeared from nowhere, and the stampede down the stairway resembled the bull run at Pamplona. One of the "in" guys screamed: "It's getting up!" The crew lit the afterburners and flew out the back door, moving en masse toward camp without a peek back at the cabin. Who stood waiting for them? The scheming, conniving Leadership Corps sporting cocky expressions of "Got you, didn't we?"

We returned many times to that scene to perpetrate Halloween horrors. Over the years, the upstairs floor began to lose its stability and the stairway virtually vanished, but ol' Palmer still managed to maraud the place and scare the wits out of unsuspecting newcomers. Sometimes ol' Palmer would appear from a corner in the front room or up through broken floor boards. Once, there he was, dangling from a rope in the kitchen.

During one of the last Halloweens at Lost Creek, I escorted the kids to the cabin for our traditional after-dark graveside talk. As usual, the autumn leaves had deposited themselves into the grave's depression. In fact, they looked a little thicker than usual that year. While I spoke, something began to happen: the leaves in the grave shifted slightly. With my mouth dangling open, I stopped talking in the middle of a word and stared blankly. A sight I couldn't believe was unfolding before me. Something began emerging from the grave, gradually out from the shadows and into the faint moonlight that bathed the site. It was—no it can't be. It was a decomposed hand coming straight up out of the grave! I backed away and stood for a second in absolute awe, staring in confused astonishment. The kids were exploding out of there. Although my mind said *Go!* my legs simply wouldn't move. Then, a familiar face emerged from the leaves and, with a wide smile, said, "How'd you like that one, Sholzie?"

I wish I could have met Palmer. Our antics certainly were not meant to dishonor the man. Wherever he is, I hope he enjoyed giving shivers and weak knees to hundreds of jelly-legged city kids—and one deserving Scoutmaster who got caught up in his own hoax.

We survived Palmer, but could we survive wilderness emergencies?

10

TROOP 117 LEARNS THE SECRETS OF SURVIVING

Dark Nights on the Other Side of Lost Park

The easy entry into East Lost Park's open meadows made it a favorite locale for first-time backpacking and hand-whittled canoe races down the creek. But the meadow was also a site of a few solitary, if not scary, nights. Here we practiced the celebrated motto of the BSA, *Be prepared*, relative to surviving in the wilderness. Every so often some switch-back-short-cut jockeys or an occasional space cadet whose wit was on furlough, would mysteriously vanish from the group and spend hours—and on one occasion, the whole night—in some location other than where they were supposed to be. A whole patrol lost, if they had their equipment and a good patrol leader, didn't necessarily keep me from sleeping. But knowing a loner was out there added a few white strands to my already graying hair. On one backpacking outing, we planned to spend five days in the Eagles Nest Wilderness. Fitzy's patrol had a new transfer from California, a bright 14-year-old lad. I questioned taking him along on this long trip, since we had no idea of his capabilities, but Fitzy insisted the boy had a lot of camping experience. As it turned out, most of this experience was gained on Newport Beach.

The trail to our first camp at Eaglesmere Lake wound upward,

spawning a heart rate bordering tachycardia—1,700 feet elevation gain in just a couple of miles. We hadn't tromped out of
sight from the bus when our Golden Bear caved in. I don't ever
remember being angry with Fitz—he was a great kid—but at
this moment, I was irritated. I reminded him that if he vouched
for an unknown entity, he and his patrol must shoulder a good
deal of the responsibility to get this lad safely through the trip.
I waited while they unloaded some of the boy's belongings into
their packs and stayed long enough to ensure they were moving
again. Then I dashed ahead with several of the younger boys to
check on the rest of the troop. Before moving on, I explained
the two turns they had to make to reach Eaglesmere Lake, both
well marked.

Within a half hour of trudging uphill, I caught up with stragglers from the leading half of the group. The color of the sky was
becoming increasingly ominous, so I put the spurs to the crew.
We made the final turn into the lake just as the initial drops
began moistening the boulders bordering the tiny, mosquito-
infested body of water. Some tents were already up, but with the
sky now rumbling, the stragglers' tents popped open in haste.

A cold, mean rain coupled with corn snow pounded the
tents for nearly an hour, and I waited another 20 minutes, but
no Fitzy. It was getting dark. Volunteers to go back down the
trail with me were about as thick as the Cobra Patrol's instant
soup. Who finally emerged with a virtuous "Well, somebody's
got to do it" swagger? None other than Andy O. So off we went,
sloshing down a once-dusty trail, now a sea of muck. If there
had been footprints, they were obliterated by the new creek that
occupied most of the path. For nearly two hours, we skidded
and slid all the way back to the bus, but the four bodies we were
seeking remained missing in action. By the time we staggered
back into camp, we were beat, cold, and resembled mud wres-
tlers. Both hands on my wrist watch now pointed straight up.
"Well, Andy, they have a good leader, tents, sleeping bags—let's
worry about it in the morning."

Shortly after sun up, I rechecked my map. There were only two options: they either missed the turn onto Gore Trail or missed the turn to the lake. Send out the Scouts. As it turned out, Fitzy's fuzzies maneuvered the first turn correctly but, in the fading light, missed the lake, nestled but a hundred yards in from the trail. Fortunately, they stopped and made camp in time to stay dry. By the time we found them, they had packed up and were heading northward on the Gore Trail. In two days they could have been in Wyoming. That's why I preferred the shorter, familiar environs of East Lost Park to experience wilderness survival.

Troop 117's Spin on Wilderness Survival Training

In the early 1970s, the BSA introduced a *Wilderness Survival Merit Badge* book that would have been a belly buster if it hadn't been so dangerously misleading. This document encouraged kids to build wickiups and sweat lodges along with methods that burned hundreds of precious calories in search of a few. Experts who knew wilderness survival were livid. More accurately, the book should have been titled *Pioneer Camping*.

Wilderness training at our summer camps also lacked teeth. Kids were rationed a whole pound of hamburger, a shelter, a sleeping bag, and all the candy they could smuggle, then would spend a night in an open field with 15 other kids. It was time to get real and develop our own wilderness training program.

Each participant had to be at least a First Class Scout, have completed the Camping Merit Badge, and have had some initial wilderness experience. After several Monday-night classes covering survival basics, we backpacked into East Lost Park with its grassy meadows surrounded by wooded mountain terrain. Once there, the boys pulled out daypacks with only those items they would normally carry on a mountain hike: lunch, water, matches, knife, compass, rain gear, sweater, warm hat and gloves, and a space blanket. No tent, no sleeping bag—no pound of hamburger. At noon, we disbursed individual boys into the wooded areas bordering the meadow where each boy would spend the night alone. If they came across another Scout in their search for wood or materials to construct a shelter, they were under oath to ignore him and not speak. They were to stay by themselves until 9:00 the next morning when they could return to camp. As a safety measure, the boys carried whistles, and they knew we would keep a lantern lighted in camp. If they ran into trouble or couldn't handle the dark solitude, we encouraged them to toot or return to camp. No one ever did.

During the afternoon and early evening, adults would sneak around and peek into each site. Most kids had learned their lessons well. Space blankets were hung and secured at an angle, creating a shelter from wind and possible rain and acting as a gigantic reflector oven. They constructed their ground beds with boughs between the space blanket and a small fireplace, frequently located close to a huge boulder, making a double reflector. By nightfall, most kids had gathered enough firewood to stay through the winter. When they were finally enveloped in darkness in a land complete with bears, mountain lions, bobcats, and other critters of the night, were they afraid? Some were afraid for awhile, but we would debrief them in the morning and uncover some interesting facts:

Biggest problem:	Hunger? Thirst? No, boredom.
Biggest fear:	Letting the fire go out or sleeping too late and missing breakfast.
Biggest surprise:	All the great thoughts that drifted in when you're by yourself for so long. As one lad put it, "I got into my own head."

No one reported being cold, most rationed the minimal food they had, and no one came running out of the woods at 9:00 a.m. Most important, they all seemed confident and ready to go back and do it again. Kids do adapt well to new situations. We advanced to conducting this exercise sans sleeping bags in midwinter. I pitied any kid they encountered who bragged about passing wilderness survival at summer camp.

Snow Caving at a Glacier:
A Close Call on a Subzero Night

Colorado boasts over 50 mountains exceeding 14,000 feet. Regardless of possessing all these "Rocky Mountain highs" and the distinction of having the highest overall elevation of any of the 50 United States, Colorado is weak on glaciers, thanks to its more-or-less southerly latitude. The Rocky Mountain National Park region offers a few insignificant rivers of ice, but no glaciers to match the Canadian Rockies or the states of Montana and Washington. Yet, just off Interstate 70 and west of Idaho Springs, one little glacier and its surrounding terrain provided an abundance of happenings for the Scouts and adults of Troop 117. Some escapades proved somewhat paradoxical to the glacier's sacred name, St. Mary's.

The first time we visited St. Mary's Glacier was for a little early-summer skiing. Of course, we weren't alone. Dozens of slat fanatics were showing up like empty-handed deer hunters trying their darnedest to extend the season. We learned something from these fellows, however. The snow buildup in the winter at the glacier's base was of storybook depth and quality—ideal for snow caving.

That year, winter couldn't come fast enough. Real snow caving was truly advanced camping, and this gang was ready to give it a try. Nearly two-thirds of the troop was up for this activity after we coached them on digging methods, clothing, and living comfortably in a cave. We stressed one key factor: chances are you'll get wet digging your cave, so have ample dry clothing along. Also, a water-repellent ground cloth and pad are essential.

The sun was its usual bright self as we packed up the narrow trail leading from the parking area to St. Mary's Glacier.

After about a mile, we found excellent snow. Some drifts were six- to eight-feet high and well settled, ideal for caving. The guys broke into teams of two, three, or four. No Scout was allowed to cave alone. Soon shovels hummed, and snow flew. One four-man team attempted to create a three-room mansion. After an hour and a half of digging, they came face-to-face with frozen earth—the side of a hill. They started again and, this time, seemed satisfied with a simple one-room cottage.

By late afternoon, when the west wind picked up, most of the teams completed their caves, removed their wet clothes, and sought the warmth of their new dwellings. It was amazing how much heat one small, backpacking stove could generate. Some teams became concerned that their caves would become too warm and slowly turn into dripping shower rooms. After dinner, the adults made another check. Everyone reported being just fine and toasty. New Assistant Scoutmaster Jim Colburn, who was leading this trip, checked two of the younger boys who had come into the troop together. They said they had already eaten when Jim poked his head into their cave, and both appeared to be comfortably snuggled into their sleeping bags.

Jim had an amazing sixth sense. Before he crawled in for the night, he pulled on his boots and warm parka to make one last check. He headed into a full-blown windstorm—a total white out. All the packs and tarps serving as entrance covers were now camouflaged with wind-blown snow. I've experienced this, and it's a tough situation. Add darkness to blowing snow, and depth becomes a lost dimension. Finding a cave is like locating King Tut's tomb. It's nearly impossible to identify a cave location unless you actually stumble onto the entrance. Plus, the blowing snow quickly conceals your tracks. Suddenly you're standing in subfreezing temperatures with an egregious wind-chill factor and you've lost your own cave! That's more than embarrassing, it's downright frightening.

With blind luck and his native skill, Jim located most of the caves, especially the ones containing the least experienced kids.

When he found the two boys in question and flashed his light into the white cavity, both sleeping bags resembled a conclave of Mexican jumping beans. Both kids' voices were vibrating so badly they couldn't speak clearly. He crawled inside the cave, took off a mitten, and felt inside each bag. These boys were wet and reaching the business end of third-stage hypothermia. He didn't stop to ask the whys and wherefores. Hustling them out of their damp bags, Jim helped each into dry sweat shirts and sweaters and into boots and jackets, then pushed them out of the cave entrance. The two shivering lads nearly panicked when they faced the wind and snow, but there was no time to dwell on that. Jim ran them down the trail toward the parking area and threw them into his old VW van that was complete with bed and an exceptional heater.

That was the closest call our troop ever encountered. I fear that those boys would have been ice cubes by morning. Jim was able to deduce what went wrong: Like nearly everyone, they became wet and cold building their cave. But when they finished, they hurried into their sleeping bags—still wearing damp clothes—and didn't take the time to lay out a ground cloth and unroll their pads. I still shudder at the thought of the potential outcome. It was the last time our troop allowed young, inexperienced boys on a high-adventure winter activity.

Avalanches, Snow Mansions, and Girls at St. Mary's

For the most part, winter trips to St. Mary's Glacier were relatively placid. Well, other than the time Greg Schroer caught an exhilarating ride down the glacier on a room-size block of snow that broke loose and slid with a convoy of other segments in a full-blown slab avalanche. While most trips were tame, they certainly weren't boring. Take the time Troop 117 built the four-room, eight-man snow cave monstrosity. This was snow caving at its finest. It featured a low tunnel entrance to maintain the heat, a living area complete with carved-out benches, and tunnels leading into three sleeping areas. A handful of candles jammed into the snow produced enough light to nearly blind you. Inside the cave a light sweater kept you warm. Outside, the wind-chill factor dropped to nearly 65 degrees below zero. How cold is 65 degrees below zero? One kid swore that when he dashed outside to make yellow snow, he nearly ended up with a yellow icicle!

Caving at St. Mary's became an annual activity. When the Patrol Leaders' Council put together their camping wish list for the year, St. Mary's was high on the list. One year the Girl Scouts snow caved with us at St. Mary's. Naturally, we had to arrive on cross-country skis, but as usual, the thrust of the day was consumed in digging. And dig they did. Combining the creativity of the girls with the guys' strong backs resulted in a near Frank Lloyd Wright design: rooms in all directions. Creating an ice palace may have been fun, but it ultimately left about a half dozen girls without a separate cave of their own. My son waltzed up and said, "Hey, Dad, you know the girls worked all day on this cave. It's only fair that they get to use part of it." My mind danced back and forth between, "Hey, this isn't totally kosher" to "They worked all day on it, and I trust these kids; plus, there's ample sleeping space so the boys and girls can have their own areas." Don't ever tell the GSA, but you can guess which argument won out.

Just Dropping in for the Evening

St. Mary's Glacier hosted a particularly bizarre snow caving event the year Norm Tuccy joined us as Assistant Scoutmaster. Norm was a taciturn, mild-mannered guy who drove an 18-wheeler for a large grocery chain. He was a good guy, and the kids liked him. Norm never came across as a rough, tough trucker. He fit into the reserved, shy, stay-home-at-night-and-whittle category. So it wasn't surprising that Norm decided to dig his own cave and sleep in there alone.

The snow was exceptional: deep, well-packed powder. Norm picked a spot on the edge of the good stuff. Not wanting to feel cramped, he dug a narrow, exceptionally high cave that you could stand in. We completed all the digging earlier than usual, but then the weather was unusual. It was a sunny, reasonably warm day with a slight breeze. The troop spent the remainder of the day having fun—skiing on the glacier and along the trails between the glacier base and St. Mary's Lodge, a little hostelry that included a downhill ski area (if you want to call it such).

Norm ate dinner and retired early to his cave. I suspected that after a week of barreling over the high, snowy, mountain passes with his truck, a full night's sleep might have climbed near the top of his Things To Do list. Hopefully he dozed off quickly that night, because smooth slumber wasn't destined to last long.

The moon was at a waxing quarter, yet it still bathed the trees and the snow with shadowy illumination. At the lodge, a sweet, young thing and her boyfriend, fortified with antifreeze, decided to steal away for a romantic, moonlight stroll up to the glacier. The caves were silent. Old Norm Tuccy was sawing logs while huddled deep in the recesses of his warm sleeping bag. It was a perfect night.

The sweet, young thing was romping around in the snow ahead of her dawdling boyfriend when she stumbled onto a thin patch of snow and disappeared from the face of the earth. Frantic, the boyfriend heard her muffled screams, but didn't have a clue to her whereabouts. Meanwhile, down in the cave, Norm felt a sizeable weight topple onto his bag, followed by screams reminiscent of high-school girls watching an old Frankenstein movie. When he began to grunt and move in the bag, the screams hit their apogee. From her perspective, this gal had just dropped in on a hibernating bear. Norm now realized he had a female thrashing around on top of him. He must have thought he had died and passed on to some crowded, frosty place in heaven.

Either that or hell had just frozen over.

As they say, all's well that ends well. Norm was able to halt the hysteria of the frenzied female and reunite her with her baffled boyfriend (who had gone completely bananas stomping around in the snow in a frantic but fruitless search). Norm returned unscathed to his roofless hideout, probably shaking his head in dismay, to spend a relatively comfortable remainder of the night.

Of course, the rest of the troop slumbered though this entire comic opera in the peace and solemnity of our well-insulated isolation booths. Troop-wide jealousy hit that morning when shy, reserved Norm unfurled his outrageous tale.

11

WANDERING THE WILDERNESS: FROM MOUNTAIN SUMMITS TO DESERT CANYONS

Ascending Mount of the Holy Cross

Weeklong expeditions into wilderness areas simply whetted appetites for more. In unison, we yearned for endless acres of aspen and Douglas fir, vast granite outcroppings, sparkling lakes, and gushing creeks with the hope of encountering few other human beings. Come spring, we invaded standard forest service campsites when most peoples' sleeping bags were still slumbering deep in the basement. But with the warmth of summer, we tapped our Vibrams into locales with *wilderness area* for their surnames, such as Eagles Nest, Holy Cross, Rawah, and Flat Tops. Our expedition into Holy Cross Wilderness Area was the first time we combined a long pack trip with the ascent of a 14,000-foot mountain.

Mount of the Holy Cross is distinctive. It's not a tough climb, yet it has claimed lives. On the eastern face, a huge vertical trench descends sharply from the summit, bisecting a horizontal gully several hundred yards down, thus forming a cross.

Snow tends to linger in these depressions well into the summer, which makes the huge cross visible from great distances. For years, the cruciform of ice and snow attracted organized pilgrimages to an area directly below the cross known as the *Bowl of Tears*. Disabled people climbed to this viewpoint on crutches, some on hands and knees, seeking special powers from this special mountain.

The journey up Cross Creek and the eventual climb of the mountain had a spiritual significance for several of our boys. But for most, the joy of being in the wilderness; the pain of the steep, switchback-laden trail; the climb itself; and the relief of arriving at a campsite with the subsequent fun and friendship overwhelmed any metaphysical sensations. As one remarked, "You know why I like to backpack? It feels so darn good when you quit." Amen, brother.

We discovered our camping sanctuary at the base of Holy Cross by blind luck. The main trail veered away from the creek and, after miles of switchbacks, our energy levels dissipated. We bushwhacked through low-growth brush and followed a faint deer path in the direction of water. The dense undercover gave way to a flat, clear expanse bordering both sides of Cross Creek with ample space for tents. Here we relaxed, enjoying a king's view of Mount Jackson and other rugged, snowcapped peaks to the west. A huge log straddling a narrow section of the creek provided easy access to the other side.

By morning the aches and pains of the long journey had evaporated from the kids' legs; dads Dick Theis, Bill Grabou, and I could have wallowed away another day in the serenity and scenery before attempting the ascent, but the laddies were up early, the sky was clear, and it was time to go. There was no way we would lead them up the cross route. That was a difficult rope-up ascent. Several years before, two climbers descending the cross (including one from Littleton) lost their footing, slid out of control on mushy spring snow, and tumbled over a drop-off. A third climber, roped to the other two, stopped abruptly at the drop and probably had thoughts about how fortunate he was—just before the yank of the rope catapulted him into space. The Littleton man, father of several children, didn't survive.

We chose a northerly route and worked our way up a boulder-laden ridge to the summit, taking care to avoid huge snow cornices still overhanging the ridge toward the leeward side. Cornices produce exceptional excitement when you're inadvertently on one and your ice axe penetrates deep into the snow, creating a hole through which you see nothing but clear, mountain air. Back with the Wisconsin Norskys, such an incident qualifies as an "uff da."

The final ascent to the summit was the usual high-altitude puff—pounding one foot ahead of the other over granite boulders. And then you're on the summit, chest pumping for more oxygen out of that rarified air, yet standing in awe of a seemingly endless view. I surveyed my cast of characters on the summit of Mount of the Holy Cross, all turning like second hands to make eye contact with the ocean of snowy mountain peaks in every direction: my son Scott in his green polka-dot hat, the Parsons boys and Theis brothers, Bryan Johnson, Greg Schroer, Gene Fitz, Bob Grabau, John Shorthill, and Scott Ferguson. I especially remember that Mike Johnson, a devout Christian lad, was thrilled to be standing, wind blown, by the small, wooden cross marking the summit. The view from a Colorado fourteener—with its 360-degree kaleidoscope of distant, jagged peaks—is an instant reminder of why you suffer through these climbs. "Whoopies" and "yeahs" are absent; a quiet introspection seems to supplant outward exuberance. The stay is always brief, and each one of us savors it quietly in his own fashion. I wondered what thoughts sped through the kids' minds as they silently surveyed that sight. One Scout told me years later that those experiences added to, if not compounded, his lifelong love of nature and the great outdoors. In a recent email message, he related his "short version of how you changed my life." Mount of the Holy Cross was his first fourteener, and he went on to climb all 54 of Colorado's fourteeners, plus spent three months hiking from the Mediterranean to Switzerland through the Alps. "In addition to getting 'turned on' to nature," he continued, "my Scouting adventures affected my choice of majors in college, environmental conservation, which led to summer jobs with the Bureau of Land Management, U.S. Forest Service, and National Park Service." He reported that he is now in law school and specializing in environmental law. He concluded by saying, "If you ever wonder whether your time with the BSA was well spent, know that you have touched at least this soul."

Descending from that big chunk of rock didn't punish the lungs as much. But it was a reminder that knees were still connected to the legs of these mountain masochists. Downhill travel teases your quadriceps. You step easily to minimize the jarring, which reverberates all the way up the back. I'll take going uphill any day over a descent. Although climbing uphill is a grunt, you can always stop and steal an extra breath. However, high-altitude winds usually crank up in the early afternoon, providing a threat of a storm and hastening your downhill retreat into the protection of the trees below timberline.

Finally, you encounter that majestic feeling when you arrive at camp, sink your backside onto the softness of your sleeping pad, rest your back against a log or tree, and sip ice-cold water enhanced with some sugary substance. Giardia was still a mystery, and, thankfully, no one ever contracted it. At times we used halazone tablets to purify the water, but these made the water taste like a swimming pool. Usually, we drank right out of the creek. This time our camp was directly downstream from a beaver dam and probably replete with giardia protozoa. Talk about enjoying good fortunes in our state of ignorant bliss.

That evening, Bryan, the first of three Johnson brothers, decided to pull a Copey and wandered into the beaver pond to test his endurance in the icy waters. I can still picture his eyes nearly ballooning out of their sockets, with his mouth paralyzed in the shape of a gigantic letter O. He didn't bet anything on his short stay, so he didn't disassociate himself from his money. And remember the outdoor plant eater, Euell Gibbons? We had our version of him, too: long, tall Greg Jones, who eventually became a University of Colorado football jock. Greg constantly reminded us that he, like Gibbons, could live off the land. I suppose that's why his hand was always in someone else's food sack. If he got little sluggish on the way back to the bus, I'd simply say, "The last one to the bus doesn't get a hamburger on the way home. Somehow, that would always spark Greg's afterburners. Years later, with a handful of the troop alumni now in their late 20s, we retraced our steps up the Holy Cross trail. Strangely enough, the long switchbacks had grown much steeper and our aching legs moaned much longer.

The Serendipitous Death of Bertha

In our constant quest to invade Colorado wilderness areas, our research turned to the Flat Tops, a quarter of a million acres offering a maze of crisscrossing trails leading to scores of picturesque lakes, soaring volcanic cliffs, and a seemingly endless expanse of alpine meadows and tundra. We just had to get the bus through the recently completed Eisenhower Tunnel, which eliminated the agonizing climb over 12,000-foot Loveland Pass, then drive beyond Vail to Glenwood Springs, and scoot north 20 miles to an entry point. Sounds great. Let's go!

As always, our bus angel, Ralph Shorthill, had Bertha checked out, gassed up, and ready to rumble. A bit overweight but always game, Troop Chairman Duane Newell, decided this trip would be his first major pack trip. With an ever-increasing number of older boys in the troop, Bertha's shocks would be sagging. Even old Montana, now living in his namesake state, showed up to partake in yet another escapade. Little did he know the excitement old Bertha would soon create.

Storming out of Littleton with the usual serene and docile complement of riders screaming, yelling, and singing at a decibel level sufficient to crack crystal, we worked our way to Interstate 70, zipped past the old mining town of Idaho Springs, and chugged up to the 10,000-foot entry into Eisenhower Tunnel. Bertha would never be mistaken as an Indy 500 participant, but she moved fast enough not to be cited for loitering. The few dozing Scouts came alive once we entered the mile-and-a-half-long passageway under the Continental Divide. "Hey, Sholzie," some whimsical cat shouted over the din, "this is nothing but a big bore!" Why didn't I buy a pair of those sound-dulling headsets like the folks directing jets at the airport wear?

Our chief backpack sewer, Dick Theis, was doubling as chauffeur as we exited the west portal. I pointed out Mount of the Holy Cross in the distance as Dick geared down this galloping goose to control its speed and pointed it downward for the long, steep, and winding descent that leads into the towns of Dillon and Frisco. Due to the steep descent, eighteen-wheelers often lose control on this stretch, necessitating runaway ramps at several locations. Everything was fine for the first half-mile or so, and then I heard a strange, mechanical twang. Yet nothing seemed unusual—not until Dick pushed gently on the brake pedal. No response. He pushed it again, this time with vigor. Again, no response. Then he noticed a light on the dash panel indicating that the engine had stopped. In his usual tranquil tone, he told me we'd "lost the mechanical advantage of the brakes." Whoa! If this buggy started moving too fast, we may never get it stopped!

When Dick slipped the bus onto the shoulder's rough gravel the boys began to realize something was amiss. Dick wanted as much surface friction possible. I told the crew we were having a little trouble and to sit down and hold on tight. Meanwhile, Dick strained his right leg to milk anything he could from the brake pedal. For the first time ever, we experienced total silence in the bus. Bounding through the rock and pebbles, Dick grabbed the emergency brake and finally began to feel some drag taking hold. Within 100 yards, the big, orange clunk lumbered to a peaceful stop. Turning the wheels into the mountain, Dick tossed himself against the seatback, fell into a brief catatonic state, and finally decided it might be a good idea to breathe again.

Before we could consider our options, flashing red lights of a Colorado State Patrol car were blinking in our rear window. The officer dispatched a huge, panzer-looking, mountain tow truck, and soon we were two-wheeling it down the steep grade. The tow truck plopped us in a parking lot in the little town of Frisco, 100 miles from our destination and 60 miles from home. The stark reality of our situation set in, followed by disappointment. We weren't going to see the lush meadows of the Flat Tops. But perhaps all was not lost. After phoning Ralph and alerting him to our mechanical demise, I walked into a nearby store, found a backpacking local, and asked him whether there were any entries to good backpacking trails near town. He pointed right across Interstate 70 to a dirt road. He told me to follow the road for one-half mile and then look for a trail along Meadow Creek. If we stuck with that trail, we could circle Red Buffalo Mountain and emerge at Silverthorne a short distance north. He assured me that it would be a snap to complete this route in four days.

Hoisting our packs, we trudged up the narrow, steep entry trail. For the next four days our unplanned venture transformed into an emotional high. For the first time, I watched a lad sit quietly in the pink alpenglow of sunset, nearly moved to tears by the beauty of the moment. One morning I agonized watching big Duane Newell sweating and puffing with his middle-aged belly dangling well over his belt, struggling up the rocky face of a mountain just to do something special with his son. I feared we would lose him to a coronary that day, but he made it to the top. When Duane passed away a few years later, I remembered that morning and was thankful he had shared that special moment with his son. We had no maps. We simply traversed the valleys using compass bearings and good sense, always keeping big Red Buffalo Mountain to our right. Our journey into the unknown turned out to be beautiful and meaningful—a unique adventure with no real destination, but plenty of rewards. (In fact, this trip far surpassed the Flat Tops backpack trip we finally took several years later.) Yes, let's hear it for the thrills and gifts of the unexpected.

We did lose big Bertha; all the king's horses and all the king's men wanted too much money to put her back together again.

Invading Slickrock Country—and Loving It!

During the cold-weather months of early 1975, I began dreaming of hauling the troop to the Bridger Wilderness in western Wyoming. I had worked in the Cowboy State the summer following my Navy tour, and Wyoming's mountain trails were indeed special. I bought topographic maps, studied trails, and in early June I called to check on permits. The ranger laid it right on the line: "There's still so much snow up here, you can't even find the parking lot much less the trailhead." I needed to move on to Plan B. But there was no Plan B.

A month before, I had flown to California with a scheduled stop in Grand Junction. Lifting off from this western Colorado city, the plane headed southwest and, within minutes, soared over a narrow range of mountains east of Moab, Utah. The peaks were impressive; I guessed that some topped out at over 12,000 feet. Only the summits were still covered in snow. The range was surrounded by an endless horizon of red-rock canyons and plateaus. The whole area looked mighty appealing—and it was less than an eight-hour drive from Littleton. Checking a map on my return, I saw that the range was called the La Sals; and, yes, the highest peak, Mount Peale, was over 12,700 feet high. The kids seemed game to try Utah. I contacted a National Forest ranger who seemed delighted that folks were coming from Colorado to wander in his mountains. He mentioned several possible routes and quickly mailed maps to us. When Montana got wind of where we were headed, he immediately signed on. Our new committee chairman, ardent backpacker and emergency bus driver

Dick Theis, rounded out the adults. In early June, we crossed the Colorado-Utah border west of Grand Junction, took a shortcut through the almost-ghost town of Cisco, and came face to face with slickrock country.

I can't recall how many times since then I have traveled Utah 128 between Cisco and Moab. Each time I felt the same thrill I experienced that first day. The initial dozen miles of highway parallels Cisco Wash and is the epitome of sagebrush loneliness. But a glance through the windshield toward the red-hued towers with the snowcapped La Sals to the south as their backdrop was as tempting to a nature lover as the anticipation of your first smooch. I remember wanting to put the pedal to the metal on that first trip, but the road lifts over rises and dips into arroyos and simply won't allow it.

Dropping down into the valley, the canyon walls blocked the view, but soon we ran adjacent to the chocolate-tinted Colorado River as it wound its way out of foamy Westwater Canyon and moved with the potency of a powerful spring runoff. Passing an unattended gas station, we saw a large black-and-white sign reading, "CAUTION—ONE LANE BRIDGE." Driving the lead car, I made the gentle left turn, then hit the brakes. Whoa! Directly in front of me, barely wide enough for a broad-shouldered cowboy, was several hundred yards of white-painted sideboards and a wooden roadbed—an ancient bridge suspended across the mighty Colorado by small-diameter cables connected to aging, metal towers staked on both sides of the river. Dewey Bridge. I wasn't sure if this rickety contraption was named after Thomas E. Dewey, who unexpectedly collapsed in the 1948 election; Admiral George Dewey, who effectively blew anything out of the water; or Huey, Dewey, and Louie, who could demolish everything they touched.

The kids lunged out of the cars, tossing off their auto lethargy, and dashed with newfound zest across the shaky expanse, jumping up and down either to prove their manhood or their faith in this structure. Well, I thought, at least the drivers will be the only ones becoming dunked donuts in the Colorado when this antique caves in. But we made it across. Time and time again we crossed Dewey Bridge. (Today it rests in regal retirement adjacent to a new, modern span that can't flaunt a tenth of Dewey's character or offer an ounce of the exhilaration the old relic generated as it creaked, shook, and bobbled on every crossing.)

The drive along the Colorado River through Professor Valley toward Castle Valley is one of my favorites. Every turn on the narrow, winding road seems to cry for a picture stop. Such contrasts in colors: the blue sky, its hue deepened by the absence of humidity; accents of fluffy, white balls of cotton floating eastward; lush, green spring grasses and foliage; the purple tint of the La Sals, topped with stacks of thick, white frosting; and, of course, the ever-present, rusty-red slickrock canyon walls decorated with black desert varnish—a visual feast. The desserts to this banquet are the monumental mesas and pillars shaped by millennia of constant agitation from wind and water. We all sensed it: A feeling of vastness, wonder, and the exhilaration that comes when you leave your normal world and surround yourself in raw beauty and absolute tranquility.

A weather-beaten sign directs us to the left, up a rutted, earthen road leading to Fisher Towers, a series of striated, brick-toned monoliths sculpted (as is so much of southeastern Utah) from ancient Paleozoic strata. Frustrated mountaineers like Montana, resting in his usual Chinese squat, along with Brian Parsons and son Scott, scrutinized the tallest of the towers: The Titan, a gigantic finger stretching 900 feet into the clear Utah sky. Later in life, The Titan became one of Scott's many mountaineering conquests. A hike to the top of the trail rewards a dozen sets of eyeballs with a striking panorama of the La Sals, including Castle Valley's maze of buttes and mesas featuring humanoid figures eloquently carved by nature, some hosting titles such as The Bishop, Mother Superior, and The Nunnery. We could have ingested this sight for hours, but not today. We had trails to find, miles to pack, and camps to make.

The ranger had sent a forest service map with recommended routes. Several miles from the Fisher Towers road, we headed eastward toward the La Sals on the Castle Creek Road, which led to our chosen trailhead. Cinching up packs, we started upward through lush stands of budding aspen harmonizing with an ocean of red, yellow, and purple wildflowers. Soon, clouds began to thicken, but after a rumble or two from the celestial bowling balls, the sun crept back out, igniting the snow on the jagged peaks dead ahead. By late afternoon, we tripped upon an ideal campsite: flat with a perky little creek dancing by and great protection from the westerly winds, topped with a magnificent view. Tents went up and dinner went on. The surprise of the day was when Greg Schroer (bless his aching back), as though in an act of Blackstone magic, unveiled a whole, fresh pineapple from his bright-red pack. That was a first. Never before and never since have I savored fresh pineapple on a pack trip. Combined with the view, this qualified as an epicurean nirvana. Ah, yes, the thrill of the unexpected.

For three days, we hiked the La Sals from stem to stern, from basement to roof. We worked our way up the less snowy side of Mount Takuhnikivatz to bask in the sun on its rounded summit. Behind us was the elongated ridge of 12,700-foot Mount Peale, which a few of the hearty souls took off to ascend. But to the west, far off on the distant horizon, was a life zone we had never experienced. It looked desolate and foreboding, yet tempting and exciting. Hidden out there were the desert canyons of southeastern Utah, creeping with scorpions, rattlers, and black widows. No doubt, like a wicked temptress, the desert was calling.

After another day of ascending ridges of the La Sals and hiking a multitude of trails without meeting another soul, we reached the top of Geyser Pass, at which time Alan Parsons donned his t-shirt from the famous donkey race between Leadville and Fairplay, Colorado. It read, "Get Your Ass Over the Pass." We were ready to commence our final descent to the cars—but two days earlier than we anticipated. We held a literal "summit meeting." No one chose to head home early; everyone was anxious to move down to warmer climes and have a desert experience. Dick Theis suggested, "Let's go to Arches."

We knew little of this off-the-beaten-path national treasure other than it was red-rock desert headlined by an abundance of natural arches. Within an hour after we arrived at the visitors' center, we became far better educated. (Today we also know it as the place where the cinematic Indiana Jones, as a Boy Scout, had his first run-in with archaeological thieves.) Dick and I cornered a ranger and explained that our troop had never camped in the desert before, but we were ready to expand our horizons. He led us into a little theater to watch the standard tourist slideshow and added some of his own, personal slides. The guy loved the place, and he wasn't alone. While wandering through the gift shop, I latched onto a book called *Desert Solitaire,* written by some rugged, agitated author I'd never heard of, who related his year as a seasonal ranger at Arches. Edward Abbey's first sentence said it all: "This is the most beautiful place on earth." After viewing the slides, I began to believe it. After wandering through the endless maze of arches, spires, and eroded monoliths for two days and sleeping under a cloudless sky so saturated with stars that it boggled my mind, I had little doubt that this guy, Abbey, knew what he was talking about. The ranger directed us to the Delicate Arch trail; at the arch, we were to head northeast at least a mile where we were free to camp anywhere we chose. He cautioned us about water, for there was none out there, then added a little side comment about snakes and spiders. When eyes opened and ears sprung up like a mule deer's, he had achieved his hoped-for reaction. I'm sure his comment served his entertainment needs far better than as a warning for our safety.

We drove past Courthouse Towers and along the Great Wall, turning at the Windows Section, where the kids got out and clambered around Turret Arch, Cove Arch, and the majestic

twin spans of Double Arch before the short drive to the Delicate
Arch trailhead.

Just before we left the cars, we exchanged the weight of
warm, mountain clothing for the burden of additional water.
We hit the trail at Wolfe Ranch, a time-warped site dating back
to the 1880s. The weathered, one-room log cabin, root cellar,
and collapsing corral gave the kids a peek into primitive life
in this harsh country. At 3:30 p.m. we left the ranch, crossed
a small suspension bridge over Salt Wash, and trudged north-
eastward up a long, slickrock incline dotted with trail-marking
cairns. The full fury of the summer desert sun formed beads
of sweat on our brows, trickling down and stinging our eyes.
Clusters of tiny gnats swarmed and circled around our heads
while horseflies zoomed in, took aim, and drilled away at bare
legs. The ascent of only 500 vertical feet began to feel like 1,000
when we finally rounded a bend and saw Delicate Arch on the
far edge of a huge sandstone bowl—the pride of the park. Heck,
the pride of Utah.

Troop 117's First Utah Adventure – At Delicate Arch

Dressed in its garb of red Entrada sandstone, the arch resem-
bles the bottom half of a bow-legged cowboy. The kids spotted a

lone hiker standing beneath the arch, dwarfed by its size. They instantly dropped their packs, dashing off for their own worm's eye view. I found an angle in which this stunning work of nature perfectly framed the snow-topped peaks of the distant La Sals and pulled out my Nikon. Just then a cool, refreshing breeze cut across the bowl, bringing a moment of air-conditioned relief. A unique moment. Yes, Edward Abbey, this is special country.

The trail ended here, leaving only red-rock outcroppings and sand. Sparse stands of pinyon pine and gnarled juniper added a splash of green to the contrasting red-sandstone terrain. Here and there, a group of hearty wildflowers challenge the harsh, dry environment. In the heat of the day, animals have better sense than humans—they are nowhere to be seen—yet the presence of cottontails, kangaroo rats, and other tiny rodents was revealed by numerous tracks in the red earth. Shade was at a premium.

When we hiked far enough off the main trail to be legal, we chose a spot where a cluster of junipers offered scant relief from the sun. A large, flat-top boulder provided a vantage point for the whole area, which was as desolate and remote as any we had ever visited. We sat, sipped water sparingly, and waited for the sun to creep farther westward.

The cooks got to work on supper, careful not to add too much fine-grained sand into their concoctions; unexpected breezes handled that duty. After dinner, we trooped back to Delicate Arch to view the panorama at sunset when the red sandstone, alive with color, is accented by enigmatic shadows. As I dashed a quarter of a mile to the southwest to shoot this spectacle from a unique angle in the warmer tones of the setting sun, I jumped between two small boulders. As I was airborne, I saw, directly beneath me, the unmistakable diamond-shape head on one end of a motionless reptile. I didn't wait around for his tail-end concert. I got the shots I wanted and was far more cautious on the trip back to camp.

Returning to the campsite, the sunset faded and darkness

enveloped the area. In the coolness of evening, the desert critters began their search for food. We scattered crumbs of dry rolls and crawled up on the huge boulder behind our camp. We sat quietly for a half hour, watching the stars emerge, speaking only in whispers. On a given signal, everyone switched on their flashlights, beaming them down toward the bread. It was a circus down there. A dozen shy, little kangaroo rats stood upright on their oversized feet, went ballistic, and darted and dashed with their characteristic hop in every conceivable direction, totally baffled by being bathed in a bright blanket of light. This experience was a first for us and certainly was a first for them.

By 10:00 p.m., Theis and I were wiped out and ready to hit the sack. The kids had built a small fire and were sitting around with Montana singing Indian chants. It seemed they weren't overly anxious to crawl into sleeping bags. I'm certain everyone had heard tales about rattlers slithering into sleeping bags at night seeking warmth or warnings of snuggling into your bag, only to find a lonely scorpion awaiting your warm body. By this time, I was wearing no badge of courage myself. That's why I chose to "sack in" on top of that big, rigid rock instead of on the nice, soft sand that you could easily contour to the shape of your body. I crawled into my bag and, as I faded into oblivion, I heard the chants harmonizing with the wail of a distant coyote.

At the dim glow of the false dawn, I crept out of my bag to check the whereabouts of the troops. Most of the boys were congregated together (safety in numbers), heads down deep in their bags. The morning air was cold. I crawled back in for another 40 winks before forcing myself out to walk the desert in the early morning. Pinyon jays were tuning up, and a hungry red-tailed hawk was circling in search of breakfast. The bread crumbs were gone. By 9:00, the heat from direct sunlight penetrated the nests of our nighthawks and slowly they came alive. No nighttime encounters with snakes or scorpions.

I mentioned before how rapidly kids adapt. During that day, they vanished into the desert: wandering, climbing, exploring.

Several discovered a small rock shelter hidden behind some brush, laden with lithic flakes, presumably a prehistoric chipping station. Although Canyonlands National Park to the south is inundated with sites and artifacts of the ancient Anasazi, the arid Arches region, with few dependable water sources, seems relatively void of evidence of long-term occupation other than a few panels of rock art.

The big surprise came after dinner. One by one, kids came up to me and told me where they would be sleeping that night. Brian LaGrone wandered up and pointed to a large boulder several hundred yards to the north. "I'll be over there tonight, Sholzie." When I asked him who would be with him, he nonchalantly answered, "Nobody." What a difference a day makes. They had adapted. Apprehension had dissipated; the desert was creeping into their blood. For the next decade and a half, when we asked the boys of Troop 117 where they wanted to go for a spring trip, the answer was always the same: southeast Utah. Notice that I said *spring*. We were smart enough not to try backpacking into this country and battling the gnats and heat of summer again.

12

THE END OF TWO ERAS

Final Days with the Girl Scouts

For several years we hiked, backpacked, climbed, rappelled, snow caved, and skied with our female compatriots, and word of our co-ed adventures filtered out to the neighboring Scouting community. One afternoon, the District professional called me, telling me that "a lot of people" were interested in this program we were sharing with a Girl Scout unit. After beating around the proverbial bush, he finally admitted that at a recent Roundtable (the monthly powwow of district Scouters) some leaders registered apprehension regarding our co-ed activities. He suggested it may be judicious to present our program at an upcoming Roundtable. Sure, I thought, why not? This could be fun.

Meeting with junior leaders from both troops, I asked if they would participate in a presentation to show other Scouters the advantages of co-ed Scout activities. I suggested it might be appropriate to open the meeting with a presentation of the colors in full uniform. I'd never seen any of the Girl Scouts in uniform, in fact, I wasn't certain they owned uniforms. But they showed up that evening looking very "regulation," complete with merit-badge sashes.

The co-ed junior leaders performed the flag ceremony with almost military precision. After the usual opening activities and announcements, the Roundtable commissioner introduced us. We had prepared a slide presentation to show these apprehensive doubting Thomas's the range of activities that Scouts of both genders could share in the great outdoors. Seeing images of these gals chugging up switchbacks with full packs, rappelling off sizeable walls, and digging away at snow caves seemed to impress the Roundtable Scouters, yet I sensed we hadn't won our battle yet. A chilled atmosphere still permeated the room. Following the presentation, I brought the boy and girl junior leaders to a table in front of the room, introduced each one, and invited the Scouters to ask them anything they would like to know, such as how they handle bathroom necessities on a co-ed outing. Now the ball was back in the big boys' court. Not a hand was raised, nor a question asked. The kids simply waited them out. Finally, one brave soul stood and fired off a rather inane question, but he received an intelligent reply from one of the girls. That opened the door. For the next 45 minutes questions came flying—with the kids' wit and smarts clearly showing in their replies.

When the questions began to drag, one of the girls—who was particularly shy and had said nothing all evening—slowly rose from her chair and faced the room full of uniformed men. She took a deep breath. In a firm, strong voice, she addressed the Roundtable: "I've been a Girl Scout since Brownies, and now I'm a Senior Scout. What I have experienced in the last couple of years has been the greatest. I was bored with the Scouting program. These boys helped make Scouting come alive for me. We respect them, and they respect us. I want you to know that we don't regard each other as Boy Scouts and Girl Scouts, we look at each other as outdoor people. That's all I have to say."

The room fell silent. The apprehension diminished and shifted to curiosity. One hard-as-nails Scouter in the back of the room stood, looked at me, and asked, "Well, how can a Boy Scout troop meet up with a Girl Scout troop?" That's when I knew we had won the war.

No one that evening had the guts to ask the kids if there might have been a little kissy-face going on out there in the woods. I would have loved to have heard the answer. I never saw any mischief of this sort myself, but I don't naively think our outings were complete "hands-off" operations. Heck, we were dealing with the hopping hormones of 15- to 17-year-old teenagers. I was naive enough to believe that any Scout troop could function effectively on a co-ed basis. But the girls had a change in adult leadership and that impression exploded. The boys called her "Bertha from Belsen" after Germany's infamous Bergen-Belsen concentration camp. On their first joint outing, she informed the boys that their tents must be at least 100 yards from the girls' tents and that at no time could the girls be out of her sight. Fearing deposition of land mines between the two camps, the boys promptly packed up and went home. Unfortunately, the girls quit the Scouting program.

The secret is to know your kids, set guidelines, and trust them. Troop 117's years with the Girl Scouts were good ones. I was sorry to see the end of this era. And I know the boys were, too.

Reliable Assistant Scoutmasters— Don't Leave Home Without One

Through those early years, without gentlemen like Irv Johnson, Ed Knight, the Kershaw boys, Jack Dillman, Ed Fitzsimmons, Skip Oliver, and a four-year stint by Bob Parsons, I would never have lasted as a troop leader, particularly with mischievous Troop 117. Add to those fellows all the supportive parents who served on the troop committee. It seems that when you have an exceptional troop, the Scoutmaster gets all the credit. In Troop 117, these folks were behind the scenes doing most of the grunt work. I fear that in the continuous pandemonium of leading a troop, I failed to thank them properly.

For three years times two sons, Char and I faithfully drifted down to East Elementary School for the monthly Friday night Pack meetings. As much as I loved the Scouting program, I never could have functioned effectively with Cub Scouts. Being a Cub Scout leader takes phenomenal patience. Regardless of any earthly sins, all Den Mothers should have free passage through and a dozen roses waiting at the Pearly Gates. The running, screaming, and bouncing off the walls made Boy Scout meetings look like Sunday Mass. In six years, I saw more arrow points than Sitting Bull. Young Grant Johnson, who would one day enter Troop 117, had Cub Scout arrow points going so far down his shirt, I began to think his mother must be sewing new ones on his underpants!

If those Friday night meetings weren't enough, I helped to create six pinewood derby cars. We'd whittle, sand, paint, and shellac them; adjust and readjust weights; file wheels to a razor edge; squirt graphite on the axles—and still my poor sons only reached the second heat once. (We only won the first heat because the leading car lost a front wheel!) But who was I competing against? Boy Scouts with engineering fathers who worked at Martin Marietta; they reportedly tested the air resistance of their sons' derby cars in mini wind tunnels. They probably applied top-secret lubricant on the axles. My only pinewood derby joy came one year when a lad showed up with his untouched block of wood. He had worked the weighting, wheels, and axles to perfection—and won all the heats, hands down.

I met Troop 117's future Assistant Scoutmaster Jim Colburn at one of the East Elementary School pack meetings. Jim was a short, wiry guy with dusty red hair and a bushy beard to match. He was blessed with mischievous, dancing, green eyes and a mouth that seemed to turn up at the edges in a perennial smile. When he walked up to shake my hand, I liked him immediately. A geologist, Jim and his wife, Barb, had just moved from Utah into a house only a block from Char and me. He brought his younger boy, Ted, to sign him up in the pack and had an older son, Alex, who was looking for a troop. We enlisted Alex that night, plus, Jim expressed interest in becoming an Assistant Scoutmaster. What luck. Jim became my right-hand man for the next ten years, plus, a most cherished friend. On our fall and early-winter outings that year, I learned how fortunate I was to have Jim in our troop. This guy knew the outdoors like the back of his hand and quickly gained the confidence of the boys, who were naturally suspicious of new adults. This was exciting—now we had good junior leaders, a full troop, and talented, interested adults. Then came December.

The Last Displaced "Indian" Tribe

The Navajo Indians suffered the Long Walk. The Cherokees endured the Trail of Tears. Now, in more enlightened times, whoever expected the troop's Wasechie Indians to be sent packing?

Troop 117, sponsored by the First Baptist Church of Littleton, was one of the first Boy Scout units established in that community. (It was initially established in 1928 as Troop 112.) During the years immediately following World War II, the strength of the unit waned with only a handful of boys participating. Adult leadership was nowhere to be found. For 11 years, Scouting lay dormant at the First Baptist Church. Then in 1959, the bear shook loose from its long hibernation. The Men's Fellowship, with the assistance of Pastor Simmons, uncovered a Scoutmaster, formed a committee, and recharted the unit with 11 boys. Soon that number grew to 18. When I arrived on the scene in 1964, 32 Scouts were crowded onto the roster. The Indian dance team moved into high gear, and the troop grew into one of the prominent units in Littleton. Troop 117 had an engaging history and outstanding potential.

A year after I took over as Scoutmaster, a new minister joined the church, Reverend Babylon. He was a big teddy bear of a man with whom I enjoyed chatting. I'll never forget his expression the first time we met. With a straight face I asked him whether his name, Babylon, had a Biblical connotation or simply alluded to the length of his sermons. Relationships between the Reverend, the church, and the troop always seemed cordial, even when one of my khaki uniformed clowns inadvertently potatoed his exhaust pipe.

In the mid 1970s, the number of Baptist boys in the troop kept diminishing. In fact, it seemed as though the congregation itself was dwindling. I wasn't a member, so I was unaware of changes that were occurring within the church's membership. Apparently, the demeanor gradually had shifted from a traditional Baptist style of worship to a charismatic, proselytizing style. My first clue came when a member of the church's Board of Deacons called and told me they were considering dropping sponsorship of the troop. I was stunned. This church had actively promoted Scouting since the 1920s. He rationalized this decision by saying that few, if any, Baptist boys were members anymore, and the troop seemed to be functioning without much association with the church. I countered with the fact that the Men's Fellowship, a group that had been so helpful in the past by providing leadership assistance, committeemen, merit-badge counseling, and financial aid over the long term of this troop, was now defunct. Even though no one from the church seemed interested in assisting the troop any longer, I felt they should be proud sponsors of a unit as large and as active as Troop 117— and as effective in providing an outstanding Scouting program for the kids in the immediate neighborhood. He suggested we hold a joint meeting.

Several days later, Duane Newell, our troop committee chairman, and I met with representatives of the Board of Deacons. They informed us that the members of the board had changed their minds and were willing to send one or more church members to every troop meeting and on all campouts. I was delighted. I suggested that, to be effective during these activities, they might wish to participate in an upcoming Scouting training course conducted by the Denver Area Council. They stated quite flatly that each man would be very well trained for his role. *Role?*

"What did they perceive their roles to be?" I asked. His answer was simple, "To bring Jesus Christ to every boy in the troop." Wow! After pondering this for a moment, I explained that the troop included several Jewish kids, and I was sure their message would go over like a lead matzo ball. Further, I defined the BSA's position, explaining that although Boy Scouting is built on non-sectarian religious principles, pushing any particular belief or dogma was simply not "kosher." We agreed to meet separately with our respective governing bodies to determine if we had any common ground and planned to meet jointly in early January.

On that day, Duane and I arrived at the home of one of the deacons. The atmosphere seemed chilled but cordial. The pastor led the meeting with a prayer—the kind of prayer that is more of a position statement than adoration, glorification, or appeal. Then we got down to business. Their first question set the tone: "Is your troop still doing Indian dances?" I indicated that we were. In fact, we had three dances scheduled that month. The deacons looked at each other in silence, their faces registering varying degrees of concern. Finally, the dominant deacon cleared his throat and stared at me with his left eye partially closed. With a tone of learned arrogance, he exclaimed, "Do you not realize that you are glorifying pagan rites?"

I glanced at Duane whose arms were now crossed, his foot was tapping, and his tongue was swirling around inside his mouth. I felt an adrenalin surge, partly from astonishment, partly from acrimony. I couldn't believe what I had just heard. *Pagan rites!* I felt ten times closer to God in a Sioux sweat lodge or on a mountaintop than I ever felt inside a church. I had never experienced this type of mentality. Rising slowly, I went eyeball to eyeball with each one of them while my mind hit the wall, seeking a solution. Their faces were stone cold, expressionless. We obviously were at the end of our rope. Achieving an agreement by compromising both groups' philosophies would prove to be a weak base on which to build a strong and lasting working relationship. I feared that time would wear away the veneer of any compromised agreement, leaving little substance with which to cooperatively conduct a Scouting program acceptable to the church, to the troop, and to the Boy Scouts of America. As much as I hated to say it, I said, "Gentlemen, I honestly feel it would be best if the troop seeks new sponsorship." They didn't appear surprised or in the least bit anguished. They simply suggested we address the issue in writing, which we did. We thanked the church for so many years of sponsorship and suggested they inform the Council that they were terminating sponsorship as of January 31, 1977.

Another era came to an abrupt end, but we parted as friends. Shortly after, the Littleton's First Baptist Church disbanded, due (I was told) to dwindling membership.

With the BSA breathing down our necks to renew our annual charter by the end of the January, we hustled to find a new sponsor. Running prospective candidates through my mind, I quickly settled on the Littleton United Church of Christ, which I knew from experience to be an open and community-spirited congregation. Plus, it was geographically centered in our Scouts' population area.

I visited the pastor, Bob Clark, and defined our Scouting predicament. We had kids, we had leaders, we had a solid program, and we even had money. All we needed was a tender, loving sponsor who would put a leak-proof roof over our heads. Space could be an issue. The church had several outbuildings, which were far too small for our large troop. Bob agreed to bring the sponsorship question to his Board of Deacons and saw no problem in allowing us to use the main chapel, which was a tiled, multipurpose room with folding chairs. Within a week of our inquiry, word came from their Board of Deacons that we were not only welcomed, but *warmly* welcomed. In fact, the board shifted their meeting night and another youth meeting to allow the troop adequate space on Monday evenings. I discovered later that one of the board members hesitated about having a Scout troop associated with the church, because he felt the BSA was too military mannered. After we spoke—and performed some "pagan" Indian dances at the Scout Sunday church services in February—that single dissenter placed three sons into Troop 117!

In early 1977, Troop 117 found Jim Colburn and a new home, and both seemed to fit like an old hiking boot. Now it was time to start thinking about summer camp, keeping advancement on track, and finally getting to the Flat Tops Wilderness Area. Plus, we still had all of southeastern Utah to explore.

13

A NEW ERA DAWNS

Rumblings at the Old Folk's Home

Our tenure at the United Church of Christ began with a nearly geriatric troop. I feared some of these guys might hang on long after their Social Security checks arrived. More than half of Troop 117's members were toting driver's licenses, and every one was an outdoor whiz. Unconsciously, we were skewing the troop's program to satisfy their fast-moving, higher-level demands. Indian dancing waned in the wake of tougher pack trips and mountaineering ascents. Many advanced to Eagle; others were losing interest in advancement but still loved to Scout—in their own fashion.

Every year we sought to advance at least half of the troop to a rank of First Class Scout or above. This helped ensure knowledgeable junior leaders. Usually we met that goal, which gave us a needed reprieve from teaching square knots and compass reading. Yet the adults were frustrated. The older Scouts, with all their outstanding outdoor knowledge and skills, lacked one key ingredient: the desire to *lead*. Instead, they gelled into a Senior Scout clique. On pack trips they dashed off like a fleet of gazelles while the little guys struggled behind. You can imagine what a game of British bulldog was like to younger boys. It must have looked like a fleet of Mack trucks beating down on them.

The adult staff acted quickly on this situation. During a fall committee meeting, we set a goal to encourage older boys to lead and interact with younger Scouts. The goal was notable, but how would we accomplish this? It was apparent that a troop operating like an Explorer Post loses younger kids. Quickly, we pulled together a handful of committee members and, along with Jim Colburn, assigned each dad to four younger Scouts to help them advance and feel more comfortable in the troop. Meanwhile, I drew a bead on "geriatric attitude adjustment." But to solve a problem, you have to correctly identify it. After a couple of brain-busting sessions, the "old timers" admitted they were tired of working with little kids all the time and wanted to be challenged at troop meetings. Fair enough. Maybe we can negotiate a new challenge in turn for better leadership. I'd had something in mind for months.

Although the BSA's first aid skill award and merit badge were acceptable, they seemed light when considering the emergency skills needed to provide adequate care in the advanced outdoor activities in which we were now involved. I proposed a long-term emergency medical technician (EMT) type of program for the "ancients." They ate it up, and so did I. Advanced emergency training was challenging and proved to be stimulating. In fact, when my son went off to college, he landed a summer job as an EMT at a hospital, based on the knowledge and skills he learned from that program. It provided the breather they needed from constant leadership responsibilities and come spring, this whole Leadership Corps was showing off their newly acquired knowledge to their younger compatriots and even teaching them square knots again! The big transition came just in time—a dozen new Webelo Scouts came knocking at the door.

Encountering a Backpacking Stunner

Four pack trips of varying lengths and difficulty were on the docket the summer of 1977 to give all age groups an opportunity to experience the high-country aura. The toughest trip would be venturing into the Rawah Wilderness, a series of sculpted glacial valleys dotted with numerous high-altitude lakes located 60 miles northwest of Fort Collins, Colorado. Fifteen boys signed up for this weeklong adventure, plus two guests: Jim Colburn's nephew from Yardley, Pennsylvania, and my nephew who was visiting from the Twin Cities. And here comes Montana again. Many older boys were now working, which opened the trip to more "middle-agers," including the next generation of Johnsons, Newells, and Shorthills, Alex Colburn, gentleman Jimmy Mitchell, Jay Tuccy, Ian Zahn, Karl Nyquist, and a half dozen more.

A 20-mile loop trail caught our eyes, commencing at the West Branch trailhead and leading well into the midsection of the Rawah. Here was country roofed by snowcapped peaks pushing upward from dense aspen groves ringing both sides of the valley. We signed in at the trailhead and ascended the trail, following the west branch of the Laramie River. Chatter soon gave way to tranquility. The combination of heat and a steep trail makes conversation cumbersome, if not impossible. Three miles up the trail, a wooden bridge crosses the river. We veered south and continued another five miles, climbing to Blue Lake, a jewel of an alpine tarn nestled at timberline just below the Rawah's most towering peak. After making camp in the trees, Jim and I opted for a brief *siesta* while the corps, already rejuvenated, circumvented the lake and got their jollies chasing hoary marmots in the nearby rocks.

We shook out of our sleeping bags early the next morning, since we would backtrack five miles along Fall Creek, and then face a 1,600-foot ascent to reach Grassy Pass. From there we would descend into the spectacular Rawah Lakes basin. Both Jim and I had an eye on his nephew, "Yawrdley," as we called him, due to his Mid-Atlantic intonation. As we moved higher, this young lowlander began to resemble a scarecrow with a hay deficiency. His head was down and feet were dragging.

Unfortunately, he was being grounded by an ultra-painful, high-altitude headache.

At the top of 11,200-foot Grassy Pass, we stopped to catch a breath, and it was time to work on Yawrdley. Normal pain killers did little to improve these high-altitude head rattlers. At the time, I was communications and training director for a respiratory equipment company and dealt with people suffering from chronic obstructive pulmonary diseases (COPD). Over time, I perceived an interesting correlation in symptoms between someone suffering from emphysema, for example, and a person encountering altitude trauma. These symptoms included shortness of breath, headaches, lack of appetite, disorientation, and sleep depravation. The classic COPD patient, for a variety of reasons, tends to encounter an abnormal buildup of carbon dioxide, which—when blended with water in the body—produces carbonic acid. This acid buildup causes a shift in the acid/base balance of the body and creates myriad problems. Logic told me that the high-altitude sufferer, who faces lower oxygen pressure and may not breathe deeply enough to sufficiently exchange gases may also drift in that acidic direction. Why not counter with a simple alkali substance, such as Rolaids or Tums? It worked then, a dozen times after that, and still works today. I'm never at high altitude without a good supply of antacid "tummy pills" for headaches.

The vista from Grassy Pass was only surpassed by the view from the basin where the rugged peaks of this northern range of the Colorado Rockies shove skyward, straight up from the azure Rawah Lakes. A smattering of other lakes such as Camp, Rainbow, and Sandbar also lie within a mile. We set up camp near the second of the four Rawah Lakes, and then everyone headed off to do their own thing. The fishermen went fishing, the bird watchers went birding, hikers went hiking, and the climbers started climbing. (And some nappers went napping.) My Minnesota nephew, Eric, had never stood on top of a "real" mountain, so he and I and a few others chugged our way to the naked, rocky summit of North Rawah Peak. Even though this wasn't a fourteener, the panorama of rugged cirques and tarns matched anything I had ever seen in the Colorado mountains. The Rawah Wilderness offers a truly robust feast for eager eyes.

We lingered several days in the basin and camped one night in a beautiful, flowered meadow on the way back. The vistas throughout this trip were rivaled by one final vista on the last day. As usual, I was lollygagging in the rear, prodding young Jimmy Mitchell and making sure we didn't misplace anyone, especially since we had taken an unscheduled shortcut through a crag-lined meadow. There had been another attempt at "weighting" my backpack that day, but I had discovered the two boulders tucked halfway down in a towel before we started. I was bombarded with as many "I'm totally innocent" statements as you'd expect during a parole hearing.

Everyone was nearly at the cars, and I was less than 50 yards from the sign-in station when I spotted a lone gal with a backpack in her mid-20s, apparently reviewing the register. I knew she wasn't signing it; she must've had her arms in a strange position, because both of her elbows were sticking out in front of her. Then I got closer. Wow! From all the anatomy books I had read, I immediately knew that those weren't elbows. This young lady was as topless as a Buick convertible. She turned around, smiled, and asked me for directions. I knew darn well she was checking my reaction more than she was seeking travel assistance. I didn't blink, and I didn't stare. I simply told the young shocker what she wanted to know, wished her well, signed out, and went on my way.

A hundred yards down the trail toward the cars stood gentleman Jimmy Mitchell with his lower jaw well on its way to his navel. "Sholzie!" He was nearly breathless. "Did you see what I saw?"

"Yeah, Jim, I reckon I did."

His astounded expression quickly traversed into a serious glare, complete with squinched nose and wrinkled brow. He leaned toward me and whispered, "Is that legitimate?" I assume he meant *legal*.

"Jimmy, they looked awfully legitimate to me."

I motioned him on and, as we neared the cars, the commotion, resembled a convention of frenzied magpies. "Hey, Sholzie…" and they all came rushing. Jim Colburn, laying with his head in his arms on the roof of a car, was oscillating with laughter. Even if the week had been a total flop, it would have blossomed into a triumphant, memorable adventure thanks to one backpacker, sans shirt. I think Yawrdley even forgot about his headaches!

Wild Times at Peaceful Valley

Back in the '60s when our dancers helped dedicate Peaceful Valley Scout Ranch, we, like many troops, still sought our summer camp experiences at Camp Tahosa high in the Rockies. Due to its limited size and upkeep cost, BSA eventually closed Tahosa as a long-term summer camp. We shifted our summer camp sights to Peaceful Valley, the 2,500-acre, high-plains spread 50 miles southeast of Denver near the little town of Elbert. I knew we would miss the mountain environment, but no one would miss subjecting his body to the ice-cube reception offered by Tumblesome Lake. Among the vastness of huge meadows and dense stands of ponderosa, Peaceful Valley (PV) sported a new swimming pool built, like much of the camp, with the assistance of the Seabees U.S. Naval construction force. Spacious troop campsites dotted forested areas, all isolated from each other. Home for a week was a two-man, sidewall tent with cots, plus picnic tables with rainflys. Since it was a working ranch, PV offered horseback riding along with a full range of merit-badge classes. Although PV lacked a lake, a promise of an artificial one was in the offing.

I could never understand the kids who didn't want to go to camp. Some of my most memorable times as a boy were at summer camp. Back then, extended family vacations were not common, especially during World War II. Heading off for a week with friends to Boy Scout camp in the woods was a special treat.

As a Scoutmaster, I realized at summer camp you had kids in tow for a much longer period of time than you did during a whole year of troop meetings, plus you had a talented camp staff at your disposal. Kids usually waltzed home with at least three merit badges. I say *usually* because those deficient in advancement motivation could find scores of hooky happenings, such as living on the rifle range, sneaking to the old Indian burial cave on private property south of camp, exploring the canyons on the north end, or roping cows feeding in the upper pastures. I'll never forget my irritation the day my son Scott and his partner in crime, Fergie, came back from camp one year when I wasn't able to go, toting nothing but dirty clothes and two partially completed merit badges between them. Later, the in-camp leader told me that the only place he was sure to find them that week was at the mess tent.

Back in the early days of PV, the mess tent was just that. It was centrally located adjacent to a modern kitchen, one of the many small buildings composing the camp. Rows of long picnic tables were sheltered from the hot, prairie sun by a huge, canvas roof. Before breakfast and dinner, troops met at a nearby flag pole for the usual announcements and the ceremonial raising and lowering of the colors before the mad stampede to chow. The camp staff tried to make this an orderly transfer of bodies. They probably would have had better luck slowing up Crazy Horse's warriors at the Little Big Horn. The staff called troops to the outdoor food tables by a variety of ingenious criteria: quietest, best uniformed, most merit badges completed, most Eagle Scouts, or the most kids who had changed their underwear that day. Then the Boy Scout version of *Animal House* began.

PV, as with most of eastern Colorado, was prone to late-afternoon storms in the summer. When the wind kicked up, the sand blew, and meals got gritty. Sheets of rain would whip the dropped side awnings and drench the poor souls who chose windward seats. It was fun. It was camp.

Troop 117 was beginning to emerge as a troop to watch, not only for the kids' knowledge, skills, and advancement prowess but for their antics. In retrospect, they were simply laying the groundwork for the real experts who showed up in the next decade.

One evening I watched curiously as a handful of boys worked on a half dozen flashlights, inserting a red-plastic cutout in front of each lens. The next morning at the daily Scoutmasters' meeting, one rather piqued Scoutmaster explained, in protest, how the night before boys in his troop had been scared out of their wits by "red-eyed monsters" that appeared and disappeared around his camp. Some kids were so frightened they asked to sleep in his tent. The program director offered an appropriate response but had to set his lips to seal off the grin when he glanced over at the stone-faced 117 staff.

When it came to campfire skits, Troop 117 shone. This was an opportunity for creativity; most skits had been run and rerun so many times they would put a caffeine-drinking insomniac to sleep. This seldom was the case with the 117 theatrics. One evening, one of our troop's junior leaders stepped up to the stage area and announced a new discovery that could prove extremely useful to Boy Scouts everywhere. Our troop, he explained, had discovered a unique creature called the *gorpopiller*. A 10-foot "mammalian reptile" inched onto the stage, comprised of a bunch of kids on hands and knees covered with a huge piece of canvas. The emcee explained that by feeding the gorpopiller food it liked, the creature automatically produced Boy Scout camping equipment. Petting the head of Gorpo, he proceeded with his demonstration. First, he rolled into its mouth a can of whole kernel corn. The creature grunted, bounced, vacillated, and eventually spit out a brand-new canteen to the cheer of the crowd. Next he fed the creature canned peas, a Gorpo favorite. The animation became even more pronounced, and out came a backpack and frame. He continued the demonstration several more times, with Gorpo producing a pocket knife and sleeping bag. The emcee asked if anyone had a favorite type of food with them. A staff member with a prearranged can of pork and beans stepped forward and rolled his donation into Gorpo's mouth. The gyrations became violent; the grunts were raucous. Then the canvas tail end of the monster lifted, and the tail-end kids cut loose with a sizeable fire extinguisher. The campers exploded in laughter.

One guy didn't laugh: the camp director. The next morning, he informed everyone that, from now on, all skits would be cleared through the program director. It seems that several members of the Council's Board of Directors had been invited up for that evening and had witnessed Gorpo's explosive response to pork and beans. It's too bad the camp director felt this crackdown was necessary. I find it hard to believe that even bank presidents would be offended by such innocent fun. After all, the "Viper," a guy holding a roll of toilet paper, has been running across campfire stage areas for generations.

As autumn approached and summer camp closed, PV was available for weekend outings. Each September we took the junior leaders to a cabin at the camp to develop the program for the coming year. Friday night and Saturday morning involved real work. By noon Saturday we completed a comprehensive month-by-month, week-by-week program based on the troop's needs and preferences.

Now it was time to play. After lunch, the cars rolled in for a family weekend of hiking, games, superb food, and campfires for the entire troop. During these family outings, one of the great traditions of Troop 117 evolved: the Toilet Bowl Football Game.

I have suffered cracked ribs in a mountaineering accident, departed over the handlebars of a mountain bike, performed some acrobatics off a step ladder, and survived the bottom layer of a wrestling pile. But on three occasions, my ribs took a severe beating in the Toilet Bowl. The original game, before it received its dubious title and bone-bruising ferocity was played by moonlight in over two feet of snow at PV. Bundled in heavy winter clothes, we chose out-and-out tackle, but spent most of that bitter-cold, moonlit evening locating the darn football after an overthrown pass. Soon the fall classic became a yearly event, held in the daylight—with or without snow and the protective layers of winter clothing. As you would expect, the adults ended up on the disabled list. Thinking back, perhaps this was the kids' insidious plan, a payback aimed at their aging leaders. Entire families participated in the Toilet Bowl tradition. The best punter turned out to be one of the guys' sisters, Lori Banister. And the trophy for the winning team was a little engraved porcelain potty.

The Great 1978/79 Avalanche of Kids

Early in 1978, nearly every month saw another new face or two, and they, in turn, pulled in their friends. With so many older boys moving on, it was time to recruit. I knew the principal at a neighborhood elementary school, and she allowed us to recruit 5th- and 6th-grade boys during school hours. Harvey Atchinson joined Jim Colburn as an Assistant Scoutmaster. During those years added nearly 30 new names into our roster book, such as Richardson, Slaten, Green, Borger, another Theis, another Sholes, and another Mitchell. We were back to a full house, but with too many deuces and treys. We'd spun full circle, returning to a large, young, inexperienced troop with few older Scout leaders.

The dance group, which had fallen into disarray for several years, found new life. After hearing stories and seeing slides of the colorful Wasechies, this younger gang was eager to slip on the moccasins. Déjà vu. Beads and feathers flew on kids who danced more with their heart than they could with their feet.

Jim Colburn and I decided to put all these young cats on a fast outdoor track, yet one that would be within their capabilities. In February, most of them had their first handshake with cross-country skis on a memorable daytrip up Scott Gomer Creek, a reasonably gentle uphill trail off Guanella Pass Road that skirts behind Mount Bierstadt between Grant and Georgetown. What a day. A deep-blue sky hovered over perfect snow. The air was crisp and cold without being nose-biting frigid. The initial mile of the trail was steep, but our first-timers chugged up it with minimal instruction and little bellyaching. I was impressed. Then we hit the flats where we could work on gliding. The snow consistency changed a bit, and looking backward I noticed young Ricky Mitchell, gentleman Jim's younger brother. His glide seemed a little shaky; in fact, he looked as though he was balancing on short stilts. After scraping away an eight-inch buildup of snow under each ski, plus a quick rewax, Ricky's frown moved upward, and we were off again.

I knew Ricky and his antics from son David's Cub Scout pack, so I had a vivid picture of the immediate future. Ricky was the antithesis of his somber brother. He was a clown, a goof-off, a performer, funny but frustrating, foolhardy but bright, with an oafish smile that could shift to a frown or snarl then back again in a matter of seconds. No doubt, we had acquired another never-ending source of amusement.

We broke for lunch near iced-over Scott Gomer Creek. Ahead was a wide open, U-shaped valley leading to the base of 14,264-foot Mount Bierstadt. The trail was gentle for another mile, and then twisted up a rugged, rocky section that even seasoned skiers walked. I knew this trail personally. Years ago with a handful of older Scouts, we cross-country backpacked from Guanella Pass several miles to the north, camped a night in the snow, then pointed our skis down this rock-laded route carrying full packs.

This time, the trail, the hour, and the lack of skier experience sounded the gong to reverse direction and head for home. Naturally, the return route would be downhill. This sounds much easier and a lot more fun. And it is, if you know how to maneuver downhill on a narrow, tree-lined trail on cross-country skis. Jim corralled the group and explained that heading downhill is difficult, but their attention was on the anticipated fun ahead. These were Colorado kids, already good alpine skiers. Alpine skiers, whether kids or adults, seem to enter the initial phase of cross-country skiing with enormous overconfidence. Soon they discover there is no room to traverse with oodles of big, mean trees crowding the narrow, winding trail. In addition, whereas your heels are solidly locked into downhill bindings, your heels are loose and wobbly on skinny little cross-country slats. Confidence evaporates. I've seen expressions shift from cocky to that of kids who just discovered the math test was a day earlier than expected.

The group stormed off like a jet fighters—let 'er rip, devil may care, ride 'em cowboy! A few gentle 20-yard slopes that led onto 100 yards of flat trail generated even more confidence. In their own minds they were already cross-country experts. We caught up with the younger ones just before they reached the knoll that commenced the long, narrow, winding run through the forest. Grant Johnson, Mark Newell, and several other older Scouts were already nosing their skis down this segment when Colburn reached the knoll, turned, and commanded, "Now listen to me. If you lose control on a trail like this and smash head first into a tree, you could kill yourself. So listen!" That grabbed their attention.

Jim explained several methods to control speed, mainly the snowplow and using poles as a drag. He cautioned the boys to keep a good distance between each other so if someone went down, the others would have time to stop. "And," he emphasized, "if you lose control, lay it down. Bail out, and do it before you're going too fast, okay?" With that we sent them on their way, one at a time, and well spaced. Soon a variety of screams floated up from the trail below, ranging from exhilaration to scared out of their wits. On one spot they were stacked up like bowling pins, belly-rolling with laughter. Several took off their skis and decided walking was the better alternative to valor. And where was Grant (whom I usually called *Grunt*; he referred to me as *Mr. Shoes*)? It seems that during his scorching descent, Grunt experienced a "memorable event" and now had three skis: one regular size and two shorties. I don't remember if he had rental insurance. Eventually everyone arrived at the cars tired and happy, and with all their body parts still intact.

A Freezing Night Near Webster Pass

With the exciting tingle of the downhill trails, the freshness of the cold air beating against your face, added to the soft drone of waxed wood sliding through powder snow still firmly embedded in our minds, Jim and I decided to challenge the older Scouts. Several weeks later, we hauled two carloads of the more experienced types with backpacks over Loveland Pass, pulling into Montezuma Basin east of Keystone Ski Area. The old, mining town of Montezuma looks about as tired as the miners who used to work the mines. This ghost town consists of an array of dilapidated buildings housing a few ragtag remnants of the hippie era. These folk are probably smarter than they look seeking peace and quiet in a sanctuary far from the hustle of cars and people, smog and noise that is enveloping the front range of the Rockies. A short distance down the road, a snow-packed, four-wheel-drive route wound its way 2,000 feet upward through spruce and pine into the tundra near the top of Webster Pass. The topographic map of the area showed a little, black square near timberline that we hoped was an old barn or cabin and would provide some protection from the high-altitude elements.

The trip up Webster Pass on skis with backpacks required concentrated effort. The road is steep in spots, and the vision of skiing down this hummer with a 50-pound pack kept my attention off of the immediate agony of hauling that pack uphill. Within 15 minutes, everyone removed layers of clothes to stave off the perspiration that eventually could provide greater cooling than you wanted. Most of us were attired in wool army pants with crude gaiters and goose-down, hooded jackets covering layers of cotton underwear, shirts, and sweaters. Removing and replacing head covering was our usual temperature-control method. Out here it was easy to teach the old axiom, "If your feet are cold, put on your hat." Jim, who was not tall (in fact, I used to tease him about suing the city for building the sidewalks too close to his hind end), always wore a green, wool elf's bonnet that was so long it could nearly keep his feet warm.

By the time we neared timberline, Jim's beard and my mustache were adorned with Lilliputian icicles, and became the brunt of snide commentary by Ian Zahn, Jay Tuccy, et al. "Refugees from the Siberian ice caves," they called us. Soon we spotted the "black square," an ancient cabin just left of the trail. It was a tiny, wooden frame structure but still looked solid. With luck, it might sleep six guys who at least liked each other. The others were destined for dug-in tents, which, we thought, may prove warmer than the cabin. While the kids found a slope on which to ski, Jim and I skied toward the top of the pass, which straddled the Continental Divide. Plumes of powdery snow resembling great white feathers blew eastward from the nearby summits. Skiing up the road and out of the trees, we realized how much protection the thick forest had been providing us. Contemplating that howling gale driving the powder snow into a near white-out condition, we looked at each other, nodded, and reflecting the wisdom of our age, bravely retreated back into the trees.

Tom with Jim Colburn on Webster Pass

Teller Mountain loomed just to our west, and the bright sun, which we had appreciated all that day, took an early nosedive. And so did the temperature. The cooking stoves went on early in the cabin. Everyone had arranged their sleeping quarters, except for Jim and me. After dinner, Jim suggested giving our new down sleeping bags a test. Digging out a trench about ten yards from the cabin, and instead of pitching out tent, we stretched it over the snow and placed our pads and bags on top of the flat tent. Snug in our bags, we covered ourselves with a small tarp and fell asleep listening to the howl.

Even in the isolation of the snow, the wind bursts jarred me from deep sleep. The kids' tents above us were rattling like shutters in a cyclone. Soon, the weight of the windblown flakes multiplied in layers, slowly burying us under a blanket of frigid snow. I banged the tarp, but we were in a trench, and the snow had few places to go. I was relatively warm, as long as I didn't suffocate. My ol' buddy, Jim, was sawing logs loud enough to compete with the roaring wind. Out of sheer exhaustion, I finally capitulated to sleep. Come morning, Jim nudged me to see if I was still alive. Other than near our heads where we had unconsciously been knocking it away, snow depth on the rest of the tarp was pushing eight inches. I'm not sure if the kids were impressed or thought we had lost our minds!

If you've never put on a full pack and headed your skinny, little skis down a steep, mountain trail in a near blizzard, you've missed another one of the insane exhilarations of life. It's one of those "what the heck am I doing here?" experiences, especially when you have to safely escort a dozen teenage kids down the trail. The road was covered with the freshly fallen snow, but fortunately it was wide enough and distinct enough to follow. Trail skiing out of control with a backpack can be disastrous. "Bailing out" becomes a sophisticated maneuver with that much weight on your back, so your best choices are snowplowing and braking with the poles. Using the "Norwegian brake" method, you position both ski poles between your legs, hold the top of the poles with your left hand and push into the center of the poles with your right hand. This positions the baskets at the bottom of the poles for greater drag and tends to slow you down. But this maneuver can ricochet. If the poles hit a rock or otherwise spring back into your crotch, you could quickly be propelled into the soprano section of the boys' choir. Preferring to remain a baritone, I tend to use this brake method outside of my skis.

The snowplow is the initial method of choice, because it helps regulate your speed and allows you to control your turns. Virtually every beginning downhill skier learns the snowplow but most advance to other techniques quickly. Why? Because snowplowing kills your legs. If you've hoisted a 50-pound pack on your back, skiing in that squat, knock-kneed position makes your legs feel as though they're on the down side of a five-mile duck walk. Add blowing snow spanking your eyeballs (if you neglected to bring your goggles), plus a drippy, freezing nose, and it all adds up to a real junket.

Why do we drudge up a mountain trail with 50-pound packs, on skis, sleep in a snowy trench, and risk a downhill catapult?

Well, what's life without a few hardships and a little adventure? Plus, it's great fun! And we know that a whole summer of adventures is just around the corner.

14

THE DAWN OF THE GOLDEN YEARS: TROOP 117 MEETS "THE MAN"

We Finally See the Flat Tops— With a new Flock of Fledglings

Still waiting north of Glenwood Springs stood that quarter-of-a-million-acre wilderness called the *Flat Tops*. (Bertha Bus had met her untimely demise attempting to reach this destination.) A bundle of unused maps nagged and challenged our curiosity, plus we had a covey of younger Scouts surging to try something "really exciting." Late June would be a logical timeframe for the foray; we hoped most of the snow would melt from the higher plateaus by then. I selected a kinder, gentler, loop trail so the "bath of fire" into big-time backpacking wouldn't scorch this covey of first-timers. (I always feared I'd butcher the desire of a potential lifelong backpacker with an utterly miserable first experience.)

Sixteen kids, plus Jim Colburn and I, composed the invading horde. Several parents helped transport but couldn't stay for the trip. A passable dirt road off Country Road 8 led us to the Marvine Lakes trailhead where we began our climb through a narrow valley 2,000 feet below the Flat Tops rim. This was my first Scout backpack trip with my younger son, Dave. It was a special moment. I never thought I'd see this day. When Dave was nine months old, he was diagnosed with cystic fibrosis. His estimated life expectancy was only five years. Today, Dave is pushing 40, married, and has a little girl. Watching this little ragtag team churn up the trail brought visions of the old movie *Boys Town* in which Spencer Tracy spent years shaping Mickey Rooney and his tough cronies, only to have another load of toughies dropped on his doorstep. Here was my new delivery of neophytes. What was my first clue? After lunch, Dave *lay down* to put on his backpack, and then couldn't budge, and Ricky was more concerned with brushing his teeth than moving on.

But each great civilization had what anthropologists and archaeologists call their Classic Period or Golden Years. Little did I know that hiking before me was the vanguard of what would become Troop 117's Classic Period: Lane Slaten, Dave Sholes, Chris Theis, John Tuccy, Jay Stogsdill, Matt Borger, Gary Atchinson, led by Grant (Grunt) Johnson, Ian Zahn, the Newell boys, and tall, lean Andy Green. Of course, there was Ricky Mitchell with his pea-green jacket with his ever-present tooth-brush. In time, this vanguard would be part of largest troop that 117 ever fielded, produce the most Eagle Scouts, become the best Indian dancers, and experience some of the greatest adventures in the unit's long history.

We unloaded our packs and set up camp below the rim of the Flat Tops plateau that night, amazed by the endless vista of dead trees standing silent as far as the eye could see. *Widowmakers*, they're called, and all night their report echoed as one after another crashed to the ground. During World War II, pine bee-tles infested the area; and manpower was lacking to clean them out. New growth now infiltrated the lifeless trunks, but the kids learned an important backcountry lesson regarding where *not* to erect a tent. (In fact, a friend had a harrowing experience in a desert area when a huge cottonwood branch tumbled down and decimated his daughter's tent moments after she had gotten up in the dark for a midnight bathroom break.)

Huge amounts of snow still lingered on the steep faces of the plateau, prompting us to stay one more night and explore our planned route. Meanwhile, the morning sun worked its magic on the remaining snow. The air remained cool as we forged our way to the top. The upper flats were an ocean of white with hundreds of rivulets creating miniature canyons in the snow, ushering the ice-cold runoff toward the larger creeks below. Soon snowballs flew with the density of migrating geese. A gentle slope to the north looked enticing and, after a long, sloppy climb, screams of delight echoed off the walls as the renegades glissaded hundreds of yards downward on foot, fanny, and belly. This was wilderness all right, and everyone, including Jim and I, relished it.

The next morning, after Ricky brushed his teeth, we broke camp and packed upward across slush and snow and found enough dry space to camp adjacent to a small lake with its ice just beginning to think about departing. The climb took only a couple of hours, but with the elevation gain and the slick footing, this was enough for the younger contingent. That afternoon we discovered a craggy overlook offering a spectacular vista of frosty lakes and endless forests. Puffs of tiny clouds accented the deep hue of sky above. I watched Lane, Dave, and Andy sit and gaze in silent awe. You could spend the summer here and not see it all. Later in the afternoon, the magic tranquility exploded when Lane and quiet, meek, and mild Chris Theis broke loose with the most flagrant fanfare of fisticuffs this troop had ever witnessed. Theis's eyes were sparking and his fists were a blur as he attacked Lane, who was bigger, stronger, and older. Fortunately, big Lane, who may have helped provoke this incident, took it all with a mild sense of humor and didn't level him. Ricky even stopped brushing his teeth long enough to take it all in. The controversy was corked long before any permanent disfigurement resulted. Not that Chris cooled off that quickly. I can still see him lying motionless for the next hour, his head resting on two tightly closed fists, glaring, with hardly a blink, into the emptiness of space. Riled as he was, I'm glad he was still small. Mixing several dozen volatile teenage personalities in the same bowl under somewhat stressful conditions creates an ideal breeding ground for flare-ups. Fortunately, discord was minimal and normally remained verbal and short lived. I monitored disputes from a distance, mediated if necessary, and only jumped into the fracas if it became violent. In a troop setting, kids seem to solve their problems best without constant adult involvement.

Snow lingering in the Flat Tops inhibited our planned "great circle" route, so we retreated to the dryness of the lower elevations for several days. We hiked, explored, and watched beavers slap their broad tails when we approached their ponds. Jim, Grunt, and I conducted a variety of outdoor classes on maps, compasses, and nature to help these little guys start moving up the advancement ladder. But best of all, we broke them into the joys of backpacking without breaking their spirit. In time, these kids would see the West like none of their predecessors ever experienced. Now, it was time to head home because summer camp was waiting.

A Flock of Nesting Eagles

Only 20 boys from Troop 117 went to camp the summer of 1978, but their accomplishments set a precedent for years to come. Like my gang in Minnesota, these guys were fish. For years, the Littleton High School swim team crawled and breast-stroked their way to the State Swimming Championship. With some of these swimmers on hand, the troop followed suit, winning every waterfront activity, including the big night of King Neptune's Court. They achieved the highest percentage of completed merit badges in camp, won all the Boy Scout skill contests, and members of the staff told me they were by far the sharpest Scouts in camp. It's no surprise that over half of them eventually became Eagles.

Each new Tenderfoot mastered swimming, pioneering,

and horsemanship skills while the older boys moved to more advanced topics. As a troop they successfully pocketed over 50 merit badges. At the rifle range, the number of bull's-eyes in Jay Tuccy's targets won him an NRA sharpshooter medal. I presumed he was learning to protect himself, since I hadn't forgiven him for selling me a bag of hot chocolate—the contents of which I learned (too late) he had dropped in the sand on a pack trip and had gently scooped it up (sand and all) before he sold the mixture to me. I didn't see his expression when he saw me mix the "chocolate" into my hot water. I'm sure he remembers my reaction when his sandy mixture hit my pallet that morning!

What excited me most about this era of Troop 117 was a new feeling of troop spirit brought about by the all-important relationship between the older and younger boys. The older guys were not only conversing with the younger ones, they were *leading* them, thanks to the warmth, humor, genius, and natural leadership abilities of my old buddy "Grunt" Johnson.

With a half dozen new boys, summer camp segued into fall and winter activities: a Mountain Man Klondoree in October, a big District Winter Klondoree, and a cross-country ski day in February. Then came March and the search for the elusive "Man" hiding somewhere, deep in the desert.

The Search for the Icon of the Desert Southwest: All-American Man

Marshall Field's department store in Chicago is a strange place to learn about the great American Southwest. On a business trip to the Windy City, I noticed a book about the Anasazi, the mysterious, so-called cliff-dwellers of the Four Corners region (the meeting place of the Colorado, Utah, New Mexico, and Arizona state lines). I read the entire book on the flight back to Denver and was mesmerized by one photo: an ancient pictograph of an anthropomorphic figure called *All-American Man* hidden deep in Utah's Salt Creek Canyon. I sought more books and maps of the area. The specter of the Anasazi culture piqued my curiosity. Where did they come from? Where did they go? They left such a wealth of archaeology behind. This was my introduction to a topic destined to evolve into an expensive, time-consuming passion that would lead me to visit archaeological sites around the world.

That spring, my youngest daughter, Leda, became over-stressed with schoolwork at Littleton High. I felt she could use a change of venue. So we played hooky for three days and a weekend, which gave us five days to get to Utah, find "The Man," and return. The trip was a story in itself: a night at Arches National Park, driving back roads of the Abajo Mountains in an Oldsmobile station wagon, and the look on Leda's face when, from the edge of a sheer, 1,400-foot cliff, she absorbed the vista and perused the maze of canyons we would enter with little idea about where to go or where to find water. Everything spelled failure. Even the words *All-American Man* stretched a mile and a half across a 15-minute topographic map. This was looking like mission impossible.

After several hours winding down a narrow trail on the steep, rocky wall and adjacent flats, we finally located Salt Creek. The descent was successful, and our water problem was solved. Early the next morning we hiked north, knowing we had until 2:00 in the afternoon to find "The Man" and trudge back to our camp before dark. We must have resembled first-time tourists to New York City. We gawked, necks craned upward. The natural beauty of the canyon coupled with magnificent ruins, both historical and prehistorical, left us in a daze. At ancient sites, the ground was speckled with pottery shards and chipped lithics. We needed more time to explore this canyon, but time was our limiting element.

It was already 2:00 p.m. when we stopped for lunch. I knew we were close, but the hands on my watch said it was time to turn back. While Leda munched on a sandwich, I backtracked 100 yards and found a well-worn trail heading eastward toward a red-sandstone wall that looked like it harbored a small cave. I called to Leda, and she followed, sandwich in hand. She was the first one to spot "The Man" as I worked my way up the wall into a small alcove. I emerged next to a small, stone structure and now stood face to face with a strange and ancient humpty-dumpty figure whose round body, painted in vegetable dyes, presented red, white, and blue patterns and stripes reminiscent of the American flag. From his head emerged a long stem or antenna. Leda climbed up and I threw my arm around her shoulder. It was a moment neither of us will forget. We were truly in the company of an ancient man. I knew the troop had to see this enigmatic pictograph, and I wanted them to discover it the way Leda and I did.

Spring is the best time to visit southeastern Utah. The stifling heat hasn't descended yet onto the canyon floors, the beloved gnats and deer flies are still planning their summer attacks, and, most important, precious water is running in the creeks. For months before our departure, we introduced Troop 117 to the Anasazi culture, commonly called *cliff dwellers*, who inhabited such places as Mesa Verde and Chaco Canyon and who lived and farmed this arid Four Corners area well over 1,000 years ago. The boys were excited to explore southeastern Utah, see Anasazi ruins, and search for All-American Man—and so were their parents. By departure time, 30 boys and several parents signed up to visit "The Man."

For the first time, ladies joined a troop trip. Lane's mother, Barb, cornered me one evening and informed me that it simply was not fair that moms couldn't go along on our trips. I told her that no mom had ever asked. "Then I can go?" she asked excitedly. I told her it was no problem. Then came her second question: "Can my mother come along?" I don't know how many troops have taken grandmothers on desert backpacking jaunts, but Grandma Eagle joined this pack trip. Other adults and guests included Andy Green's mother, Bernice, and his sister, plus new Assistant Scoutmaster Harvey Atchinson, and Committeemen

Jack Zahn, Leroy Moberly, and Jay Williams (who tried, unsuccessfully, to break in his new boots by walking around the block for a week).

We approached via Interstate 70, down the Cisco cutoff to Moab, over Dewey Bridge, and camped across from Newspaper Rock. Large, flat, and protected by a projecting overhang, Newspaper Rock is a palette of 1,500 years of petroglyphs etched into its dark desert varnish. Many of the early glyphs are squiggly lines known as *eccentrics*. The more artistic work may have originated with the Fremont people or perhaps Basketmaker Anasazi. Newer entries such as images of men mounted on horses probably were added by Ute artists within the last several hundred years. Some personalized graffiti, notably by someone named Gonzales, prompted the metal fence that now keeps viewers at a distance. This enigmatic wall was a precursor of exciting discoveries to come.

Early the next morning, we moved this small army to the north end of Salt Creek Canyon and loaded and lashed 30 packs into and on top of Harvey Atchinson's International Scout. With day packs and plenty of water, 29 of us began the 12-mile trek to the next campsite near Angel Arch. Once our eyes became trained to spot the camouflaged remnants of the ancients, a ruin or a stunning panel of etched or painted rock art seemed to await us at every turn. The adventure already far exceeded our expectations, and we were still miles from our goal.

Harvey waited at the campsite where the road officially ended. He had successful evaded the many insidious quicksand traps we had sighted along the hike. After 12 long miles, no one was dancing to trek another two miles to view Angel Arch. We decided to take in that sight on the way back. Shelters went up, meals went on, and as darkness rolled in, so did we—interrupted only by a skunk who meandered harmlessly into Barb's tent!

Come morning, we hoisted our packs and began the eight-mile trek following the creek bed, which was dry in spots and loaded with water in others. The trail shortcuts wide meanders, which turned out to be an easy way to lose a kid who stayed with the creek. Knowing others were behind him, one guy suddenly discovered that everyone was well ahead of him. Not long after passing the Upper Jump, a small waterfall with a drop of about 25 feet into a refreshing plunge pool surrounded by a dense growth of willows and cottonwood trees, we arrived at a larger pond—our camp site and water source for the next several days. Nearby, we discovered a wall of ruins decorated with four large and unusual pictographs of four faces. The next day, without even a hint from me, Troop 117 discovered "The Man."

This pack trip was such a great adventure that I decided to write a story for *Boys' Life* magazine. It contained all the elements of a perfect Scouting story: adventure, challenge, discovery, history, companionship, and rugged, colorful scenery. If it was well written, I felt they'd print it. What an accomplishment this would be to appear in Scouting's own magazine, one with an astronomical circulation. My aging body nearly unloaded cartwheels the day the acceptance letter arrived. "Now, send us the pictures," they requested.

And did we have pictures: kids hiking, jumping in and out of quicksand, backpacking through the red-rock wonders of the canyon, exploring ruins, marveling over intricate panels of rock art, examining shards of ancient pottery, and, of course, the whole gang proudly posing in front of All-American Man. But you know what? No one was in uniform. "Thanks for the great story," the editor wrote, "but we are returning it because it is our policy to show Scouts in appropriate uniform whenever possible." I realized that it was true. You never saw a Scout in *Boys' Life* carrying out the garbage unless he was head to foot in an official Scout uniform, topped at the time with that silly, red beret. But, come on, that isn't the real world. Who in their right mind would tramp through these muddy or dusty canyons in their nice, clean Scout uniform? Didn't the editor ever see what Scouts look like after a week in the wilderness? Getting dirty is what Scouts do best. I've brought kids home whose mothers made them take their clothes off in the garage! We were in a desert wilderness, and we were supposed to wear full uniforms topped with useless red bonnets that were a standing joke among the boys and offered no protection from sun or rain? But policy is policy. So the world of Scouting never experienced the thrill and excitement of one of our greatest trips. But now, you can.

THE SEARCH FOR ALL-AMERICAN MAN
by Tom Sholes
Scoutmaster, Troop 117, Littleton, Colorado

It was only 9:00 in the morning, yet the late March sun already beat heavily on the desert canyons of southeastern Utah. Four patrols of Colorado Boy Scouts trudged slowly through the deep sand and juniper bushes, staring apprehensively at a tired, weather-worn sign cautioning "QUICKSAND IN SALT CREEK CANYON." High above, a turkey vulture floated motionless on a thermal, back-dropped by a clear-azure sky, while the horizon was alive with weird-shaped sandstone creatures knurled and carved by untold ages of wind and water.

Our goal lay two days away. Somewhere in this Chinese puzzle of twisting and turning canyons hides an image of a man that archaeologists believe to be nearly 1,000 years old. Painted from vegetable dyes by a prehistoric cliff dweller, this humpty-dumpty shaped figure rests on a sandstone wall inside a remote desert cave. He's known as *All-American Man* and for a good reason. On his shield-like body, his ancient artist created a red, white, and blue resemblance of the American flag! The troop's objective: find "The Man."

Within a few short miles, the Scouts of Troop 117 discovered that the desert was much different than most of them had expected. Vegetation near the creek bed was lush, and fresh tracks of deer, mountain lion, and scores of smaller mammals were everywhere. Even quicksand was nothing like in the movies; although the boys approached it with apprehension, everyone was soon jumping up and down in the squishy water-laden sand, convinced that someone would rescue them before their hand finally faded beneath the surface of that oozing, brown mire.

At Peekaboo Springs, the Elk Patrol discovered the first Indian pictographs, paintings of animals and human figures stretching 20 feet across a smooth-faced, red-sandstone wall. Soon, every turn in the slickrock ravine meant a new "find"—an Anasazi granary, stone dwellings, and colorful pottery shards. If you were really observant, you might uncover an ancient stone tool carefully sculpted from a core of chert or chalcedony. But the rule was to discover and enjoy, then leave the items for others to do the same.

The tall cottonwoods shading Camp One were a welcome relief after the hot 12-mile trek, and as evening drew near, the fragrance of fresh-baked rolls and seasoned meats drifted from the patrol kitchens. But then came the best show of all: the desert at sunset, a dazzling display of reds, pinks, and oranges fading gently into lengthening shadows and stillness.

As a chorus of larks and thrushes greeted the morning sky, a new bouquet, sizzling bacon and grilled pancakes, infiltrated the air. Soon packs were hoisted, and the troop's search continued, snaking farther southward following the crazy meanders of Salt Creek. By noon, the trail turned into a wide valley enclosed by canyon walls hundreds of feet high, guarded in the distance by the imposing ridges of the snow-peaked Abajo Mountains. Ruins became more numerous with screeches of joy announcing another find, such as ancient corn cobs lying dormant in fields Anasazi farmers tilled over 750 years before.

At mid-afternoon, a quick peek at our topographic map showed us to be within several miles of our destination. Yet finding a small cave in this maze of rock and desert shrub was still a sizeable challenge. A party Scouting the east side of the valley sighted a series of dwellings, neatly constructed rocks and stones chinked together by clay, one of which was adorned with four elaborately painted faces that stared in silence as we quietly pitched our tents beside a nearby, rippling creek. As evening drew near, anticipation grew, impatiently waiting for tomorrow to arrive.

Following a good night's rest, the search continued. Although packs were now off and hiking was easier, thick prickly undergrowth hampered the movement southward. Each tiny bend in the rock walls required careful investigation, but still no hint of a cave.

Less than a mile from base camp, a faint footpath intersected the main trail. "Hey!" someone ahead yelled with a trill of excitement. "There's some sort of an opening over there in the wall." Jogging along the narrow path and through clusters of thorny plants, the patrols hustled to the site. A large opening in the wall stood some ten or 12 feet above the desert floor. Inside, the roof was blackened by ancient smoke, and a granary or small dwelling stood to one side. A long, vertical crack in the rock provided foot jams as the first of the group edged slowly upward toward the entrance, hands searching and stretching for solid holds. Then, there he stood!

All-American Man measured over four-feet tall, commanding a rusty-hued sandstone wall that was now bathed with the rays of the sun. From his head emerged an antenna-like stem. Hand prints, perhaps those of his ancient artist, small and looking nearly spray-painted, also adorned the wall. One by one, the boys edged slowly up the rock ledge to stand and gaze in amazement at this round-bodied man, painted some 500 years before the arrival of Columbus, and adorned with a blue field accompanied by red-and-white stripes. There were no cheers, no celebration; the boys stood silent and in awe of their discovery. The search was over.

The moon that night broke through a cluster of clouds to cast an eerie light on the nearby ruins. Younger Scouts were already asleep, victims of the long day's search. But scattered in two's and three's, others sat in near silence, feeling the magic of this place and absorbing its rugged, spectacular beauty. How unchanged it must be from the time the ancient Anasazi roamed this very canyon wilderness before vanishing mysteriously. And the painting. Why the antenna? Why the flag? Was it a mere coincidence?

Oh, so many questions without answers. But then eyes were growing heavy, and tomorrow starts the long journey home.

Troop 117 Meets All American Man

All-American Man, the ruins, the artifacts. These desert canyons had everything: history, natural beauty, mystique. This was the ultimate adventure. If Arches National Park turned us on to the desert, "The Man" and the nearby ancient dwellings ignited our yearning to experience much more of this culture so shrouded in unknowns. Troop 117 became avid Anasazi aficionados, vowing to return to this canyon every three or four years so that every boy who entered the troop could savor this experience.

Does Anyone Listen to the Kids?

The *Boys' Life* decision frustrated me. I personally felt that if Scouting was going to keep pace, such a rigid, pointless, and outdated policy needed revision. By the end of the summer, I was convinced of it when the Denver Area Council conducted its first (and only) Senior Patrol Leaders conference, thought to be the first of its kind in the country. The purpose was to determine from the top Scout in each troop what boys want and expect from Scouting. I was one of eight Scoutmasters chosen to host a discussion group on topics including camping, uniforming, advancement, training, and more. My assigned subject was, "Why boys don't join?"

On a warm Saturday morning in August, the senior patrol leaders divided into eight "troops" of about 15 boys each. The council president and council executive welcomed the group and explained the program and ground rules. Then each troop of SPLs, with their itinerary in hand, began vividly expressing their opinions.

The objectives of my station were:

1. To determine the image Scouting has in the eyes of non-Scouts.

2. To identify the origin of these impressions.

3. To determine the reaction of SPLs to that image.

4. To explore avenues in which the image could or should be modified.

The concern that these older boys might not participate and could simply "clam up" was totally unfounded. In their own words, "This is was the only time anyone ever asked us what we thought." And they didn't mince their words.

To the initial question, "What do your friends and classmates think of Scouting?" they replied:

1. An organization of sissies, goody-goodies, and squares.

2. Scouts don't do anything fun.

3. Too structured and controlled by adults. Too military.

4. Don't like the idea of wearing uniforms.

5. Takes too much time.

6. Works you too hard—just like school.

Their next question was, "Where do friends and acquaintances get their impressions and opinions about Scouting?"

1. Disenchanted Cub Scouts.

2. Disenchanted Boy Scouts.

3. TV shows and movies that portray the "wait around and help the little, old lady across the street" mentality.

4. Scout-sponsored ads. Showing former presidents or aging movie actors in Scout uniforms and shots of Scouts picking up trash do little to encourage boys to join.

5. And my favorite response: *Boys' Life* magazine. It's in every school library. But it fails to show Scouts realistically. For example, they show every Scout doing everything in full uniform, and kids make fun of it.

Most of the Senior Patrol Leaders felt Scouting was getting a bad rap, it was fun, it didn't take that much time, and, sure, you work hard, but it was fun work. And most definitely, they objected to the "sissy syndrome." They knew that real Scouting was rugged.

When asked how Scouting can make its image more favorable to more boys they really came alive, giving me writer's cramp as I filled page after page of ideas, including:

1. Improve the quality of Cub packs and Scout troops to reduce the disenchantment of kids who did join.

2. Improve local visibility using the media and shopping centers to show what Scouting is really like.

3. Action ads in national magazines, such as *Sports Illustrated*.

4. Camping with Camp Fire and Girl Scout units to achieve a mutual respect that will carry over into the schools.

5. Portray Scouts in *Boys' Life* more realistically, with fewer pictures of berets, full uniforms, etc.

Plus, these kids were critical of themselves for not being friendlier to new Scouts, not inviting boys into Scouting, and for not standing up to the school crowd and admitting that they were Scouts. They agreed it was time to "come out of the closet" and show pride in being a Boy Scout.

I was impressed with these Senior Patrol Leaders—with their openness, honesty, love of Scouting, and insight. We sent the final report to the Denver Area Council's Executive Board and to national headquarters. I hoped the Scouting organization would take this information seriously, because if you don't listen to your customers, you lose their business.

The council billed this event as the *First Annual SPL Conference*. That was in 1979 and, to the best of my recollection, the council has yet to hold the *second*. How unfortunate.

15

KAMIKAZE CANOES: TROOP 117 CHALLENGES THE SAN JUAN RIVER

Meet Our Illegal Assistant Scoutmaster

Ready for another confession? In the early 1980s, Troop 117 had everything going for it: a great sponsor, superb junior leaders, the Wasechie Indian dancers were again tapping moccasins, and a canoe trip on the horizon. But our membership numbers jumped beyond my comfort zone. The solution: patrol dads. Get a great dad for each patrol and register him as an Assistant Scoutmaster.

Three dads signed on for the Bear, Buffalo, and Elk Patrols in a week. Plus, we had the ideal candidate for the Eagles Patrol. This person knew how to handle kids, loved the outdoors, was a hiker and backpacker, was a stickler for solid advancement, and would run a tough ship. But *he* was a *she*! At that time in Scouting's history, the BSA remained staunch male chauvinists when it came to Scoutmasters and their assistants. We simply registered Barb Slaten as *B. Slaten*. And what a "patrol dad" she became. In her tenure, she moved virtually every kid in her patrol to the rank of Eagle, and they were not "cheap Eagles." She brought a new level of cheer (and good eating) to every outing she was on, which was most of them. Annoyed by teenage boys given to dabble in colorful language, she conducted classes in "creative cussing" and taught the Gabby Hayes style of expressing disdain. This gal knew boys, and she knew Scouting. Every troop should be blessed with an "illegal" Assistant Scoutmaster like Barb Slaten. But was she ready for the river?

"Love Many, Trust Few, and Always Paddle Your Own Canoe"

With spring and summer closing in quickly, the troop began to finalize its summer program. A canoe trip seemed high on their hit parade. Still suffering from Upper Midwest mentality, I thought, "Where in the world would a troop canoe out here in the land of mountains and deserts?" Rafting I could understand, but canoe country was northern Minnesota! Then I tripped over a book called *Canoeing Western Waterways*. It was loaded with trip ideas. Paddling from Dewey Bridge down the Colorado River to the confluence of the Green River looked interesting, but there was no easy, inexpensive way to return. If you continued farther down the river, you shook hands with a series of rapids in Cataract Canyon that make experienced float boaters quiver. The Green River from the town of Green River, Utah, to the take-out location at Mineral Bottoms was a possibility, but the older guys were seeking whitewater. On top of that, the 12- to 13-year-old boys were bent out of shape, because they wanted to canoe too. We decided to tackle the San Juan River, which trickles out of the high mountains of southern Colorado, drops down into New Mexico, and meanders across southern Utah before pouring into Lake Powell. We could put in near the Four Corners with the younger crowd and give them 50 miles of paddling experience without white water. Then we would switch passengers and pick up the older group at Sand Island, near Bluff, Utah, and continue an additional 90 miles to a take-out spot at Clay Hills Crossing. That stretch would challenge us with

18 "canoeable" rapids—at least we hoped they were "canoeable." To participate, a boy had to be at least a First Class Scout and hold both swimming and canoeing merit badges.

The placid South Platte River running through Littleton was our classroom, giving everyone much-needed experience with moving water. From this, we hoped the canoeing neophytes would at least recognize a draw stroke from a breast stroke. The South Platte's flow rates had become placid since the Chatfield Dam was built. (The dam building was prompted by a flash flood in June 1965. A 20-foot wall of water roared down that vapid little stream.) Yet this river's obstacles turned out to be far more challenging than anything we would encounter on the rough-riding San Juan.

On one practice run, Barb Slaten and crew sailed around a bend in her new, "indestructible" fiberglass canoe—if it gets a dent, you simply push it back out. Immediately ahead, a freshly fallen tree blocked most of the narrow channel. Fortunately, the paddlers were able to escape onto the tree rather than face the disaster of being pulled under it. The canoe wasn't as fortunate. Indestructible? If it had received one more twist, this little paddling machine would have resembled a street-vendor pretzel. Nearby workmen agonized for over an hour, even used a hydraulic hoist, to free this decapitated dinghy, so Barb could mount the tangled wreckage on her vehicle, return it to the sporting goods store, and ask for a dent removal demonstration. She drove home with a new, aluminum canoe.

Meanwhile, the Zahn father-son team successfully maneuvered farther downstream and paddled through an area bordered by a country club on the port side and ancient light-industry companies on the starboard. Stroking paddles with good, German vigor, the Zahn team was generating velocity when the canoe ground to an abrupt halt—so abrupt that the bowman resembled the buxom figureheads that adorned the prow of old, English sailing ships. A half-inch reinforcing rod firmly attached to a huge chunk of submerged concrete protruded several inches through the bottom of their vessel. We hoped our trial runs were not a harbinger of disasters to come.

Meanwhile, we began organizing the logistics of moving 21 people, canoes, food, water, tents, and sleeping gear to the Four Corners area and shuffling vehicles once we got there. By late May, we had appropriated eight canoes with three paddles and three life jackets for each canoe. We lined up cars, adults, and kids. We established canoe teams by considering strength and experience, and we gave each boy a clothes/equipment checklist. And we imbedded the following safety instructions into their sometimes dense, little skulls:

- Life jackets will be worn on the river at all times.

- Each canoe must carry one extra paddle and jacket.

- Canoes will stay in sight of each other at all times.

- Whistles will be used to signal problems.

- All gear will be securely lashed.

- The minimum liquid carried will be one gallon per person per day.

- Be prepared for lots of sun and heat.

Friday, June 20, 1980, was departure day. The parking lot at the United Church that morning resembled a depression camp. And it was an exercise in disorganization. As cars pulled in and unloaded kids and gear, I stood in disbelief. There was no way we could carry all that stuff: coolers full of ice and pop; an army of five-gallon water containers; ammo cans filled with cameras, film, and binoculars; mountains of waterproof bags; plus people! If each canoe ended up with an inch of freeboard above the water, we'd be lucky. We rejected unnecessary items on site and, somehow, managed to fit the rest into the vehicles and eventually into the canoes. Now, the two canoeing groups—younger boys and older, more experienced teenagers—headed southwest, with Scout tour permits in hand, toward the great unknowns on the San Juan River.

Our first sight of the San Juan was east of Pagosa Springs, Colorado, where this brown, little river meandered back and forth across U.S. 160. The brown hue was nothing compared to the chocolate soup it became after it ventured into New Mexico; joined up with the Mancos, Piedra, and Animas Rivers; and met us a little more than a mile from the Four Corners Monument. It was no longer the little rivulet we had crossed in Colorado. This baby was wide, high, and moving fast. Plus, it turned out we would venture into and camp on Navajo land without a permit. Why? Months in advance I had written the Navajo Tribal Council requesting permission to camp several nights along the river on tribal land. When a response never came, I called tribal headquarters in Window Rock, Arizona, numerous times before our departure date, but no one ever answered the phone or returned the call. After many experiences with native people, I was certainly aware that their clock ticks a little slower than mine, which I appreciate. I'd just as soon set my clock to theirs. It was no surprise that I received a nice letter giving us the permission we requested—two weeks after we returned home.

Group 1 Meets the River and the Navajo

We loaded gear into our canoes, safely secured it, and waved goodbye to Group 2 as they headed to Bluff, Utah. They would camp there for several days and move vehicles to Clay Hills Crossing, the terminal point for their segment of this adventure. Clay Hills lay some 140 miles downstream from the Four Corners put-in point. When son Dave and Steve Richardson, in the first canoe team, pushed off, we received a vivid portrait of how fast this river was moving. We just needed paddles to keep the canoes going straight or to backpaddle so we didn't arrive at Bluff two days early.

Dave and Steve had been neighbors and buddies since preschool, yet each had a mind of his own; plus, they were competitive with each other. If one said "right," the other said "left."

It would be interesting to see what direction their canoe would travel. Grandma Eagle and Barb were along, determined to stay away from trees. The Borgers and Onsagers had father-son teams, while Big Red Conway and Andy Green, both carrot tops, were easy to spot. Andy was quiet; loquacious Big Red helped achieve verbal equilibrium in that vessel. Brian Moberly drew the short straw to see who would have to try to control a canoe with Ricky Mitchell's predictable outlandishness. Art Gillson, Committeeman Jim Haines, and I rounded out the first group.

The scenery during that initial day fell shy of spectacular. This upper segment of the San Juan runs through open country. Much of the river is dotted with sand islands but no rapids and hardly a riffle. The vista included some reddish bluffs to the south and a few cliffs but lots of foliage, mostly pesky tamarisk covering the side flats, which probably was a flood plain when this river danced prior to the construction of Navajo Dam in New Mexico. Tamarisk was imported from Eurasia in the early 1800s to control erosion on the lower Colorado River. It has an unwavering ability to reproduce and maneuver upstream on any tributary at a phenomenal speed. It does control erosion by protecting the banks from water, yet it becomes a vegetal Great Wall of China, making it virtually impossible to land a canoe.

Sightseeing on that first day was on hold. With canoes moving rapidly in that current, the banks became a blur. About every half hour we would call for a pull-in onto an island, just to give the lads practice landing their overloaded vessels. Any concerns that the fast-moving water, coupled with their neophyte skills, might have exceeded their ability to handle the supply-laden canoes were soon dispelled.

The San Juan produces a strange phenomenon: sand waves. Every so often calm water up ahead began to churn, and three- or four-foot waves seemed to appear from nowhere. Supposedly, sand waves are caused when the water is supersaturated with silt and mud. Before the Navajo Dam blocked the river, sand waves reportedly rose eight to ten feet high. The kids darted their canoes back and forth across the river like dragon flies as they tried to catch a wave and enjoy a little "whitewater" action.

A canoe ride from the Four Corners to the first Navajo town of Aneth normally takes eight hours without stops. With our mid-afternoon start, we had no intention of going that far. Instead, we chose an isolated, sandy island several hours down-stream. At 4:00 in the afternoon, the desert sun was still high and hot, encouraging a late-afternoon dip. Always clean, Ricky (adorned in nothing but a towel) headed to a shallow inlet between two small islands for his daily bath. Instantly, the tow-el was zapped from him, but dad, Jim Haines, saved the day by providing Ricky with a broad-brimmed cowboy hat with which to maintain some semblance of modesty. When I approached with a camera, Ricky scampered off through the shallow water, but the long lens captured him and his bare behind, featured in a show-time story at the fall Court of Honor.

A small, driftwood fire provided heat for hot dogs. Though eyelids were feeling heavy, the summer-solstice sky fought off stars until nearly 10:00 that night. The day's heat dissipated, but not enough to enclose yourself in even a light sleeping bag. Soon the soft ripple of the water splashing gently against the beach did its magic, and the crew dropped into deep slumber.

I awoke that morning to unfriendly taunts from the north side of the river. Lifting up, I could see a half dozen cars and a group of young Navajos standing near the river's edge. The din was definitely aimed in our direction. As the Scouts got up, I told them to ignore the shouts, get on with fixing breakfast, and pack up. No need to irritate the Navajo youngsters any more than they seemed to be. They were probably good swimmers! We encountered more resentment to our intrusion again dur-ing a brief lunch break on the beach beneath the low bluffs at Aneth. Four Navajo men stood, arms crossed, at the top of the bluffs—peering down and saying nothing. Several of the kids gave them a friendly wave, but received only angry stares in return. The kids were baffled by this display of Indian animosity. "Hey," I said, "sometime I'll tell you the story of the Navajo's Long Walk. Our Anglo ancestors didn't treat their ancestors with much warmth and compassion. I guess they haven't forgotten."

Soon we encountered several large islands with multiple channels encircling them. Also, more and more downed trees blocked our route. Trees scare me. They are a far greater threat than rocks. You can bounce off rocks, but getting tangled in a tree and pulled under the water could be the end of the road. Ricky and Mobe did shake hands with a rock, and Ricky busted a paddle, but all in all, everyone stayed out of trouble in that thick, brown, swift-moving water. The biggest on-river chuckle came when one of the dads broke out an umbrella for sun shade. From the acid comments, you would guess that a sun umbrella just wasn't a kosher 117 approach to the great outdoors.

The town of Montezuma Creek was only a three-hour paddle from Aneth. That stretch of *terra firma* lacked charm. Why is it that areas rich in oil and gas development may have the money, honey, but they don't have the looks? A highway bridge crosses near Montezuma, and less than a mile downstream we came upon a reasonably good camping spot, but our umbrella-sheltered dad spotted a red ant hill and was adamant about moving on.

The camp we finally chose was much more alluring, featuring green grass and tall cottonwoods that hopefully wouldn't lose any big branches during the night. Now in late afternoon, we were enclosed in an envelope of heat. Larry Borger grabbed a cool can of pop and plopped, clothes and all, into the shallows of the river. Soon the whole gang splashed around in a gigantic water fight, while Grandma Eagle sought shade and snored herself to sleep. With everyone soaked to the skin, Ricky suggested a wet t-shirt contest. Barb was the only female participant, but she lost to Brian Moberly! Well, we always said Barb was just one of the boys.

Following our typical hearty breakfast, the hollow, metallic reverberations from coolers and ammo cans being loaded into aluminum canoes competed with the raucous magpies and crows. Soon, Group 1 launched its final day on the river. The rocky bluffs bordering both sides of the San Juan began developing more character. Wind and water erosion created cave-like indentations in the pinkish sandstone. This looked like Anasazi country, but the thick stands of tamarisk blocked the view of any ruins that may have been constructed in the bluffs. We were on the lookout for a suspension footbridge crossing the river. From a guidebook, we knew it would lead to a major Anasazi dwelling on the south shore.

We couldn't have missed that bridge. Its suspension lines sagged so badly we would have been hanged if we hadn't ducked as our canoes passed under. We beached the boats on the north side to enjoy the fun (and trepidation) of crossing this expanse. That little bit of innocent fun soon became a problem. Big Red, we learned, suffered a hang up about walking across a river on a wobbly suspension bridge. The other clowns jumped on it and swung it, which just added to his phobia. He stood at the north entrance of the span like a cow at a cattle guard. Finally, after the others disappeared into the thickets on the other side, the big, red-headed hulk started inching his way across, his knuckles white from clinging securely to both sides. He dashed the last five feet and shook like an aspen in the wind when he hit the south shore.

No distinctive path to the ruins jumped out, so the kids spread out, moving across an open meadow toward a sizeable overhang on the bluffs to the south. The noontime sun, at an angle behind the overhang, created a huge, triangular-shaped shadow shading the sizeable indentation and making any structures difficult to identify from this distance. I was confused. Most Anasazi dwellings faced south to gain the winter warmth from the sun. As we moved into the shadows, the ruin became visible: a sturdy, semicircular rampart nearly ten-feet high harbored in the enclosure three quarters of the way up the bluff wall, neatly camouflaged by a backdrop of similar-colored sandstone. Easing our way up, we entered the ruin through a wide break in the wall. Seventeen rooms were nestled, hidden in relative safety behind the formidable, front barricade. Pottery shards were strewn everywhere. The kids wandered aimlessly from room to room exploring in relative silence. Pictographs dotted the rear wall, including the now-familiar, tiny hand imprints. The view toward the river was awesome. The kids learned that this piece of real estate offered nearly everything: protection from the elements, a good defensive position, a river terrace for crops, and proximity to a reliable water source. Its one major disadvantage was that it faced north. As one boy casually observed, "Gee, these people really must've had a tough life." You can bet your air mattress on it.

After coaxing Big Red back across the Golden Gate, our rendezvous point at Sand Island campground was a mere three-mile downstream ride, chasing sand waves and ducking paddle-pushed splashings. Group 2 cheered our arrival at Sand Island with a boisterous welcome. (Nearby campers must have thought it was the arrival of Lewis and Clark.) Did we have enough San Juan water for that day? Oh no. Group 2 revealed their favorite pastime. For two solid hours before dinner, the whole ensemble walked a half mile upstream and jumped in with their life jackets, yelling, giggling, and riding the swift current to the boat launch near the end of the island. There, they pulled themselves out and hiked back up for another ride. I was all for this. It was good training, since I knew that more than one guy would "hit the surf" once we collided with the big whitewater downstream.

The fatigue of young Group 1 and the restlessness of Group 2 showed that evening as they relished a feast of burgers, dogs, and trimmings. The feast satiated the bellies of the hungry incoming crew, and it helped line the cavities of those tigers heading out on their 90-mile, whitewater journey in the morning. The younger contingent deserved to be proud. They handled a fast-moving river in heavily loaded canoes with ease. Maybe in a year or so, they could hone these new skills on the Class III rapids awaiting us downstream.

16

BIG WATER AHEAD

Group 2—The "Submariners" Take on the San Juan

In 1980, the San Juan River had yet to be "discovered" and made popular by river rafters. For the next five days, we encountered only three or four humans. Today, you must enter a lottery to gain a permit; so many river-hungry applicants are vying to win this lottery, you might be better off betting on the state lottery.

The canyons of the lower San Juan are a geological wonderland: sandstones, limestones, shale, anticlines, synclines, monoclines, diatrenes, and rock formations so old they make the dawn of man look like yesterday. Navajo Sandstone, the Kayenta Formation, Wingate Sandstone, the Chinle Formation, Moenkopi formation, the Cutler group—you name it, the San Juan River canyon seems to have it all. The first 50 pages of our guidebook, published by the Four Corners Geological Society, detailed the geology of the area, but our main interest was the river log. The log reeled off, mile by mile, an account of the geology as well as locations of ruins, pictograph panels, old cabins, and other prehistorical and historical sites. But we really wanted to know: Where were the rapids, and how big were they?

Along with location, the guide indicated the class or difficulty of a rapid. These were relative, of course, because rapids change dramatically with flow rates, but when we saw a Class III-IV we knew we were going to have a ride. An expert canoeist can usually handle a Class III (on a I-to-X scale). We had lots of neophytes on this trip and heavily loaded canoes. In retrospect, I'm not sure if we were courageous or just plain naive to take on the San Juan in canoes. But I'm sure glad we did it—and everyone lived to tell about it! What's life without adventure?

While dads Borger, Haines, and Onsager escorted the Group 1 greenhorns back to civilization, Barb, Grandma, and I eased our already sun-baked bodies back into our aluminum chariots for the big 90-mile push, assisted by our resident geophysicist, Jack Zahn. The kids included some of the biggest and strongest in our troop: Jeff Andrus, Paul Carnell, Jimmy Mitchell, Lane Slaten, and Ian Zahn. This time we were truly venturing into unknown waters, an exploratory trip to determine if this wild river would be a feasible and safe adventure for the troop in years to come.

The bridge just downstream from the Sand Island Recreation Area that carried U.S. Highway 191 south to Arizona was the zero marker for the river log. But determining distances wouldn't be easy. Few canoes are equipped with odometers. With our guidebook and topographic maps within easy reach, we pushed off into the fast-moving current. Before long, the scenery surpassed anything we had encountered on the upper river. Scores of mud swallow nests clung tightly to the red-sandstone walls, many of which carried the dark stain of desert varnish, also called *patina*, which often became the "canvas" for ancient desert artists who, about a millennium before, called this canyon home. A little over a mile from the launch site, the river made a brisk turn to the right, but the current kept pushing our canoe straight forward toward an undercut in the red-rock cliff. I yelled to Paul Carnell, my bow man that it was time to quit lollygagging on the paddles. We averted a rocky collision then yelled a warning to the gang behind. One boat came within inches of shaking hands with the wall. The next several miles brought a smattering of small ruins. We stopped to investigate several, plus one large and impressive panel of petroglyphs that included many anthropomorphic figures, some with a series of "power strips" rising above their heads. Strangely, these same symbols of rank appear with frequency in the rock art of ancient India, Pakistan, and China. Rock art was beginning to intrigue me, but trying to watch the river and spot signs of the ancients keeps the eyeballs hopping. On more than one occasion, I turned around and looked upstream and sighted a ruin we had already passed.

Until now, the river remained flat with a riffle here and there and lots of pillows (near-surface boulders) to work around, but the first, full-blown rapid didn't show until 11 miles after we launched. Just before entering a rapid, rivers can become quite subtle and sedate, as though they're lulling you into tranquility before slapping you across the face. The calm before the storm. From our topo map we determined that Four-Foot Rapid was just around the next bend, so we beached our canoe. Barb, Jack, and I scrambled over boulders and brush to check the rapid's ferocity and determine the best route through it. While we were engaged in a high-level technical discussion on the most cautious, judicious, and tactical route to safely traverse this swirling mass of moisture, along came a canoe with one lone guy, totally unconcerned, stripped to the waist, lounging back on the rear seat, and applying suntan lotion as his canoe bobbed effortlessly through the rapid. We looked at each other, got into our canoes, and ran Four-Foot!

What a thrill! You feel an adrenalin surge before you nose your cigar-shaped paddling machine into the foaming broth, but once the initial splash hits your face the experience is pure exhilaration. To better control a canoe, you keep it moving faster than the current. That's the main reason you paddle. The person in the stern usually can maintain direction, but occasionally, especially when you're heading straight into a rock, a little crossbow rudder from the bow man is always appreciated. We didn't get through Four-Foot Rapid totally clean. All of our canoes took on extra water, and our gunwales loafed only an inch or two above the surface of calm water. After pulling over to the bank and congratulating each other for surviving, the bailing buckets came out, then we popped open the ice chests and tossed down well-deserved cool drinks. The first campsite was still six miles down the river, right at the top of Eight-Foot Rapid, which sports an eight-foot drop and is classified a big Class III.

From Four-Foot, our guidebook became quite geological, listing abandoned meanders and explaining how the cherty dolomite marks the lower Ismay cycle, algal bioherms, and leached oolites. Jack, the geophysicist, ate this up, but it was a bit weighty for those of us who had to stretch to tell Pikes Peak granite from speckled jaw breakers.

As late afternoon approached, we began having visions of food. Because of our limited number, we cooked as one group. Once we made camp, two double-burner Coleman stoves made things happen quickly. With Barbara in charge of the menu, we knew we would chow down in style. Plus, the ice chests provided the luxury of perishables, and more ice would be available once we arrived down river at the thriving metropolis of Mexican Hat.

Soon we spotted the big, sandy Eight-Foot Rapid campsite dead ahead. We beached the canoes and studied our next challenge. This rapid could usher you into a cardiac-stimulating experience. Eight-Foot could have been called *Big Foot*; it looked mean. We would save that hair-raiser for morning when we were fresh. Although situated on Navajo land, this flat, sandy campsite had the earmarks of everyone's favorite Holiday Inn. Let's hope the Navajo at this end of the river were a little more accommodating, because we never spotted good campsites on the north side. We spent our four nights on the river for this 90-mile stretch on the Navajo south bank. We did have visitors late that night at the Eight-Foot camp. A herd of thirsty Navajo ponies ventured in and clip-clopped down to the river. At first we didn't know if they were mounted or not. Historically, Navajos on ponies were a pretty tough combination. Fortunately, the horses came alone, got their drink, milled around for awhile, and drifted back up a draw with no sleeping visitors' skulls connecting with an ill-placed hoof.

Come morning, I shook myself awake and didn't even have to look around to be assured that Eight-Foot Rapid was still there. It was talking to us—it was roaring at us. To a float-boat sailor, a Class III is a bouncy, little ride. But in an overloaded canoe, this rapids looked like the Colorado River's dreaded Lava Falls. "Eat a hearty breakfast mates, for a big ride is just ahead." There was no way to mitigate its wrath. Skirting this rapid on the left side led into an impassible mine field of rocks and boulders. If you hedged as you left the campsite, the fast current introduced you to those boulders in a matter of seconds. A few guys gave serious thought to lining their canoes along the shallow south shore, parallel to the rapid. But we came to run rapids, so let's run 'em.

We lashed in all the gear, while the photographers hustled to find a suitable location to accurately record any disasters. Meanwhile, the first of the four canoes moved into position to shove off and churn for the opposite side of the river, with the hope of straightening out the bow in time for our run down the Eight-Foot. (Someone mentioned, "It's too bad we don't have Ricky with us. We could send him down first as a test pilot!") Leading the pack, Paul Carnell and I pushed off. Paul was big and strong, but, at times, this giant had a yellow streak down his back resembling a no-passing zone. (Every time we invited the "Snake Lady" to a troop meeting to introduce kids to the reptile family and pass around her slithering pets, Paul was either at the back of the meeting room or in the parking lot.) Already, this rapid had his eyes popping. And my ticker was vibrating like a five-stroke drum roll. This rapid did not look friendly.

Using basketball pads to cushion our knees, we snuggled into our respective bow and stern positions, resting our backs firmly against the seats. We hugged the near shore and paddled 30 yards upstream to gain distance to help ensure a successful cross-river traverse and, therefore, meet the rapid head on—nice and straight. Whether we would remain in that position was definitely in doubt. But as the old saying goes, "When in doubt, straighten it out." If we turn perpendicular to the current, the river could spin us over. We put some hustle to the muscles and turned our canoe into the downstream flow just in time to position ourselves into the center of Eight-Foot. Ahead, the water was boiling, offering a buffet of rocks, waves, and a sinkhole or two. The moment we crashed into the first big wave, the tense silence on the shore erupted into a cheering chorus of encouragement.

The rapid was a straight run with an abrupt rock wall on the right and a rock congregation on the left. After nosing into the first several waves, we consumed enough water to feel unstable, but we were able to keep the bow heading straight. The bow man always takes a beating; the first wave soaked poor, ol' Carnell to the skin, but he hooted with excitement, and his fast-moving paddle became a blur. We were moving, we were upright, and this was a kick. Let 'er rip!

I was never sure how long I was in a rapid. Time is obscure when you're watching walls of water rise and fall in front of you, and the force of the water is smashing against you and the boat. Everything happens too quickly. Once you emerge, it seems like it never happened—as though you weren't in there long enough to register the event in your memory bank. You're sorry it's over so soon. But this time, as we limped to shore with the water in the canoe nearly reaching the river level, we were relieved to be out of Eight-Foot and still upright.

Now it was our turn to man the cameras and lead the cheering sections as Jimmy, Grandma, and Barb, the Zahn team, and Andrus and Lane all braved their first encounter with *real* whitewater. They zoomed through Eight-Foot, showing spunk and skill way beyond their near-zero whitewater experience level. This gang was transforming into river runners on the crest of good, old, unadulterated on-the-job training. The excitement level was running as fierce as the river. The sighs and smiles were reminiscent of kids coming off their first rappel. And, yes, everyone expressed that same "Let's do it again!" exclamation. But for now, let's bail—we'll do it again just two clicks down the river.

Less than a half mile from Eight-Foot, we entered the upper Narrows where the river's width diminished to less than half of what it had been. It was quiet here, with deep, smoothly flowing water moving briskly between a series of limestone walls and ledges. After another mile a small canyon entered from the right which deposited rocks that created riffles. Riffles and sand waves used to be exciting. But after a Class III? Everything's relative.

Our marked-up guidebook, now soaked with pages sticking together, listed a Class II at mile 19.1 called Ledge Rapid, but it didn't tell us that Ledge was a come-around-the-corner surprise. Perhaps one develops a sense of false security after successfully running a Class III rapid, and then you perceive a Class II as a no-problem obstacle. Ledge was a ride. We were sailing along on the wind and a song when the river gently drew us around a soft turn to the right and—wow!—we were staring down the gun barrel of a frothing cauldron of undulating waves smashing away at a solid rock ledge. Will the current smash us into the wall? Are there rocks in this fast-moving channel? Where do we run this rapid? Can we run it? Such questions seem meaningless when you're mere seconds from being nose to nose with crashing waves and a stone wall.

Volleys of instructions nearly drowned out the roar of the rapid. "Cross bow to the left. Quick, pull that bow away from the wall. Hold steady. Now paddle hard. Pull! Harder!" Our starboard gunwale cleared the wall by a whisker, and then we made a straight shot through some tricky cross current, bouncing off the wall. And we were out. Thank goodness it was a short run. Our canoe was so full of water we nearly had to part our hair in the middle to keep from tipping, but our arms were up, our heads laid back in a genuine belly laugh. That was close. That was fun. That was a blast! Coasting into the calm below the rapid, we back paddled to hold position in case we had to grab someone or something that came floating by. Everyone zoomed around the corner wet, nearly swamped, but with the keel in the water still pointing downward. Each crew beached to bail while all mouths babbled simultaneously. It sounded like a 45-RPM recording of Tiny Tim spinning at 78.

We didn't encounter any more rapids that morning, but plenty of pillows hid beneath the surface, keeping us on our toes. At the 22.5-mile point Mexican Hat Rock came into view, a chunk of head-like shale topped by a sandstone sombrero. This put us only four miles from our lunch stop and our last source for goodies. We wobbled through a riffle or two, then soon spotted the Mexican Hat boat ramp.

Just ahead, we could see the Highway 160 bridge heading from Mexican Hat south into Monument Valley. It used to be called Goodridge Bridge, but in 1911 this structure, which was 20 or 30 feet above the river, was washed away in a flood. Wouldn't that have been a day to be riding the river? We beached our boats and devoured lunch. The noontime sun assaulted us from the top while torrid reflections rising up from the heat-saturated rock and sand scorched anything ol' *sol* missed. A dirt road led uphill across the highway to a little sheltered oasis offering food, drinks, ice cream, phony Kachina dolls, and coffee-can tom-toms. The one item we all purchased was ice. Once we floated under that bridge, we were paddling a river of no return for the next four days. And there was *big* water ahead.

Mean Government Rapid Looms Ahead

My watch read 1:00 when we shuttled under the Highway 160 bridge. On a cliff to the right, folks at a motel behind the little store waved and yelled encouragement. One man gave us his version of a papal blessing; perhaps he possessed far better insight into what was ahead than we had.

For sun protection, our crew flaunted a variety of exotic head gear. Grandma wore a blue fedora that looked like it came straight out of a Chicago gangster flick. Barb and Jack Zahn sported squishable, off-white lids that resembled sailor hats with the rims jerked down. A rainbow of baseball caps adorned the kid's heads, while Ian sat crowned with a hat umbrella. And to keep from literally becoming a redneck, I tied a big, white kerchief around my blue captain's hat, which I eventually donated to the river gods when it blew off in a rapid.

Soon we entered Mendenhall Loop. It took a mile or more to paddle around this meander, yet it's less than 150 yards to climb over it. Just ahead stood The Tabernacle, a distinctive rock formation, and shortly we were sailing into the Second Narrows—a deep, carved, limestone gorge. Horror stories abound about the rapids and sand waves in the Narrows, but we sailed through them with ease. Ahead were the famous Goosenecks, six miles of twisting, turning canyon terrain 1,000 feet below an overlook accessed by a dirt road from Highway 261. We pulled over for a drink and a swim. The kids spotted a few demented tourists at the edge of the cliff jumping up and down and waving. The equally demented river runners jumped up and down and waved back.

Exiting the Goosenecks, we staggered onto another rapid. Although it wasn't big, it was exciting enough to fill the boats. We traveled about 23 miles that day with a long noon-time stop at "the sombrero." When a sandy beach appeared, partially sheltered from the sun on the south shore, we decided to call it a day. Some previous wayfarers had created a miniature Anasazi cliff dwelling in the hardened sandstone protected by a small ledge. That evening our resident geophysicist led us up a small canyon to a limestone strata laden with fossils. I was so impressed with a large rock saturated with fossils that I carted it back to camp and put it into the canoe. Just what my boat needed: a 15-pound rock! I figured that I might as well do this myself. I could have bet the farm that someone would deposit a weighty gift in my canoe for a trip souvenir. At least this one had fossils.

In the morning the river was down several inches. We could tell by the position of the canoes relative to the water. We always made sure the canoes were well secured at night. Untold river runners wake to the thrill of seeing no beach and no boats—the river creeps up during the night and silently purloins their vessels, sending them on unmanned journeys downstream.

We launched the day with another great breakfast and a fresh start into a new batch of bubbling, brown broth. The rapid wasn't too difficult but, as usual, brought a little broth on board. Already the sun was sneaking into the canyons and sharing that warm envelope of heat with us. After a mile or two, we passed the infamous Honaker Trail, which dates to 1904 when gold hounds tried to work some placer deposits near the river. All day, the San Juan had been dropping about six and a half feet per mile. At this point, the drop became steeper. A score of creeks emerged from small side canyons, creating a few riffles. Five rapids of varying degrees awaited us before we would confront the big, bad one—Government Rapid—some 20 miles downstream.

Trying to watch the guidebook, the topo map, the river, hidden rocks, the location of the other canoes, and the spectacular scenery leaves you feeling short on eyes. After mile 50 we had a 1-2-3 crescendo: first a riffle, then a Class I rapid, then a Class II rapid. At the end of that run, we made a pact never again to tackle any whitewater river without covers on our canoes. Bailing gallons of water after each run took zip out of the trip. Next, we encountered Johns Canyon, which was listed as a Class I but turned out to be a legitimate Class II. Back to the buckets.

What an afternoon it was: warm sun, a few cooling breezes, and a river running through a dazzling, desert canyon. We had to wake up from our complacency to dive into two more Class I rapids. The last one was just a half mile upstream from Government. We needed to be alert and not lulled by the calm before the storm.

The stretch just above Government Rapid was in the shadow of canyon walls, making it difficult to read the water. Then we heard the roar. We had been briefed on this rapid. We were told we should make a sharp right at the approach, then a sharp left turn into the rapid. Once in, there was a sink hole to the right that would eat rafts and canoes. Just right of center was free of rocks, but that's where the big haystack waves were licking their chops, determined to flip you over backward. We *really* needed to scout this one. In fact, this may be a good place to camp. We would attack Government when we were fresh in the morning.

We "beached" the boats on the left side of the river and secured them. There was no beach to speak of, only rocks, and we had to rock hop around a huge boulder that blocked our view of the river and any potential camping area. Climbing over, we discovered that the camping spot was four star. Plenty of sand to contour to your body for restful sleeping and the best kitchen area we'd seen, complete with a flat, table-height boulder and a large "inlaid" stone floor. Best of all, we had a broadside view of Government Rapid. It's probably not more than 100 yards long, but the action is sufficient to cause minor palpitations. We stared in silence.

From the shoreline we couldn't pinpoint the suck hole, but the four or five haystacks directly in front of us were impressive. Heck, they were awesome. In the pit of my stomach, I knew we were going to dump some boats in this one. From atop the big boulder we located the suck hole, but its depth remained a mystery. Everyone began unloading canoes to set up camp, but it was a real grunt carrying gear up and over that boulder. Barb decided it would be easier if she and Grandma ran the rapid, then unloaded gear on the beach. I thought she was nuts, but was impressed with her courage.

Over Jack Zahn's objections, Barb decided to run Government Rapid. She and Grandma would stay near the shore to avoid the haystacks. Even the shore route was anything but easy; they had to make the turn by the sink hole, and then paddle out of the main rapid toward the less turbulent side. The kids lined the shore. You could feel the electricity. This was late-afternoon white-water excitement at its best.

We knew we wouldn't see Barb and Grandma until they made the turn and nosed into the rapid. It was like waiting for someone to drop over Niagara Falls. Finally, one of the kids yelled, "Here they come!" Grandma was in the bow pumping her paddle for all she was worth, her blue fedora cocked at an "I mean business" tilt. Barb was yelling instructions faster than her paddle was moving—and it was a blur. They were taking water, but were successfully avoiding the big haystacks. Still in the rapids, they were heading straight toward us when a large wave bounced sideways off the opposite wall and nearly flipped them, tipping the canoe 45 degrees to the left. Barb tried to point the canoe into the beach while they were still in wicked water, but she turned too early and more water poured in. Now the bathtub was full. The only portions of the canoe showing were the tips of the bow and the stern, and the ladies were still 20 yards out and heading sideways, but upright, down the river. Several guys ran along the shore, ready to dive in and help. But Barb and Grandma finally hit calm water and paddled close enough to toss a line, so we could pull them into shore. Their smiles were as wide as the rapid they just rode.

We celebrated with spaghetti and fresh sausage. Tomorrow night, our last night out, we would degenerate to macaroni and cheese, which I had securely snuggled into my waterproof river bag. The sky faded to a light blue, while the sun painted angel-hair clouds hanging over the pink canyon rim. Although heat still reflected off the nearby rocks, the air was cooling nicely. With the concert of moving water in the background and stars overcoming the fading daylight, we snuggled into our sleeping bags on top of warm sand. Sleep came easy.

The next morning, we bolstered our courage with pancakes and syrup, fruit cocktail, and sweet oranges. Finally, we would be running with nearly empty canoes, so a dump wouldn't prove quite as disastrous as with a boat full of gear. From any angle, Government was big water for an open canoe. We would run the rapid one canoe at a time, and Paul Carnell and I would lead the pack. At this stage, Paul may have traded this run for snakes!

The camera corps and rescue troops were ready on the sideline. We tightened the ties on our life jackets, pulled on our kneepads, then kneeled with our backs to the seats. Carnell was finding religion, crossing himself as we pushed out with visions of that big, unforgiving sinkhole. We made the left turn into the rapid and executed some paddle power, quickly moving a safe distance from the hole. But we played it too safe; we couldn't see in the hole to judge its depth. Ahead was a solid wall of water. I felt as though we were paddling into a tsunami. The canoe lurched up vertically, then down and over the first haystack. In the bow, Carnell was so high he could have gotten a nose bleed. The second haystack crashed over us, half filling the canoe with water. I felt a jolt on the right side. Fortunately, we were both paddling on the left side and narrowly prevented tipping over. No time to bail; we had more rapids to maneuver. With so much water sloshing from side to side, I forced my knees against the sides of the canoe to counter the water movement. We slammed through two more haystacks, and then balanced our way through the downstream rapids until we hit calm water. Nearly swamped, a sideways turn against the fast current proved delicate. We paddled safely to the shore, which was lined with excited bystanders who, in just moments, would themselves be running this caldron.

Riding High in Government Rapids

No one tipped a canoe going through Government, but we couldn't have been any wetter if we had. This might not have been a pretty run, but it was heart-stopping exhilaration. Everyone was pumped and ready for the next one. And their wishes came true: In the next mile, we ran three Class I rapids, although they seemed insignificant after meeting Government up close and personal.

Our guide book mentioned plunge pools that were a short hike up Slickhorn Gulch, but it failed to prepare us for such a refreshing surprise. This clear, cool pond stretched 40 feet across, was 12 feet deep, and was surrounded by ten-foot walls. Vegetation lingering on the downstream side enhanced its charm. Within minutes, bodies raced up the steep sidewalls and hurled downward into the instant gratification of this oasis in the midst of a hot, dry desert. That cool, clear water rejuvenated every overheated pore in my body. I could have stayed there forever. I hated to be the spoil sport, but after an hour we adults coaxed everyone out. A big rapid still waited at the mouth of Slickhorn Gulch, with another one downstream. Our final camp was still nine miles away.

Slickhorn Rapid looked mean. Maybe it was our inexperience or maybe the river was doing tricks that day, but after viewing the rapid from every available angle, we decided to let discretion be the better part of valor and line this one. There was just one problem. There was no room to line Slickhorn. Our choices were to run it or portage canoes and gear over a steep hill. We chose the latter, and would not make that choice again. Canoes and gear were heavy, it was hot, and we were pooped.

The final rapid offered little challenge and now the mid-afternoon heat was stifling. We pulled over to the south shore and slid into the shade of a large boulder to escape the relentless afternoon sun, popped open some drinks, and prepared for what should have been an uneventful paddle to Oljeto Wash, our final camp. Lane Slaten was now in my bow, and we invited Grandma to ride in the center to give her some peace and quiet for the rest of the afternoon. She soon regretted that decision. The current had slowed considerably, since we were nearing the backup from Lake Powell. We passed a room-size boulder dead center in the river. I paddled ever so gently to pass the rock on the right side. Somehow we began moving backward. We were caught in the boulder's eddy. Before I could react, the bow went sky high. Everything—and everyone—in the canoe flew out, then floated downstream. Well not everything floated: We donated a Buck knife, my eyeglasses, and a few other goodies to the river gods. River bags bobbed along downstream. Even our cooler took a swim. Like dunces, we had untied everything during our rest stop and thought, Why go through the hassle of lashing when we'll be stopping after a mile or two of calm water? The only one who didn't panic was Grandma. She floated restfully down the San Juan without a care. She didn't even lose her fabulous fedora!

For several minutes, vertical walls permitted absolutely no place to beach, but the cool water felt good, so we retrieved floating bags and ammo cans, lifted them into the canoes, and enjoyed the float. But did I hear about it all evening long, especially when we discovered that all the boxes of macaroni and cheese, the Last Supper, so to speak, got soaked. My only reprieve from deep depression was Oljeto Wash.

If you weren't paying attention, you could miss the entry into Oljeto. The camp area in the wash is 30 feet above the water line. This year the water was high, and we could easily paddle into the little harbor, pull the boats onto the rocks, and climb an easy grade up to the camping area.

Oljeto Wash features a small, red-rock amphitheater. This beautifully sculpted open-top cavern was created by the wind that blows through it and the water that infrequently roars down the wash into the San Juan River. It must be a sight to see the water cascading off the cliffs when Oljeto is running strong. But that day it was desert dry. You get a false sense of weather protection in Oljeta. Its huge, red-sandstone walls enclosing our camping area seemed to arch inward near the top like a partially open stadium. I'm sure that, in a good rain, we would get wet, but the walls and pseudo roof are beautiful. Voices echo, bouncing back and forth between the walls. It doesn't take teenagers long to discover that feature and fully exploit it.

That's why, after a somewhat sketchy supper of San Juan-red-stained macaroni, I wandered up the wash a mile or two. In spots it was tough going, but the beauty, coupled with the absolute stillness, lured me to go farther. What's around the next bend or over the next little wall? Rock, rock, and more rock, knurled and shaped. Like fingerprints, no two were alike. The ambiance of this place is like nowhere I have ever been. It's mystical. Oljeto Wash translates to *Moonlight Wash*. The solitude enhanced the moment. I returned to my senses and realized that the sun was long gone and darkness was quickly easing into the wash. I stopped my gazing, reversed my direction, and picked up my pace. Still, I trekked the last 15 minutes in darkness and had to use a stick to feel my way, like a blind man in paradise.

The kids were busy doing what Scouts do best: having fun wherever they are with whatever they find. After that walk, though, I wasn't in the mood for games or conversation, I simply wanted to snuggle into my bag, contour into the sand, and watch the stars peek through the narrow opening in the stone roof above. We called it a night. We would head out early to paddle the final 13 miles of calm water before the warm westward winds began blowing up the canyon. It was another one of those nights when you wish you could watch the stars forever.

We were up and at it early, downed a simple breakfast, packed our canoes, and paddled back onto the river. Without current, the paddling gets tougher, reminiscent of years earlier on Minnesota lakes. A few water fights emerged out of the quiet boredom. Ahead, Organ Rock showed on the skyline, and a small ruin appeared on the right bank just above the water level. It's an unusual place for a granary and a more unusual place for a dwelling, I thought. At Whirlwind Draw we knew we had just five miles left of our exploration.

Just before Clay Hills Crossing, the canyon gives way to open country. Soon we could see our cars in the distance. One by one, we pulled our canoes onto shore, unloaded, rinsed off the San Juan silt, and loaded up the cars for the long drive home.

The end of this trip was a study in mixed emotions. A 140-mile river trip is a long enough journey to satisfy my river-running urges, yet I saw so many sights and experienced so many events, it seemed as though I needed to remain there, to sit in that same environment, until my mind could finally assimilate all the happenings with all the associated feelings. Everything was packed, and I stole a few minutes to stand alone by the river and watch the breeze kick up a series of ripples. One of the boys came up to me and said, "You know, Sholzie, this is why I stay in Scouting." I slung my arm around his shoulder and, watching the chocolate San Juan lumber by, I replied, "Gosh, all this time I thought it was because of me."

17

FROM WILDERNESS TO ROMANCE: ADVENTURES INTO UNCHARTED TERRITORY

Mica Lake: A Name that Lives in Infamy

Buck Burshears, the originator and long-time leader of the famous Koshare Indian dancers in La Junta, Colorado, created a little booklet he loved to give to Scout leaders entitled *The Program of the Scout Troops that Fail*. Open it, and you found nothing but blank pages. I guess that said it all.

Developing a yearly program that challenged kids required some insight and energy, but executing good programs took a fistful of talented and devoted adults. Fortunately, Troop 117 was blessed with parents who were ready to step in when needed, A good example was the troop's first venture into the Mount Zirkel Wilderness Area.

Zirkel had been calling me for years. Over 160,000 acres of riparian forest span both sides of the Continental Divide, etched and shaped by massive glaciers that left spectacular, broad valleys and countless azure lakes. Along its backbone, a series of jagged peaks rise like sentinels on a great stone wall. The tallest, Mount Zirkel, ascends over 12,000 feet into the deep-blue Colorado sky. You bet I wanted to see that, but the week of the outing I was hamstrung by a frustrating encumbrance called "making a living." Who led the trip? Assistant Scoutmaster Barbara, of course, with the help of a few other backpacking adults. After I returned from my business trip, my son, Dave, gave me a blow-by-blow report of the five-day misadventure—perhaps working wasn't so bad after all.

The entry via the Gilpin Lake trail was a tolerable uphill hike through heavily forested terrain peppered with the usual wise-cracks and jokes. Joviality gave way to pants and groans once they trooped north onto the narrow and precipitous trail that eventually led their aching, dragging bodies to a high-altitude tarn called Mica Lake. The lake itself was quite beautiful, basking in the glow of a clear, sunny sky. Shelters went up, and the fishing brigade marched off—filled with confidence that, within an hour, they would snag enough fresh trout to feed the motley crew. Several of the resident meteorologists, observing the sky, predicted nothing but great weather.

As the tale goes, kids caught fish faster than they could land them. But fish seem to have a feeding frenzy just before a storm.

To hear it, this was Troop 117's Mother of All Storms. The sun still radiated warmth when the fishermen tethered their catch in the icy waters of the lake and rushed to dinner. In fact, peace prevailed through the evening until about 2:00 in the morning when the wind and water, nicely accented by a continuous drumbeat of hail, invaded from the west. These unwelcome visitors were determined to remain as all-night guests. The howling gale whipped tarps off hammocks and collapsed tents. Cold, shivering kids, still pooped from their long, hard climb, scurried to anything that might resemble shelter and huddled under ponchos inside toppled tents. The roar of the wind obliterated yells for help or words of encouragement. Author Cornelius Ryan called his war story of the Normandy invasion *The Longest Day*. The Mica storm would go into the annals of Troop 117 lore as "The Longest Night." The Boy Scout motto *be prepared* took on a whole new posture. After all, hail wasn't supposed to be delivered horizontally!

The storm finally decided to blow eastward and torment campers on the other side of the Divide. Frigid bodies emerged in the scant light of early dawn, searching for anything dry to burn. Most of their clothes didn't fit that category. But these guys were accomplished fire builders. As soon as tiny flames began licking the dampened wood, the masses huddled against the fire so tightly they could have cut off its oxygen supply. The fire grew, kids changed into dry clothes that had been safely protected in their packs, and, as the sun finally emerged from hiding, the thought of fresh fish for breakfast tickled their taste buds.

Camp life was slowly making a turnaround, at least Barb thought so until she looked toward the lake. The boys were carrying something small. As they approached, she could see nothing but a few fish heads tied to their line. "Hey, where's the rest of your fish?" she asked.

"Something ate 'em." Well, oatmeal is hot and filling, right?

The weather cleared, and the trip to Gilpin Lake wasn't as tough. The camping area was lush, the hikes were spectacular, the food was great, and any further rain restrained itself to afternoon sprinkles. The sojourn there might have approached monotonous if Barb hadn't opened her head on a tree branch. Head wounds love to bleed and this one did—enough to send her protective number-one son into dithers of worry. The good crew adorned her crown with a series of butterfly bandages, and soon Barb was once again orchestrating her charges with the wit and charm that made her one of Troop 117's favorite "patrol dads."

Names of places and events do trigger feelings and emotions. With Troop 117, "Mica Lake" probably competes with "Battle of the Bulge!"

A Lost Troop Discovers Remnants of a Lost Culture

The weather gods tested us that year. For our next adventure, we chose an expedition into the obscure Fish and Owl Creek Canyons on Cedar Mesa in southeastern Utah. This was raw Anasazi country that was not overrun with people, and it was laden with ancient sites.

The upper entry to these canyons—and the preferred route—is a mile south of the Kane Gulch Ranger Station off Utah Highway 261. The nine-mile road to the trailhead could become a glue pot of mud with a good rain or heavy, wet snow. In mid-March, weather is capricious on Cedar Mesa. We chose to enter from the downstream side, from Comb Wash and work our way up the canyons. We drove through the cut at Comb Ridge, an impressive 700-foot rock wall that stretches nearly 100 miles starting far south of the San Juan River. Driving south on the Comb Wash Road, we found the entry point into Fish Creek Canyon.

I ventured into this canyon once under unusual circumstances. For my medical advertising business, I needed a high-quality photo of a guy delivering a large oxygen tank to an ancient Anasazi ruin. (This was for a rather creative journal ad.) A professional photographer and I knew the first ruin was only a short way in, and we drove as far as we could. For the final half mile, he carried his camera gear, and I pulled an oxygen tank on a dolly, wearing a delivery man's uniform. Moving that dolly through deep sand tested my strength and my patience; the smooth, rocky creek bed looked much friendlier, although a light, springtime flow of water would probably dampen the delivery uniform. Solution: take off the uniform and walk in my underwear.

I was down in the creek where I couldn't see the trail above. But the photographer could and promptly hid behind some brush. Two backpackers appeared on the bank of the creek, a young guy and gal, staring in disbelief at me: a bearded fellow pulling a huge, green oxygen tank dressed in nothing but a baseball hat and underpants! With no place to hide and no way to run, I stopped and, with a straight face, asked them if the trail was this tough all the way up the canyon. With unblinking eyes and dropped lower jaws, they nodded and told me it would get even worse. Shaking my head in disappointment, I thanked them and went on my way. I wonder how many times they have told that story! When the troop reached that ruin years later, the kids hustled up to examine it, unaware of why I was chuckling.

The air hung hot and dry the morning of Troop 117's expedition into Fish and Owl Creek Canyons. The seven-mile hike into what we thought was the confluence of Fish and Owl Creeks took a toll on several of the little guys. But with three or four good Anasazi sites to explore en route, their agony (complete with moaning and general bellyaching) dissipated. By mid-afternoon, we trudged into a flat area near the creek and decided to call this home; this would be our base camp for explorations up both Fish and Owl Creek Canyons.

Somehow, this bunch of excellent map readers screwed up. Maybe because we didn't even look at the map, but we were a good mile and a half away from the confluence of Fish and Owl Creeks. We had camped at the entry into a smaller side canyon called McCloyd.

Late that afternoon, several groups headed out to prospect for ruins but came up empty handed. We knew there were ruins in these canyons, and we were determined to find them. But for the moment, legs cried out for rest and stomachs grumbled for fuel.

While cooking near a fire late that afternoon, the nose of my fuel bottle flamed up and gave me a sudden vision of it detonating in my hand like a Molotov Cocktail. Without hesitating, I heaved the fuel bottle like a grenade in the direction of the creek. It dropped about five yards shy of the creek and rolled, spewing flaming gasoline on all the foliage. Wow! Instant forest fire. Everyone dashed toward the creek to attack the front lines. We were lucky. Deserts have an abundance of sand, which works great on a gasoline fire. Can you imagine the verbal abuse this old Scoutmaster took from that act of insanity?

Dick Theis, my right-hand Assistant Scoutmaster Jim Colburn, our institutional rep Wayne Tewilliger, and I broke out of our tents at the crack of dawn to a cold, ominous-looking sky. One by one, the kids staggered out of their tents and fired up stoves to heat water for oatmeal and cocoa. In the dismal overcast, the nearby entrance to McCloyd Canyon resembled a huge, angry mouth. And it wasn't long before the mouth began to "speak." Deep in the canyon, we could detect a crescendoing groan. Everyone stopped cooking and faced the canyon mouth in utter silence. The groan turned into a roar and continued to increase in volume. In moments, a massive wind-driven sheet of white jettisoned around a canyon corner and headed straight toward the mouth—and straight for us! The blast toppled coffee pots, sent loose clothes flying, and, if we hadn't dived into our tents, we too may have departed into the next county. Inside the tent, the rattle of the canvas whipping in the wind was nearly deafening. Then, as quickly as this micro-storm appeared, it vanished. We exited our shelters and found the tents and sandy ground white with kernels of corn snow. The air temperature reflected the ice-box terrain. We shook our heads in dismay, bundled up, and returned to starting our fires. Then we heard the far-away groan again. This time we didn't wait—we flew into our tents and none too soon. Remember the lyric *They call the wind Mariah*? Well, Mariah and her white cloak danced through our camp again and with gusto. Once satisfied with her handiwork, she sailed off to the east and, we hoped, disappeared for the day. Springtime in the desert.

We were deep in Anasazi country and weren't about to sit and nurse our weather wounds. With lunches and rain gear stuffed into daypacks, the troop bravely sauntered through the jaws and into the mouth of this cavernous canyon, unsure of what we'd encounter with weather or remnants of the ancients. The sky lightened up, and so did our spirits.

Within the first mile, the canyon walls remained vertical; no granaries or dwellings were apparent. An interesting rock-strewn draw to the south looked like a possible route to higher ground and perhaps a location for ruins. Adventures into this mysterious land are exciting. Why these Anasazi chose such high and protected locations are among the uncertainties prevalent in Anasazi archaeology. As Liz Morris, an archaeologist and daughter of famous Colorado archaeologist Earl Morris, told me, "When I graduated, everyone in our class thought by the time we retired we would know everything there was to know about the Anasazi. We still don't know diddly squat!"

We carefully worked our way upward, over, and around boulders. Dick Theis spotted what appeared to be moki steps: small indentations worked into the rock that provided the sure-footed Anasazi with a route to ascend near-vertical walls. We instantly had several self-proclaimed rock wizards maneuvering up these notches, paled by nearly a millennium of weathering. Soon discretion overcame valor, and they slid down to follow the rest who were scampering up a less demanding, yet arduous route over rocks, ledges, and cacti. One ledge led to a water drainage with a series of large pot holes filled with water. Nestled in the shadow of a southeast-facing wall, a sizeable ruin rested with several small dwellings or possible granaries. Farther up the water-worn rock, another dwelling basked in the sunshine. Our excitement grew. This is what we came for: adventure and discovery. It felt as though we were the first ones to discover this site.

The experience of visiting an Anasazi ruin probably differed for each individual Scout. Some kids looked at construction methods, calculating how many people lived there, looking for possible kivas and obscure walls. Some were interested in finding artifacts: stone chips or pottery shards. Some listened attentively to our stories and information; others were happy just wandering about and snooping. A few searched the walls for petroglyphs or pictographs. Soon everyone was sharing their discoveries. But strong ethics of visitation had to prevail. We taught these kids to replace examined artifacts in the original location, not to pocket samples, not to climb on ancient walls, and not to touch rock art. We are fortunate to be able to access and experience so many incredible examples of an ancient culture. Each one of us has to be a steward, dedicated to protecting them. On subsequent journeys, the kids would see, first hand, the results of vandalism. And they didn't like what they saw.

We examined this site, letting our imaginations soar. Natural pockets in the rock harbored pools of water—one warmed from the sun, the other more sheltered and cooler. Was one used for drinking and the other for bathing? Or was bathing a low-priority activity due to the scarcity of water in this desert canyon? We backpacked out of the canyons mulling the same unanswerable questions that still baffle scores of Southwestern archaeologists.

The Muddy San Juan, Take Two

Fish and Owl Creeks join and drain into Comb Wash and eventually wind their way to the sand-laden San Juan River. In June of that year, we wound our way to the San Juan, too. This time, we splashed our canoe paddles through this chocolate-brown waterway with more savvy than we had two years before. We had spent half of our first trip bailing water out of our canoes. Now we fit each canoe with snaps and a canvas cover, which gave the canoes the appearance and protection of two-man kayaks. Plus, now we knew the river and how to play the rapids. We faced the San Juan's challenges with much less apprehension.

Not everyone arrived with less apprehension. Our "baggage" included a handful of the younger Scouts who, two years before, were relegated to the no-rapids upper section of the river. Plus, two dads faced San Juan whitewater for the first time. Red-bearded geologist Jim Colburn knew his way around a canoe. After Scouting together for over eight years, we had become crossed fingers—what one lacked, the other possessed. We were an exceptional team, close friends, and I was delighted that he and his son, Ted, would be along. Our second dad, a tall, pipe-smoking Abe Lincoln-looking guy, Roy Kannady, knew Scouting and knew backpacking, but this canoe adventure was a first for him. Plus, he and son Bryan had the only canoe without a cover. (They should have requested submarine pay!)

Much of the trip mirrored our first run. We relished the solitude of the quiet waters pressed tightly by narrow rock walls and snuggling into our sleeping bags in the form-fitted warm sand to watch the spectacular stellar display of cloudless nighttime skies. The big rides were memorable: Ledge Rapid, Eight-Foot Rapid, and, of course, Government Rapid with its bottomless sink hole and humongous standing waves that cause a canoe to look like it was balancing upright on its stern. Twice our rescue swimmers hit the water to assist persistent Jimmy Mahoney. Dumping in Government once wasn't enough. He had to go for a duet. In fact, this happy camper (who eventually became an Eagle and a U.S. Navy JAG lawyer) never made it through Government Rapid upright. Funny the Navy accepted him.

Our sun-baked skin yearned for the refreshing, clear water of the deep plunge pool in Slickhorn Canyon. We floated in the delightful coolness, letting our minds escape from the fact that big, mean Slickhorn Rapid was less than a mile away, eagerly awaiting our arrival. This time we ran Slickhorn, and it was a rush. Only a short journey downstream, nestled into the southern wall, was the quiet beauty of Oljeto Wash and its enclosed red-rock walls. I simply love that country.

The next morning, we paddled the waters quieted by the backflow of Lake Powell (a.k.a. "Lake Fowl"). Back in our vehicles, we ventured the rough dirt roads along Clay Hills, darting across dry arroyos to the paved two-lane highways through Blanding and Monticello to once-quiet Moab. We paralleled the Colorado River, crossed over rickety Dewey Bridge, breezed past Fisher Towers and the other spires of Castle Valley, and passed through the truly quiet, almost ghost town of Cisco to the 18-

wheeler-laden Interstate 70. Late in the afternoon, we joined the bumper parade of rush-hour Denver. During the stop-and-go traffic, we mentally erased the endless line of cars ahead of us and floated back to the peacefulness, beauty, and allure of the San Juan River and red-rock canyons... back to sanity.

The Invasion of the Female Badgers

What happens when you mix a concoction of 40 girl-crazy teenage Boy Scouts from the big city with 40 boy-hungry, teenage members of a precision all-girl color guard from small-town Wisconsin? We were about to find out. Troop 117 was excited over this busload of dairyland females who were heading to Littleton to participate in the annual Western Welcome Parade in August, which would be followed by a big, joint potluck picnic with our guys.

During the many years I was leading Scout troops, my hometown friend, Rich Neumann, was heading up an exceptional girls' color guard in Richland Center, Wisconsin, called the Hilltoppers. This was no nickel-and-dime unit. These kids appeared in major events, such as Gimbel's Thanksgiving Day Parade in Philadelphia, the Indy 500 parade, the American Bicentennial Parade in Washington, D.C., Frontier Days in Cheyenne, and the flag presentation at the Cotton Bowl. This troupe had a fistful of trophies to prove their talent. In comparison, the Western Welcome Parade in Littleton was small fish, but for Rich it wasn't the parade that counted as much as the travel adventure gained for a group of small-town kids.

Rich and I had a long, winding friendship. I met Rich when we received our Eagles on the same night. I ran into him later when he played drums and I played the bass in a DeMolay dance band. We became close friends when we both played in a nine-piece swing band in college. We ended up in Navy boot camp together, where Rich gave me an accelerated short course in drumming, which allowed me to join him in the Great Lakes

Naval Training Center drum and bugle corps. We even swirled the tassels on our tenor drum sticks together at the Chicagoland Music Festival at Soldiers Field.

The Hilltoppers bus arrived early evening in Littleton. We had arranged to quarter the contingent in Euclid Junior High's gymnasium. I arrived at Euclid shortly before the bus to be the first to offer a true Western welcome and watched a road-worn gang of tired, young ladies file in to enjoy a comfortable night's sleep on the gym floor.

The next day, I joined the noisy, excited busload of Badger State girls as a tour guide to see some Rocky Mountain sites in the nearby foothills. Meanwhile, the lads in the troop were eager to meet these young lasses and some did that evening when we escorted the gals to a presentation of the Koshare Boy Scout Indian dancers. Word hit the circuit that there were a couple real foxes among the Badgers. Ah, to be young again.

The day of the Western Welcome Parade was clear with a cloudless, deep-blue sky. It was early August, and the mercury was sneaking upward by parade time. For many years, the Wasechie Indian dancers tinkled their bells down Littleton Boulevard and Main Street to the resounding beat of the drum and the accompanying cackling chants. But this was a day to stay on the sideline and cheer the girls. I positioned myself near the judges' stand where I knew the Hilltoppers would perform their famous flag lift: four members of their rifle squad hoisted their flag bearer. (I was hoping their presentation would show more class than when the Wasechies, dancing a ribbon dance before the judges, danced the three colorful ribbons into a humongous knot!) The cheers and applause of the Littleton folk truly extended a Western welcome to the Hilltoppers and were truly impressed with the color guard's poise, professionalism, and military snap.

Troop moms prepared a feast for that evening when the two gender groups finally met in a local park. Tables of picnic delicacies were devoured, our dancers performed, volleyballs whizzed

across the net, and as dusk approached, the tigers began stealth-
ily stalking the foxes. While the younger contingent was "cum-
bayaing" around the fire pit, the senior high-school crowd
began wandering hand-in hand through the park. Soon arms
were snuggling shoulders, and there's a good chance that some
lips were doing more than simply whistling. After all, these two
groups had been waiting months for this close encounter. The
friendships that formed that weekend resulted in letters and
phone calls between Littleton and Wisconsin and even several
cross-country trips. A couple of my lovelorn seniors even followed the bus into the mountains the next day.

Rich took his Hilltoppers home sporting the parade's first-
place trophy and a check for $100. But I'd guess that those smiles
in the bus had much more to do with their exciting cross-cul-
tural experiences.

18

SEVEN DAYS IN JULY: REWARDS AND REVOLTS AT SUMMER CAMP

The Saga of Summer Camp

Who gets more spice out of summer camp? My experience tells me it's the Scoutmaster. I loved summer camp. It was a solid week in a fresh and frolicking outdoor environment far away from the clanging phones and computers of the office setting. Although orchestrating the whims of 30-plus away-from-home cutups and moving them as a team demanded the hocus-pocus of a tenured Houdini, summer camp proved an exercise in merriment, and kids usually wound up with a ton of merit badges. I'd convince them that if they really worked at camp, we could focus more on pack trips or running rivers—the real fun stuff— for the rest of the year. At camp, the kids came together, patrols solidified, and everyone had a chance to compare their skills and knowledge with guys from other units.

Not that we didn't have fun. As many a camp director can testify, Troop 117 at summer camp was a lesson in rollicking gaiety. If the kids didn't break rules, they certainly bent an ample array of them. Yet when placed in a competitive environment, they usually couldn't be whipped at anything, a factor that confused many camp staff members.

A Debacle at Ben Delatour

Following the famous kamikaze canoe trip, summer camp
loomed on the horizon. The previous year the kids were named
Honor Troop at our own council camp, so this year they decided
to test their skills at a "foreign" camp, one run by a different
council. Ben Delatour Boy Scout Ranch was a 3,500-acre Longs
Peak Council camp nestled near the village of Red Feather Lakes
northwest of Fort Collins, Colorado. It was featured in *Scouting*
magazine and looked intriguing from a variety of perspectives.
Bathed in natural beauty, the camp reportedly had a great staff,
and it was strictly patrol cooking with no mess hall. Outings
with Troop 117 alerted my palate to the fact that concoctions
these guys created were possibly edible, but they lacked any
sense of mealtime motivation. Their epicurean skills became
so depleted, I was backing away from one of my stronger suits:
mooching food. So with a covey of new kids and new patrol
kitchens we headed for Meadowlark Campsite at Ben Delatour.

A.C. Stutson was one of the younger summer campers that
year, along with Steve Richardson, Chris Theis, and Joel Slaten,
Barb's second boy. Joel's presence was a story in itself. This hard-
headed little backup to an older brother wanted nothing, absolutely nothing to do with Scouting. Barb coaxed and shoved, but
this storehouse of stubbornness would not align his independent nature with the BSA. One evening he consented to attend
an Eagle Scout Court of Honor. The speaker was an old friend
of the troop, Judge Don Smith, who sat on the Colorado Court
of Appeals. The Judge wasn't tall and had about as much hair
on his head as an eggshell, but he had a commanding presence.
Don was blessed with a deep, resonant, Walter Cronkite voice
with the delivery of a TV evangelist. He knew how to pontifi-
cate; when Don spoke, you listened. Our Eagle Scout candidate
that night was not the only one with undivided attention. Joel

sat with his back straight, mouth shut, and ears tuned. When he arrived at home, he announced to his shell-shocked mother that he was going to become a Scout!

The week at Ben Delatour tested everyone: Joel's brother Lane, Ian, and Andy Haines; the other ancients who were along; and the rookies like Joel. The weather was cool and gloomy much of the week. You nearly had to chip ice off the lake to swim, and this was a swimming troop. On top of that, the guys had to eat their own cooking. Heck, I had to eat their cooking. Their scrambled eggs seemed to float. Hamburgers were blackened—or they mooed. One batch of spaghetti resembled a massive orb of tightly glued, skinny, white worms. About the only thing they didn't screw up were the oranges, which were a little soggy after Andy Haines finished a less-than-perfect juggling act. Cooking and cleaning up took so long that half of them missed merit-badge classes. With the swimming classes, it was obviously intentional. A couple of guys ended up with the backhouse trots, and Steve Richardson had to be rushed to a Fort Collins hospital with appendicitis. We needed to use the rest of the summer to recapture the plethora of merit badges Troop 117 usually earned at summer camp.

And it worked. At our fall Court of Honor, 60 new merit badges went on sashes and over 20 boys advanced in rank.

Tipis at Peaceful Valley?

The early 1980s brought an influx of impressive kids into the troop: smart, hard workers, hard players, and ready for action. Fortunately, they came equipped with super parents. Duane Zentner took over from Jay Williams and Jim Haines as troop committee chairman and stayed in that job for five years. He was rewarded in time, though: three Zentner boys—Mark, Greg, and Todd—achieved the rank of Eagle, a troop family record. Leroy Moberly and Jeff Andrus, along with my red-bearded, right-hand-man Jim Colburn, were our Assistant Scoutmasters.

We also had "Ma" Conway, Big Red's mom. This lady knew how to make a sewing machine dance—and not just on fragile fabrics. I'm convinced she could have stitched aluminum if we asked her.

During this era, our Wasechie dancers truly hit their stride. Nearly three-quarters of the troop danced with enthusiasm to the big drum. One day, Ma Conway asked if the dancers would like to have a tipi. "A tipi? Where in heck are you going to find one of those?" I asked. In her matter-of-fact way, she informed me it would come right off her sewing machine. It came off all right, and so did four more. With a smidgen of help from the kids, Ma Conway sewed five 15-foot tipis, one for each patrol and one for the Leadership Corps. Meanwhile, dads and kids went to the mountains and cut and stripped 75 lodgepole pine trees. This year, by golly, we were storming to summer camp in style!

While the kids added finishing touches with their paint brushes, I contacted council headquarters and proudly told them we would not need tents at camp, because we would bring our own tipis. But I was informed that our tipis wouldn't be allowed; we would have to use camp tents. What!? After all this, we can't use our tipis? Why not? Safety regulations stated that tents in camp must be fire retardant and include a notice on the inside wall stating that no fires were permitted in the tent. So we marched down to the fire station! The smoke eaters at the Littleton Fire Department saved us. They provided a fire-retardant material to spray on the tents and attested to that fact with written documentation. Off we went to camp with our brand-new conical houses!

Tipis are not easy to erect. In fact, as one story goes, Indian students at the University of Colorado wanted to set up a tipi for Native American Awareness Day, so they laid out the poles like spokes, tied them together and had engineering students design a hoist. I mentioned this to an Indian friend of mine, and he roared. When we loaned him a tipi for his wedding ceremony, he couldn't set it up either. His excuse was that the women always did it. Erecting five tipis at camp that Sunday afternoon was an exercise in incompetence. Twenty-two-foot poles were going up and falling down like a giant game of Pickup Sticks. Several lodges tilted like inebriated pyramids. One canvas ended up so high on the poles that it resembled the bottom half of a Victorian matron in a mini-skirt. At times, I thought we would lose a half dozen kids for a week—they were lost inside the canvas while attempting to wrap a tipi around its frame. What started out as a race, ended up as an endurance event. Staff members who came to escort us to the Health Lodge for physicals stood silently in awe, forgetting the purpose of their visit. We showed up a little late for physicals and swim check, but, by golly, we had erected five tipis, reasonably straight and standing proudly. I and a handful of parents were mentally and physically exhausted. Uniqueness has its price.

While the kids were at swim check, a camp official paraded over to examine the colorful lodges. He promptly asked for documentation proving these edifices had been treated with fire-retardant chemicals. I whipped out the fire department papers from my briefcase. He examined them, nodded, then bent down and entered one of the lodges cluttered with piles of unpacked gear from an entire patrol. With a degree of arrogant puffery, he called me in and expressed concern that a necessary sign relative to fires in a tent was missing. I pointed to a few words painted on the canvas near the entry. Staring at them for a moment he asked, "What's that supposed to mean?"

"It simply says 'No Fires in the Tipi.'" He scrutinized the words, then turned and gave me a "Whose leg are you trying to pull" expression. Hunching my shoulders, I said, "So... it's written in Lakota Sioux."

"Now, sir, how am I supposed to know what that gibberish means?"

"You really don't have to. You won't be using the tipi. Those who will use it, know exactly what it says."

We faced no further difficulty erecting our lodges at Peaceful Valley Scout Ranch.

On the Waterfront

During most of the years at Peaceful Valley, the "waterfront" was simply a good-sized swimming pool. The heating system was uncomplicated: the sun, with a tarp tossed on at night in hopes of retaining a little heat generated by that daytime solar furnace. An early-morning dip in there could generate golf-ball size goose bumps in seconds. But compared to Tumblesome Lake in the mountains at Camp Tahosa, PV's pool was a hot tub.

Scouts always became intimately acquainted with the pool shortly following their Sunday afternoon arrival. After tents and tipis were up, everyone grabbed towels and swim suits and made a stop at the Health Lodge for a cursory check-in physical, where they sent these guys off to the pool for swim checks and buddy tags and with explicit behavioral instructions. Scouting takes waterfront activities seriously, and for good reason. The results of Scouting swimming and lifesaving programs, coupled with general water safety, have saved countless lives. Expect minimal tomfoolery at the pool, unless, of course, it's the evening of King Neptune's Court.

This event was a mid-week extravaganza replicating the flavor of a beach scene from *South Pacific*. One year Jimmy Mahoney showed up as a ravishing bathing beauty, complete with wig and a smashing, somewhat bolstered purple swim suit and was serenaded by whistles and cat calls from animals who hadn't seen a real girl in four whole days. The old king was always portrayed by some unsuspecting Scoutmaster who was destined to become very damp before the evening was over. He would emerge from the staff room sporting a mop head for hair with a broom serving as his scepter and regally adorned in a cape fabricated from well-worn burlap sacks. One year his royal sovereignty was enthroned with a crown created out of a series of toilet-paper rolls. Yes, King Neptune was always made to feel exceptionally important. But rule he did over the festivities, seated with pomp and circumstance on a throne situated in a rather precarious location: on a diving board or in a high lifeguard chair rigged for a "surprise" pool-bound ejection.

The evening was a blend of the sublime and the ridiculous. Hard-nose races and a diving competition contrasted with efforts to nearly drown the good king or each other in greased watermelon contests. So much water was inhaled during the knockdown, drag-out efforts to successfully swim the big, green oval to the edge and launch it out of the pool that you would expect the water level to decrease a full two feet. Bathed in a noise level that would put a rock concert to shame, arms, elbows, hands, and feet flashed and splashed. Rules were loose. Nearly any method of attack was permitted. Some guy would grab the melon and swim with confidence to the side when suddenly he and the melon would vanish, as though they were sucked down into a gigantic whirlpool. Both the guy and the melon would bob to the surface. Again, the melon would be attacked like a plump pig by a swarm of piranha. Some guys exited the pool looking like they had just enjoyed a back scratch from a cougar. This was water war at its finest. And seldom did the boys of Troop 117 come home without the battle-scarred melon for a late-evening snack.

Their victories in and around water were nearly a given. For some reason, these land-locked Littleton kids could swim. During many of those years, Littleton High School traditionally walked away with the state swimming championship. And we had a couple of these fish in the troop. Naturally, a troop that won the four-man relay was always invited to face the camp's swimming staff. This was a great ego-builder for the staff. "Bring us your best!" they would yell, then prance out to the pool and leave those poor kids in their wake. But that competition was a great motivator. In the early '80s the troop was powered by an abundance of swift swimmers. In fact, they took the camp championship in the four-man relay by nearly a pool length. Within moments the staff foursome stomped out in their Speedos, thumping their chests and thirsting for blood. On cue the staff vocally thundered their challenge just moments after the Scouts' championship race was completed. The staff was fresh; the champs were winded.

I was King Neptune that evening, and I called for a diving contest before our champs raced the staff to give our guys a little breather. Finally, all eight lined up: four staffers and four fish from Troop 117. This was great. It was the only time a troop had the whole camp behind them. Everyone wanted to see the staff eat crow or suck water, whichever came first. The pool staff knew they were pitted against speed that night, so their lead man left the board at least a half second ahead of the gun. Was he called back for a restart? No way. A staff guy was the starter. Each swimmer had to swim down and back. The staff team member was a body length and a half ahead when our number-two guy hit the water. The staff team held the lead going into the third heat, but they were only a half man ahead when our anchor man launched off the edge.

Old King Neptune got dunked that night, but not with the vigor that the staff normally puts into that pageantry. They seemed to have misplaced their normal enthusiasm. I suppose the fact that our anchor man standing at the finish line—waiting for their last swimmer to arrive—had a little something to do with the staff's dampened enthusiasm. There's nothing more satisfying than whipping the weeping waterfront staff in their own water.

A Revolution in Elbert County

Camp directors, like Scoutmasters, come in an array of management styles ranging from Gomer Pyle to General Patton. I left the strict, rough, tough, line 'em up, march 'em, inspect 'em military approach to Scouting leadership back in Minnesota. It simply wasn't my style. For me, broad guidelines that give kids room to think, act, and develop individuality—that still keep structure and a relatively safe environment—work the best. I've never been much for absolutes, for people who see the world only in black and white when it's an endless myriad of grays. I have strived to build citizens, not robots. Independent thinkers, not sycophants with braces on their brains. I never demanded blind obedience, but I did demand responsibility. In fact, if I had my way, I would change the word *obedient* in the Scout Law to *responsible*. I feel a responsible person will be obedient when appropriate and necessary but may choose a relevant level of disobedience when such behavior is justified. After all, how could the birth of this nation or the Civil Rights movement have been achieved without a little disobedience? What happened when this covey of free thinkers encountered a General Patton?

Peaceful Valley rested quietly in rural Elbert County, but that year PV wasn't peaceful or quiet. The camp director had the personality of a sour pickle. I never saw the guy smile. With beady eyes, this black cloud would maraud through camp anxious to malign any unsuspecting camper or staff member for some inconsequential breach of his rigid rules. The normal juvenile joviality that would crescendo to its apogee at chow time seemed to fall into a pit whenever he approached the mess tent. Naturally, "Patton's" program director reflected a similar arrogant demeanor, but due to his youth, he wasn't as intimidating.

One midweek afternoon when strolling back toward our campsite, Troop 117's entire Leadership Corps charged out to meet me. Elation and joviality were not what I detected in their expressions.

"Sholzie, you wouldn't believe what they're going to have at the flag ceremony this evening!"

I studied their fiery eyes, wrinkled brows, and locked jaws. "A hanging?"

"Worse than that. A uniform inspection! Can you imagine

that? Us in a uniform inspection?"

"Well you have uniforms, so what's the big deal?"

They were nearly all talking at once. "They want us to have regulation pants and socks and hats. All that stuff we voted against and don't have."

"So you get gigged, so what?"

"But we don't think there should be uniform inspections at summer camp."

"Well, then don't show up."

They looked at each other for a moment. Several were pacing. Finally one spoke up. "I don't think that's a strong enough statement." The others grunted a general agreement.

"Hey," I retorted, "you know my position on uniform inspections. I don't dig 'em either. But I show up for dinner in a complete uniform, even with my sexy campaign hat. If you need to make a statement, make your statement. But do it in a gentlemanly manner, okay? It's in your hands."

I had a late-afternoon meeting and walked straight from there to the flag area fully expecting not to see Troop 117 in attendance. Wrong! They were there, in uniform, standing rigid at attention, in straight lines by patrols, their eyes straight ahead, ready for inspection. One slight discrepancy: They had their uniforms on inside out!

I stood in the trees emotionally bouncing between pride and shame. I watched the combined agitation and confusion on the face of the young program director, Mr. D. This troop had won every contest in camp that week. These were sharp kids, and he knew it. What in blazes were they up to? Meanwhile, the other troops wandered slowly into the area, buzzing, chuckling, and agog. Obviously, Mr. D. had to do something official. Finally, he asked Troop 117 to step back. He conducted the uniform inspection of the other units as planned—rapid and perfunctory. Troops were dismissed to the mess tent relative to how closely they resembled the Boy Scout uniform catalog. Meanwhile, the insubordinates of 117 continued to stand motionless back in the trees.

Mr. D. finally paraded up to the troop and stood silently for a moment. In a quiet, firm voice, he demanded an explanation. The senior patrol leader promptly explained the troop's position. A discussion ensued between Mr. D. and the junior leaders. He turned and paced briefly, obviously in deep thought. Finally he turned, and with a lowered head, asked them to put on their uniforms correctly and go eat.

I still feel mixed emotions about this event. I'm not sure why. It must be something lodged in the deep, dark recesses of my gray matter, a remnant from another time and place when uniforms were acceptable and respected and tolerance to choice was limited. Troop 117's revolt effectively made its point. We never again encountered another uniform inspection at PV Scout Ranch.

But there was a sticky burr under their saddle: young Mr. D's demeanor, his arrogance, and the way he dealt with kids. With my approval, they signed up for a skit at the Friday night farewell campfire. This is always a big event with lots of songs and stunts—an all-around fun time. The skit was cute. A sergeant showed a "slow" recruit how to use a new automatic weapon, a *br-oom*. Our troop had presented this skit at other summer camps. A boy would aim the broom like a rifle and shout "bangity-bang-bang" or "stabity-stab-stab," and an enemy instantly would drop. Eventually, the littlest kid in the troop, unaffected by the shooting and stabbing, would walk right up and over the recruit and turn to the audience and, in his high squeaky voice, would say, "Tankity-tank-tank." Funny and harmless, right? Lane Slaten, wearing my campaign hat, was the tough Sarge. Big Red Conway, who was anything but stupid, could play the dumb recruit's role with vigor, and that evening he did. During the skit, I realized that Lane was not playing the normal sergeant. His arrogant behavior and his dialogue was a dead ringer for young Mr. D. In fact, at one point during a chewing out, Big Red answered, "Yes sir, Mr. D., sir." I doubt if many others caught this. Mr. D. did.

After the campfire program ended and the kids hit the sack, I had a visitor. Mr. D. asked if we could walk and talk. "You have a unique troop," he said, "I've never encountered one quite like it." I told him I didn't know whether to take that as a complment or not. We talked a bit about leadership style and Scouting in general. He stopped, cupped his hands in front of him, looked down, and said, "I learned a lot about myself this week, especially tonight. It's amazing how kids have a way of teaching you much more than you ever teach them." He stood motionless for a moment, then looked up and said "Thank you." He shook my hand and disappeared into the woods.

The Day the Penguins Marched

To combat the uniform dilemma at summer camp, we decided to design a troop t-shirt. This would have greater appeal in the warm months, give some uniformity to the troop, and make life easier when attempting to spot one of our renegades in a crowd. The first design was a basic, white t-shirt with a red neckband, complete with an Indian head and troop number on the front. Trouble ensued when some of the kids washed their shirts in hot water. The red turned pink—not a hue a teenage boy is comfortable wearing. The shirts evolved into a bright, nonfade, red t-shirt and a matching red baseball hat. (We could spot them from even farther away.) Both sported a feathered shield emblem and troop number. Now we were in some form of uniform all day, and we shifted into shirts and neckerchiefs for dinner. But one year, uniform creativity didn't stop there.

The ever-alert Eagle Patrol came upon a deal on a specialty item: classy, long-sleeved t-shirts that resembled snappy tuxedos, some complete with vests, white ties, and tails. The cerebral light bulbs ignited—all of Troop 117 could show up for dinner dressed in tuxedos! Troop 117 hadn't spawned an idea that had achieved such a degree of instant, universal support since the idea of playing British bulldog with the Girl Scouts. I'd guess a half dozen kids who hadn't planned to go to camp that year signed up just to get a tuxedo shirt and join the parade to dinner.

And quite a parade it was. The Leadership Corps decided to wait for a mid-week evening free of a pending rain storm and a day when the chow was going to be especially good. After the last merit-badge classes concluded, everyone retreated to the tipis situated in the ponderosa forest just east of the huge mess tent. A dirt road circled the camp site through open meadows to the mess area, affording a marvelous view of the spectacle that would soon unfold. Boys slicked back their hair, snapped a few pictures, and some donned cool shades. Just as the final troops were being seated in the mess area, the march began.

The troop had skipped colors that evening, so they wouldn't give away their impending wacky behavior. A staff member in charge of delivering a "Where were you guys?" dissertation stood on the east side of the mess tent awaiting their arrival. He spotted a sight that had never been seen and has never been replicated at PV. Out from the ponderosa pines marched 35 penguins, ranging from Andy Green and Big Red, who both hit the tape measure at over six-foot-five inches, to a rash of Tenderfoots whose lack of altitude failed to hoist them as high as the older guys' waists. In a column stretching back into the trees they moved as a body—slowly, silently, straight and stiff, dignified, and with an air of elegance emblematic of *The Great Gatsby* era. As mess tent inhabitants spotted the incoming menagerie, the murmur crescendoed into a minor roar. Undaunted by the cheers, laughter, and cat calls, Troop 117 moved methodically to the assigned tables, noses elevated at an angle appropriate to their current demeanor. This was 117 tomfoolery at its best. At dinner, the best dressed, best behaved unit was the first troop invited to retrieve its food. A faint smile cracked on the faces of a couple of 117 guys when they were invited to lead the camp to the chow windows. Today, I'm sure those tuxedo shirts are stashed away with other Scouting memorabilia, representing a dressy dinner date to remember.

A Man Called "Two Blankets"

Some professional Scouters and volunteers get so strung out with the image of what a Scout should be that they forget the single element that brings kids into the program: fun! If a boy doesn't have fun, he doesn't stay in Scouting. And if he doesn't stay, you can't mold him into the kind of lad that fits the image of what a Scout should be. It's that easy. Mike "Two Blankets" Sulgrove obviously understood this concept and understood kids. Like myself, I felt he too was an overgrown kid.

I liked Big Mike from the first time I met him. He sported a warm smile, dancing eyes, and a genuinely happy demeanor. This guy was comfortable with himself and comfortable with kids. And now Big Mike was going to be the new camp director of Peaceful Valley Scout Ranch. Finally, PV had someone with whom the mavericks of Troop 117 could honestly relate. This will be an interesting encounter, I thought.

Did I say he was an "overgrown" kid? Big Mike could truly test the stretchability of XXX Large pullover shirts. His mountain men compatriots didn't call him *Two Blankets* for nothing. They calculated that it would take at least two *big* blankets to cover his frame. But inside that big body beat an exceptionally big heart.

Mike helped make things happen at this high-plains camp. Seabees had constructed much of this 2,500-acre retreat, which was part of a working ranch. During Mike's era, PV added an artificial lake; a huge, indoor mess hall complete with training facilities; and showers for leaders. Plus, he was a master at running a superior program. He also became a master at dealing with the unpredictable antics of 117's monkey farm.

I don't remember if Mike came up with the idea of Coulter's Run, but he sure made it a special event. If you're a little light on Western history, John Coulter did a tour of duty with Lewis and Clark before he departed to the upper Missouri country to hunt and trap. When he and a partner encountered a hoard of Blackfoot Indians, the partner ended up riddled with so many arrows he must have resembled a porcupine. Meanwhile, the Blackfoot stripped John of all his clothes and told him to run for his life. Run he did, and he survived to tell about it. Mike's version, thankfully, lacked that level of high adventure, but it combined all the elements that turned kids on to this camp-wide challenge.

With ten activity stations to visit, each troop fielded a team of ten Scouts. One runner would race a quarter of a mile to the first station, perform a specific feat, and then send the next runner to a new station. Kids had to saddle a horse and ride it around a corral, properly lash poles together, swim a series of laps, identify animal tracks or scat—all Scout-related activities. In Coulter's Run, both time and quality prevailed. Troop 117 ate it up. In the years that Mike was camp director, 117 never lost this race. One year, the troop's "brightest and best" split up and entered two teams; they took first and second places. This was the kind of spirit and know-how Mike relished, so when it came to their mischievous moments, he showed exceptional tolerance.

It seemed that each night a covey of 117ers would be on the prowl, like a pack of wolves, leaving their calling card in some creative fashion. The tags on the swimming pool's buddy board would be arranged into a huge *117*. Logs at the pioneering area would be positioned to read a giant *T-117*. At the mess hall, at the corral, wherever people gathered, the number *117*, like Kilroy, was there.

Mike's cabin, complete with the sign *Trail Boss,* was situated so his bedroom window overlooked the new lake. He was proud of that lake with its new swimming and boating facility and especially proud of his racks of new aluminum canoes. Early each morning Mike would rise and proceed with his wake-up ritual of opening his window shade to gaze at the lake and distant mountains and peruse his domain. One morning, some-thing in his blurred vision looked unusual. Hastily, he slapped on his glasses and peered out again. His jaw must have descend-ed down to his protruding paunch. Between the sage brush on the ground and the magpies in the sky were all his new alumi-num canoes propped against the dam reading: *T-117.*

I knew nothing about this and was puzzled when he tromped his big body, adorned in super-size Scout shorts and mountain boots, up to Troop 117's breakfast table. He transported an expression blending irritation, indignation, and exasperation. What in blazes did they do now? I wondered. His head scanned like a radar antenna, and his eyes diminished to mere slits as he moved slowly from one boy to the next in a staredown. No one revealed the slightest hint of guilt, not a peep. If I read their body signals accurately, they said, "Maybe, just maybe, this time we went too far." Slowly he hunched his massive frame over the table. His scowl faded into a sinister smile, and he uttered, "Clever."

The Biggest Feet in Camp

During the final summer of Mike's tenure at PV, the kids heard, with regret, of his upcoming move to Indiana as a professional Scouter. There was instant agreement (which was unique in this unit) that Troop 117 should do something special for Big Mike. A horde of ideas were batted around before we finally hit on the winner. Ol' Two Blankets enjoyed the mountain man scene. We would give him a pair of fully beaded Indian-made moccasins. He'd love that, and I knew just the gal who could make them.

In the early years of our dance group, a pair of Crow moc-casins I danced in for years wore so thin that I could step on a dime and tell if it was heads or tails. I needed a new pair, and I had heard of a Lakota lady in Denver who did magic with moccasins. I contacted a friend at the Western Trading Post on South Broadway where many local Indians bought supplies, and

I asked about her. Unfortunately, I was too late. I was told this particular lady had passed on, but the trading post promised to find me an equally talented moccasin maker.

Several weeks later my secretary walked into my office and, with a quizzical twist to her face, stated, "I have a Holy Elk something or other on the phone." It turned out to be Debbie Holy Elk Face, a lovely, smiling Rosebud Sioux who knew the secret to making and beading hard-sole moccasins. Hard-sole moccasins feature rawhide on the sole and soft buckskin or elk skin on the top where they are beaded. The first time you place hard-sole moccasins on your feet, you would swear you were stepping on a board. But after an hour or two of wearing them, the rawhide sole molds to your feet yet remains tough enough to protect you from pebbles, prickly pear cactus, or whatever may be laying in wait during an outside dance performance. The moccasins Debbie made me were so beautiful and so comfortable that I asked her to make a pair for both of my boys. So we knew where to go for Mike's mocs. But how could we get the outline of his feet, which were practically the size of cement blocks, without him knowing it? We had to come up with a valid, believable reason that would fool a guy who was not easily duped.

Kids paced around the campsite like expectant fathers. One idea would surface, then someone would promptly shoot it down. "Why not have a contest?" someone suggested. "We have some big feet in the troop." (Big Red must've pushed size 14.) "Better yet, let's try to figure out who has the biggest feet in the entire camp." Great idea! Mike will love to compete in that match. So off went a couple of our grand champion straight facers, the ones who wouldn't crack up in the middle of this perjurious process. Dubious at first, after all he knew the group with whom he was dealing, Mike suggested the guys just draw the outline of his boot. Naw, they said, they weren't comparing boots—they were comparing feet. So like the gentleman he was, he acquiesced. His hesitation might simply have been due to the fact that he had no one washing his socks!

The guys swore the monstrous sketches were accurate. Big Mike did, indeed, sport some Big Feet. When I showed the outlines to Debbie, the price went up. "I've never made moccasins this big. But I tell you what, a guy this big must be a chief. I'll make chief moccasins." That's just what we want, I thought.

We promised to return to camp with the dance group for one of Mike's final Friday night campfires. Debbie was feeling good and completed the mocs in time for us to take them along. Feeling good played a major role in her moccasin production. When she failed to meet a completion date, she would frown and tell me she doesn't work when she doesn't feel happy. "If you work when you feel sick or sad, that sickness or sadness goes into your work. That's not good." (I tried this approach once in the business world, but no one bought it.) Fortunately, a lot of happiness went into Mike's mocs. And happiness prevailed the night of the big campfire. Troop 117 put on an extra-special dance performance. We even brought along our girl dancers, who recently had joined the group. We invited Big Mike out to dance, which gave us the opportunity to present him with his chief's moccasins. If he had figured out what we were pulling off with the surreptitious foot contest, he never let on. That night we said goodbye to a friend who we knew would continue to walk tall, especially in those beautifully beaded, hard-sole moccasins.

19

NEVER-ENDING ESCAPADES IN THE 1980s

Enter the German "Redskin"

One autumn evening in 1982, a handsome blond lad, a German foreign-exchange student attending Heritage High School in Littleton, came to one of our troop meetings. Marc Behm was a Boy Scout in Germany and had already joined a troop in Littleton when he learned about Troop 117's Wasechie Indian dancers. In an instant, Marc made the switch. This boy wanted to dance. At the time, I didn't realize the level of interest many Europeans had regarding American Indians (*red Indians*, as they were called, to distinguish them from residents of India). Germans had Indian social clubs, powwows, and even camped in tipis, where they would doll up in war bonnets and beads. Marc would stay only a year, so he wasted little time learning steps, various dances, and constructing a costume. In ten minutes I taught him lazy stitch beading; a week later he waltzed in proudly carrying a fully beaded apron designed around a sketch of an eagle's head (the mascot of Heritage high school). Marc's handiwork even included a red spirit bead, the intentional error Native Americans frequently include in their beadwork to show that only the Great Spirit is perfect.

Was I impressed? I was flabbergasted, not only with his beadwork but with his speed in learning dances and his ability to perform them. Plus, I was pleased with the warmth and friendliness he displayed to his fellow Scouts, his curiosity and interest, and, most important, the skill and knowledge that propelled him forward in Scout advancement. If we could have kept Marc another year, he would have flown home an Eagle Scout—and a proud and exceptional Eagle at that. As he was dancing his heart out one evening, I realized that if this German lad had been born a few generations earlier Marc would have been the kind of Scout at whom American troops would have been shooting.

Troop 117, February 1983

Rediscovering "The Man"

It was 1984, one year from the 75th anniversary of Scouting, and we planned a full slate of adventures. The next level of leadership moved into place. My youngest son, Dave, became a senior patrol leader, and I had to use caution so I wouldn't expect more from my own kid than I would from the others. Our patrol dad system was running smoothly with Herb Banister and Roy Kannady in place. Doug Ayres, along with his wife Christy, became indispensable with the dancers and took over the Bear Patrol. Our secret weapon, Barb Slaten, who maintained the Eagle dynasty for so many years, gave way to Assistant Scoutmaster Jim Colburn. Big Red Conway and Mark Zentner were in the wings ready to be elevated to Eagle Scouts, with another six ready to burst out of the nest. As junior leaders go, it was tough to beat Mark Zentner, the first of three Zentner brothers who, in their own ways, left their brand on this unit. When Mark first joined the group, I thought he must have suffered some type of stroke that paralyzed the facial muscles used for smiling. We tagged him the *Great Stone Face*. I can't recall what eventually brought a smile to the GSF, but, smile or not, this lad became a mainstay of leadership, friendship, and companionship to virtually every kid in the troop. We decided that in the spring we would introduce new kids to the All-American Man.

This journey into Canyonlands that year offered a few different twists. Twenty-one of us headed west on Interstate 70, across Dewey Bridge, and past Moab. We camped one night across from the mystic petroglyphs at Newspaper Rock. Driving my new wide-tire International Scout that resembled a big, green Sherman tank, I led Colburn and Banister into the first section of Salt Creek. Our vehicles carried the packs while the kids hiked the initial 12 miles. We followed what appeared to be the road, and I came face to face with an anemic-looking little stream. Engulfed in vehicular power-based confidence, I charged in. I quickly found myself and my new International Scout at a 45-degree angle with brown, mucky water oozing onto the floorboards. I was stuck. High on a road to my right, sat Banister. Hanging out his window, he smiled and spewed snide comments on my choice of routes. I crawled into the backseat where I could exit without threat of drowning, while Herb and Jim pulled their vehicles into position for a major extraction exercise. It took two mighty, four-wheel-drive vehicles to pull the Mean, Green Machine to dry *terra firma*. Thank goodness the troop was not yet here to guffaw my buffoonery, but they soon learned about it. They found my tracks—and my tailpipe!

After our ritual visit to The Man the next morning, we hiked farther south to examine pottery shards, attempt a little chimney climbing, and explore the valley. Across the creek we discovered a four-exit enclosure formed by several massive, black boulders. By the tracks and scat, it looked suspiciously like a mountain lion lair. We had some new tender meat with us—Doug Kixmiller, Troy Terwilliger, Jeff Jurgenson, Ken Caldwell, Jeff Rallo, and Jason Ayres—who treaded gingerly as we entered. Fortunately, the owner wasn't home. But he may have just left, we realized, when we discovered three other exits.

It was great to be back in Salt Creek Canyon again and discovering things we hadn't seen before, such as granaries in the middle of open fields that once provided precious corn for the long-lost inhabitants. We promised to re-explore this area every four years, so new kids in the troop could experience The Man and his vast, foreboding terrain.

A Super Leader Is Anything But Young and Green

In 1985, we were long on adventures but short on adult leadership for summer camp. I decided to put recent high-school graduate Andy Green and his six-foot-six-inch frame in charge of summer camp that year. And take charge he did—leading the largest number of Scouts any troop sent to Peaceful Valley that summer. Andy maintained discipline, ensured participation in all camp events, and monitored the daily progress of his troop in myriad merit-badge classes. In testimony to his leadership, here's what this troop accomplished:

- Completed 99 merit badges, plus 12 nearly completed badges
- Seven Scouts completed a one-mile swim—a camp record

- Won the King Neptune's Court swimming and diving competitions
- Won the Weefel Chase—a contest of skill and speed
- Won (at record time) Coulter's Run, the Scout skill relay
- Entertained the camp with a colorful Indian dance performance at the final campfire
- Received the camp "Oscar," the PV Ranch Award as the outstanding troop

Summer camp could have been exceptionally difficult that year, considering it was extended to 10 days, plus the high number of first-year campers who attended from our troop. Andy faced some tough moments, but he worked out the problems. The result was one of the most successful summer camps in Troop 117's long history. Andy's performance reinforced our feelings about our junior leadership training and the important role of maturity that only comes with experience—and takes years to develop. Eagle Scouts who are only 12 or 13 years old just don't cut it in my book. I never let one fly from the nest under the age of 16. And how did we keep boys interested in the Scouting program long enough to become full-fledged Eagles at the ripe, old age of 16? This copy from our promotional brochure in 1984 reveals the "secret" to Troop 117's success:

- Average of 24 nights of camping annually
- Spring break backpacking trips to Utah or New Mexico
- Monthly overnight campouts
- Summer camp each year
- Extended summer backpacking trips in the Rockies
- Whitewater canoe trips
- Cross-country and downhill skiing trips/snow caving
- Field trips to nearby locations of interest
- Well-planned, fun-filled troop meetings

- Membership in eight Scout patrols

- Experienced patrol leaders (Star or Life Scouts)

- A Leadership Corps of older, experienced Scouts

- Tipis used for drive-in camping for each patrol

- A complete array of patrol equipment

- A troop Indian dance team—the colorful Wasechies

- A Scoutmaster with 25 years of experience

- Three experienced Assistant Scoutmasters

- Adult patrol advisors for each patrol

- An experienced and active troop committee

- Steady, but not easy advancement—you're proud of what you earn

In addition, we included the boys' families at the Courts of Honor, orchestrated fun-filled family campouts and potluck dinners, and parents were welcome on extended trips. We recruited as necessary to maintain four patrols of eight boys and a Leadership Corps of eight older guys. Patrols were assigned a Cub Scout pack to maintain constant recruiting. The entire troop fully supported planned community activities, especially projects that were designed and supervised by older Scouts heading to Eagle.

That's what our program was all about: developing guys like Andy Green. He was definitely mislabeled. This lad was anything but "green" when it came to leading and functioning safely and effectively, whether in town, in camp, or deep within a wilderness environment.

Too Many Older Scouts? A Brief Pontification

We faced many years where I could have simplified the program by sending older Scouts to Explorer units. I chose not to. Twice in my career I tried this, and both times it failed. One time we started an Explorer Post. The second time, I encouraged older boys to move into a post, because I felt we had too many older boys in the unit. In Minnesota, we had started an Emergency Preparedness Post for older Boy Scouts. However, that plan didn't fly, and, of 17 boys who left the troop as Life Scouts for the post, only two returned to complete their Eagle when the post folded within a year.

If the troop does its job, it develops an *esprit de corps*, a special pride in belonging to that unit and wearing its number. The older boy loses this important identification when he moves into Exploring. In addition, older Scouts encounter greater time restrictions than younger boys. The idea that an older teenage boy returns to his troop to teach Explorer-learned skills sounds good, but, in reality, few young adults have the time to participate actively in both units.

Traditionally, advancement grinds to a near standstill in many posts. Young adults who have not been in the Scouting program and join posts are there for the specialized activities; few will start up the advancement ladder at that point. Consequently, merit-badge classes or individual merit-badge counseling, which should be a pertinent part of a troop's program, is sadly lacking in a post. Posts seldom, if ever, participate in long-term summer camps where rapid advancement occurs. Therefore, the potential for achieving Eagle diminishes rather than accelerates in the normal post environment.

A major objective of Scouting is to teach leadership skills and provide boys with opportunities to practice these skills. It takes an average boy two to three years of troop Scouting to build his knowledge and skill level to be an effective leader. Transferring him to a post at that time—when his knowledge and skills can benefit himself and his troop—is simply not judicious.

Finally, the Boy Scout troop is one of the few places where 11- and 12-year-old boys can develop close, personal relationships with 16- and 17-year-old boys. These older Scouts can have far greater influence on the younger boys than adults. Why remove older boys from the opportunity to be important role models?

How do you keep these older boys interested? High-adventure programs. Younger boys don't need to participate in all of the troop's programs, especially if they're not yet prepared for that level of skill. But the younger boys are aware of these programs within their troop, which provides the motivation to acquire the necessary skills and experience so they, too, can participate in unique, high-adventure programs. It's the old carrot game. More important, everyone—older and younger Scouts—stays challenged and has the opportunity to work together in a junior leadership environment.

A Girl in our Midst? And Who's the Mystery Man?

Each September we shifted junior leaders. Teddy Colburn took over the Eagle Patrol, Eric Zinc led the Buffalo, Jason Ayers headed up the Bears, and Trevor Banister led the Elks. Dave Sholes, Steve Richardson, and Andy Green became junior assistant Scoutmasters. Mark Zentner became the new senior patrol leader, assisted by Chris Theis and Joel Slaten. Grady Holder was our new scribe, Brian Kannady the Quartermaster, and "Unsinkable" Jim Mahoney the Wasechie dance chief. The patrols kept busy with their own programs, in addition to participating in troop campouts. We headed into Scouting's 75th year with a full complement of adults and kids. Plus, we had a girl in our midst.

A year after Marc Behm returned to Germany, he phoned and asked if we could arrange for his sister, Marfa, to come to Colorado for a year's schooling. She arrived in August, moved in with our family, and commenced school at Littleton High. Marfa was a Scout in Germany where the troops were co-ed, an idea I had long championed. Being placed in a Girl Scout unit did not really meet her fancy, so she became an unofficial "guy" in Troop 117. Her first camping trip was the District Klondoree near the town of Castle Rock. This annual winter get-together was a fun time for kids and included building sledges to race in a variety of events. That year, we camped in the snuggly confines of our tipis. Marfa was running with the Eagle Patrol, and it took someone from another troop over five hours to figure out that the "he" bundled in winter clothes was a "she."

That winter brought a couple of cool outings, cross-country backpacking, and, in late February, the long-anticipated 75th Anniversary Court of Honor in which my son, David, received his Eagle award. Judge Don Smith again did the honors. His presentations always reminded me of the minister who conducted the marriage ceremony for my wife and me. Both men dispatched a no-nonsense presentation. I knew I was married when that pastor, who tended to spit lightly when he lectured, was finished. I'm sure that, with the honorable Judge at the helm, Dave knew he was an Eagle Scout with life-long responsibilities. I was puzzled that evening to see so many Scouts and parents from past years in attendance. I felt this was a nice tribute to both Dave and me. But, I wondered, who was this distinguished, mystery gentleman complete with cowboy boots and a handlebar mustache sitting near the front? Shortly after Dave's ceremony, I found out.

I was nearing my 25th anniversary with Troop 117, and someone had decided to combine Dave's Eagle ceremony with a thank-you presentation to me. I felt honored and extremely grateful. That's why so many people whom I hadn't seen in ages were there. Parents and former Scouts had intended to present me with a beautiful Indian painting. But how do you buy a painting for someone? Instead, they bought the painter! I was finally introduced to the strange face with the handlebar mustache, Western artist Bill Duncan. His assignment was to paint me in my Indian costume. We agreed to meet later at his ranch near Sedalia, Colorado. He was a friend of Herb Banister's, so Herb accompanied me to Bill's studio to converse with me during the sitting. This would allow Bill to capture the type of expression he sought.

Another confession: My hair had started to turn pure white around age 40, and my kids had been badgering me to "let it go" to see what color it really was. I *knew* what color it really was. But I thought I'd be a nice, compliant dad, so I dispensed with the Grecian Formula right at the time I had my first sitting for the portrait. Due to commitments on both sides of the canvas, Bill Duncan and I didn't link up again for several months. When we did, Bill took one look at the canvas, one look at me, another look at the canvas—and out came the white paint. This routine occurred through the final sitting. There must be four coats of paint on that hair. He never once made a comment, such as, "Is something stressing you?" Upon completion, Bill brought his work to the house for final approval, and he signed it on the spot. Several weeks later, the troop formally presented it to me at another Court of Honor. I fear I never expressed the depth of my gratitude to all those who made this possible. I do now.

A Gulch that Proved Simply Grand

While perusing a Utah guidebook, I tripped over a location that had Troop 117-style adventure written all over it: Grand Gulch, Utah. A 25-mile loop trail combined all the key ingredients Troop 117 yearned to experience: natural beauty, remote wilderness, spacious camping locations, wildlife, and, best of all, superb Anasazi rock art, artifacts, and ruins. Here lies one of the finest outdoor museums of the West and only a day's drive from home. Near the end of March 1984, 22 Scouts and adults entered this vast, mysterious maze of sandstone walls in two groups. Due to group size restrictions, Herb Banister and Terry Terwilliger led Group A, which entered via Kane Gulch. Roy Kannady and I headed Group B and entered via Bullet Canyon. Our plan: meet halfway and exchange car keys.

The desert sky didn't disappoint us that morning, deep blue and totally uninterrupted by clouds. The air was crisp, and magpies and rufus-sided towhees darted briskly from tree to tree.

With packs snugly attached, my group followed a ridge trail for a short distance before we dropped into the upper reaches of Bullet Canyon. Here the canyon is narrow and snakes westward through scattered stands of scrub oak, willows, and occasional tamarisk. The reddish sandstone walls bordering us on both sides grew taller with each descending step.

Before long, we faced our first obstacle, a 12-foot water-fall in a stepped narrows with no apparent way to end run it. After we carefully worked our way down, without somersaults or impromptu cold morning showers, we trudged through the growing heat for several more hours. Shade was sparse for our lunch break. Finally, in early afternoon, we reached Jail House Ruin, which sits high on a ledge and overlooks a spring-fed creek. Kids tossed their packs, and the rush to the ruin began. Jail House Ruin is a quality site, probably named for the stick-barred window in one of the dwellings. The sticks seem to have no utilitarian purpose other than to block entry into the small window. Several large, white painted circles, one with two round "eyes," adorn the ruin and are rumored to be hex symbols. Like most ruins we discovered, Jail House has multiple levels. The upper level, more than likely a defensive position, is difficult to reach. Due to the "tumble potential" as well as site preservation, we discouraged high climbs.

Following supper, evening exploration was in full force, and I soon heard that familiar holler: "Sholzie!" But this time it was followed by, "Come quick!" My first thought was that someone fell or, heaven forbid, a snakebite. I scampered up the red-sandstone wall in the direction of the alarm. Running along one of the ledges, I turned the corner of a huge monolith and was greeted by, "Look what we found!" I could see a large dwelling, and when I climbed closer to the ruin I spotted the kiva ladder. A full, covered kiva with ladder access. Wow! The sounds emanating from the kiva were simply pure exhilaration, Approaching the ruin, I encountered pottery shards, miniature *metates*, and tool-sharpening features in every direction. This was truly an exciting bundle of discovery. In the kids' eyes, and for Roy and me, this was already a successful trip. I've visited Perfect Kiva six times since that discovery, but the intoxication has never matched that first evening.

In the morning we wound our way through the wide, flat mouth of Bullet Canyon, seeking the juncture with Grand Gulch. Initially the trail closely parallels the water. Thick vegetation conceals the trail in spots, and backpackers can follow animal trails and accidentally wander off and into tiny box canyons. This is when we pull out the whistles. One toot: Where are you? Two toots: Here I am. Three toots: I'm lost, I'm hurt, I'm in trouble. The kids knew if they used three toots, they better darn well be in trouble! A smattering of ruins and rock art play hide-and-seek in the thick vegetation along this segment. Each successive trip we saw more rock art and even a three-story ruin we aimlessly had wandered past before. But this first time, we were overwhelmed by sites so large we tripped over them. That day was a poke-along day, so we investigated several smaller ruins before we finally found a wide spot near the mouth of Sheik's Canyon, sheltered by a rock wall and trees, to call home for the night. The rage that evening was sticking handkerchiefs in the rear of hats a la French Foreign Legion. But little did we Legionnaires know that a short hike up that tiny canyon would have uncovered some of the finest rock art in Grand Gulch, plus a massive rock shelter in which over 30 Anasazi remains were once found.

Our destination the next morning was Split Level Ruin, which was less than a five-mile hike from camp. With luck, we would meet Group A sometime that day. And we did—around noon at a pour off where a little pond had developed. The kids were genuinely excited to see one another and, with a buzz of verbiage echoing off nearby walls, each group exchanged adventure stories for over an hour. Finally we passed car keys and information on sites and routes and said our "so longs," hoping we'd all be safely together again in two more days.

It was mid-afternoon when we moseyed into Split Level Ruin. Built on a series of terraces, the camping area lies several hundred yards away from the ruin site. Those who dashed into the ruin were awed by what they found. The rest of us who were putting up tents quickly finished our tasks to share the excitement. Split Level is a museum of Anasazi architecture. The entry to one large stone structure is the traditional T-shaped doorway. Another structure is a waddle-and-daub construction (a stick base covered with adobe mud). A huge, unexcavated midden (trash heap) extends along the front and side of the structures, which deserves protection. Fortunately, backpackers don't seem as intentionally destructive as those with a gun mentality who can't seem to keep their trigger fingers dormant when they see an imposing piece of rock art. And then there are the pot hunters.

The following day near Turkey Pen Ruin, we learned a major lesson about pot hunting. A helicopter hovered over us for several minutes and set down on top of the ridge. Two men in yellow jumpsuits exited the chopper. With 22 Scouts and leaders in the Gulch, I was certain they sought us out due to an emergency, so we waited while they cautiously worked down a steep section of the adjoining wall. Reaching us, one of them immediately apologized for the noise and commotion, but he said they needed to repair the transmitter at Turkey Pen Ruin. Transmitter—at Turkey Pen Ruin? Wow, maybe these Anasazi were a little more advanced than we had figured.

It seems that in the mid-1980s, pot hunting had become high tech. This new breed of vermin came into the canyon under the cover of darkness by chopper, used respirators to dig quickly into ash-laden middens, tore down walls to access substructures, and, we were told, were heavily armed, like a drug operation. I questioned the economics of all this and learned that well-healed folk, especially in Saudi Arabia were paying a quarter of a million dollars for a Grand Gulch pot! Now, government officials positioned metal detectors with transmitters throughout the area. "They can pick up the metal eyelets on your boots," we were told. "But we simply don't have the manpower or budget to patrol this whole area." The Scouts were all eyes and ears listening to these stories. Lesson well learned. The gross lack of respect for these spectacular antiquities hopefully made a lasting impression on our young Legionnaires.

Moving on, we spent the next hour ogling dwellings, granaries, ghost rooms, the turkey pen, and the wealth of rock art adorning the walls. (During a later visit I spotted the initials of John Wetherill, the first white man to discover Mesa Verde, painted on the sandstone wall.) The late-afternoon sun was quickly retreating as we staggered into our last camp at the junction of Grand Gulch and Kane Gulch. This is the site of Junction Ruin. Water was plentiful in both creeks and, as usual, the last dinner on a desert pack-in was a bit bland, but we knew that Hogie's Hamburger joint waited with open arms just down the road in Monticello, and we would be shaking hands with those greasy, mouth-watering concoctions tomorrow, topped off with big, thick chocolate malts. But we still had one gorgeous ruin to explore and a five-mile uphill climb out of there tomorrow.

Come morning, I slipped out of my sleeping bag early and walked the short distance to Junction Ruin. Nestled into an overhanging alcove, it sat quietly in its old age, soaking up the early rays of the morning sun. A gentle breeze momentarily kicked up a cloud of dust and whistled like a tiny flute, triggering my imagination. White hand prints on the rust-colored walls nearly came alive. In the flats below, I could almost see fields of corn bending in that breeze as men with wooden hoes were cultivating between the rows. In my mind's eye, two women near the front of the dwelling, hunched over their *metates*, were busily grinding corn for the morning meal, while near a roofless kiva an older man was mixing water and clay to repair a short section of wall. In the distance, a young girl was returning from the stream, carefully balancing a beautifully decorated *olla* filled with cool, clear water. Wow, I thought, if this is what five days in here does for my imagination, I know I have to return.

I walked out 25 yards to see the upper level of dwellings. Access looked impossible without a ladder. What was happening here 1,000 years ago? Why did these people live in fear? Who was their enemy? Finally the silence and my dancing imagination were disrupted by the cackling of a sassy magpie. Looking below, I saw that there was finally movement in our camp. The long, hot climb and the Hogie burger lie just ahead.

The Wild River, One More Time

In early June when the water was high, we headed back to the San Juan River with covered canoes. Plus, we added a girl. Before sending Marfa home to Germany, we decided to give her a little thrill, a wild river trip with 15 guys. She loved the idea. Instead of heading straight to the river, we spent several days exploring Mesa Verde National Park. Our crew wandered through Cliff Palace, up the ladders to Balcony House, through Spruce Tree House, and camped at Morefield Village. That first evening after supper, I talked most of our gang into a hike to an awesome overlook to watch the sun go down behind Sleeping Ute Mountain near the town of Cortez. The conversation that evening was special, and so was the sunset. We knew there were rattlers in the park and had forewarned the gang. Sure enough, as we wound our way down to the road someone heard that distinctive buzz and wisely yelled, "Snake!" That means *stop, look, and listen.* Two feet from my left foot sat a coiled, diamond-headed package of poison. "Here it is," I cautioned. "Its tail is going like mad, but it isn't making any noise."

A high-pitched voice from the rear spit out, "It's making a hell of a lot of noise back here, Sholzie!"

This was a defining moment in my life. For years, both my wife Char and my secretary Carol had told me I simply didn't hear well anymore. Carol even sent me on a business trip with a *Newsweek* magazine in which she had pasted a dozen ads that read, "Think of them simply as contact lenses in your ears." Granted, at times it may have been advantageous not to hear your wife or your secretary, but hanging out so much in the desert, I would appreciate hearing a rattlesnake! This prompted a trip to the audiologist upon my return and a life of wearing hearing aids.

The San Juan was running high in early June. We loaded boats at Sand Island and paddled our way toward Mexican Hat. I shared my boat with son, Dave, and we placed our precious cargo, Marfa, in the able care of Jimmy Mahoney. Marfa was looking for excitement and Jimmy did not disappoint her. He narrowly missed hitting the wall at Ledge Rapid, looked like a submarine in Eight-Foot, then came within a hair of visiting the sink hole in Government Rapid that went halfway to China. Jim had flipped twice in this rapid several years before. Marfa not only enjoyed one bath that morning, but Jimmy suckered the poor girl into running Government a second time to prove his manhood. Sure enough, the big haystack waves ate them up again. Yes, this is the same guy who later joined the U.S. Navy, fortunately as a lawyer, not as a helmsman!

That evening, I again shared my sacred hideout at Oljeto Wash. We escorted Marfa safely to Clay Hills Crossing, home to Littleton, then a week later to a plane that would return her to Hamburg. We all hated to say *auf wiedersehen* to our little German *madtchen*, the first and only unofficial girl member of Troop 117.

20

DRUMS, TRAILS, AND A PAINFUL FAREWELL

Our Fine, Feathered Friends

Those frenzied foot-tappers, the Wasechies, were delighting crowds all over town and growing both in stature and in size. We ran two promotional ads, *We'll Be There with Bells On* and *An Invitation to the Dance,* targeting local Scouting units and a variety of clubs and organizations. The phone was ringing. Jimmy Mahoney, our dance chief, now had a lineup of dancers divided into three clans:

Sioux Clan	Arapaho Clan	Cheyenne Clan
David Sholes	Mark Zentner	Joel Slaten
Ted Colburn	Jeff Zink	Trevor Banister
Mark Stubbert	Greg Zentner	Lauri Banister
Jason Ayres	Scott Kannady	Jeff Rallo
Ken Caldwell	Davin Zink	Ron & Steph Clark
Paul Adams	Lance Caffrey	Dan Conway
Joe Conti	Todd Zentner	John Bowman
		Robert Hill

Within a year we added Doug and Darren Kixmiller, Curtis Weibel, Bret Finnell, Darren Brinker, Sarah Ball, Dee Conti, Kyle Marquand, Christopher Lawhead, Rob Lewis, and Jon Adams— all guided by our in-house squaw and buck combo, Christy and Doug Ayres, plus our new Assistant Scoutmaster Bob Finnell. Adding girls expanded our dance repertoire, plus this made life more interesting for the guys. The number of dances they learned numbered nearly 30. Dad Jim Clark constructed two boxes of colored lights that added a mystic aura to the dances, and Bob Tharp's huge van became the mode of transportation. Cub packs clamored for Wasechie performances and became our primary source of income, but our moccasins were in motion for everyone from service clubs to foreign students. The yearly income from the dances topped $1,000.

Some Native Americans object to Boy Scouts doing their dances. This is understandable, yet unfortunate. The Wasechies; the Koshare Indian dancers from La Junta, Colorado; and the Order of the Arrow dancers would never intentionally ridicule Indian cultures. We were, in our perspective, honoring them. I witnessed a demonstration in Denver when a Koshare performance was held up for nearly an hour by a group of angry Native Americans, while Buck Burshears, the legendary leader of this small-town phenomenon, refused to put his "brats," as he called them, into harms way. The only time the Wasechies encountered that experience was at the Denver Coliseum when dancing for the Rodeo Cowboys fund with Iron Eyes Cody.

Wasechie Dancers with Iron Eyes Cody

Iron Eyes, a Cherokee movie actor, gained fame as the "Crying Indian" in a series of anti-pollution television ads in the 1980s and early '90s. His acting credentials included over 80 films. I met Iron Eyes quite by accident in Casa Grande, Arizona. As I walked past a white Caddy convertible while waiting for a parade to begin, I spotted him sitting in the back and blurted out, "Hey, you're Iron Eyes Cody." He smiled, motioned me over, shook hands, and we talked. Our conversation was cut short when he was told that the parade was beginning. He was leading the parade as Grand Marshall.

"Meet me at the powwow at the rodeo grounds in about an hour. We'll talk more," he yelled. I gave him a high sign, and then, after the parade, I headed for the powwow grounds while Char investigated a craft fair. When she came looking for me, I was nowhere to be found until she finally gazed over to the powwow and saw me dancing while having a deep heart-to-heart conversation with Iron Eyes. When I learned that both Iron Eyes and the Wasechies would be at the Rodeo Cowboys benefit in Denver, I was pleased.

He walked up to meet the kids before their performance, and we renewed our acquaintance. Standing nearby were eight not-overly-delighted Indians. Iron Eyes apparently spotted the situation—and its potential for discord. He asked if he could join our performance and perhaps drum and chant a bit. We made our arena entrance with our usual subtlety of attacking a buffalo herd and then moved immediately into our first dance. Nearby, on the sideline, stood the group of disgruntled warriors. During the dance, Iron Eyes nudged me and asked if he could have the microphone for a moment after the dance ended. When the drum beat subsided, I introduced Iron Eyes Cody to an appreciative applause. "Folks," he said, "I just recently met these young boys and girls, and I must admit that I am impressed. Imagine the time it has taken them to construct such beautiful costumes and learn the dances of our people. As they honor our culture, I am honored to be here with them." More applause from the crowd. The tension evaporated.

Interesting commonality and compatibility exist between Boy Scouting and the Native cultures: the love of the outdoors, the respect for nature and the environment, the art and handicrafts, and the emotional response of the drum and the flute. All of this is Scouting; all of this is Indian. Native people should not despair when non-Indian kids gently tap their moccasins on Mother Earth, too. I know that my life since I was a young boy has been tethered to the Native cultures and Native spirituality. Over 200 books in my library expound on Native cultures and religion. On many occasions, I benefited from a visit to a sweat lodge. Plus, I took one of my Scouts, a deep thinker named Joe Conti, to a multi-week course on Native American spirituality, which terminated in a sweat lodge. Each time I exited a lodge and had experienced the stories, chants, and nearly unbearable heat, I would wander alone into the nearby woods with a mind so clear and uncluttered it was like a mental rebirth. My times with Lakota medicine man Wallace Black Elk were priceless. One evening after a sweat, we were sitting in the woods and talking.

I'll never forget how a gentle breeze started whispering through the trees. He held his hand to his mouth to interrupt our conversation and tuned his aging ears to the breeze. He smiled and nodded. "I wish you could have heard that," he whispered. I'm convinced Native American spiritualists know and understand phenomena that most of the rest of us don't.

"Practicing" First-Aid Skills in a New Canyon

During the cold months, the older guys in the troop mastered survival skills and outdoor safety while the younger guys digested the finer points of wilderness backpacking. Each winter, they'd survive a backpacking trip on skis and take their tipis to the Arapaho District Klondoree. Putting squad stoves in the tipis and venting the smoke kept the troops snuggly warm.

Now it was springtime 1986 and the thoughts of Troop 117's boys lovingly turned to Utah. This "call-of-the-desert" mentality was becoming a tradition. This year, everyone wanted to explore a new canyon, and we chose a fairly easy one, because nearly half of the crew would be making their Utah debut. We drove to the mouth of Arch Canyon, due west of Blanding, Utah, and camped at the entrance before entering the canyon for a five-day exploration. Our exit out of the canyon would end with a motel night in Glenwood Springs and a highly anticipated dip in the hot springs pool before heading home. As always, we distributed a fact sheet several weeks before departure stressing pack weight. Adult help included Herbie Banister, Roy Kannady, and Andy Green. Former illegal Assistant Scoutmaster Barb Slaten was a welcome last-minute sign-on to this junket.

A new Scout, Kyle and his dad Kermit, were among the 24 kids and six adults who would trek the seven miles into Arch Canyon. Kermit, an Eagle Scout, attended the same Scout camp I had as a kid, old Camp Decorah, in western Wisconsin. But Eagle Scout or not, when Barb saw Kermit's pack and felt its weight, her authoritative personality clicked in. "Kermit," her voice resonated like a drill instructor, "do you plan to stay through the summer? What the heck do you have in there, anyway? Has someone finally brought the kitchen sink?" Our rule of thumb was to keep your pack weight within 20 to 25% of your body weight. Kermit was no little guy, but that was no little pack. With military precision, Barb emptied Kermit's pack and his son's and methodically tossed out unneeded items. Kermit wisely kept his mouth shut. As Barbara's old patrol knew, she meant business. Later, on the trail, both guys appreciated her hard-knuckle lesson in weight reduction.

Arch Canyon, much like a blind date, starts with a wealth of false promises. Several hundred yards into the canyon, we encountered a sizable ruin, now fenced in. We hiked a short distance and uncovered a better Anasazi site. But that was it—the extent of ruins we spotted on the entire five-day trip. But we can't blame the canyon. Later ventures into Arch unveiled a host of dwellings scattered high on the canyon walls camouflaged by distance and by building material that blends perfectly with the background rock. On this trip, we moved far too quickly to spot these hidden treasures.

Trudging seven miles in the warm desert sun was a grunt that first day in the canyon, even on a Jeep road, since our trek included splashing through 59 creek crossings. Fortunately, the creek, which flows constantly, was not running even ankle deep. Along the way, Mother Nature outdid herself sculpting pillars, towers, windows, and arches, and then dressed the scene with a wardrobe of green riparian plant life and occasional cottonwoods near the creek. On the bordering slopes, pinyon, juniper, plus an abundance of rabbitbrush, mountain mahogany, and Mormon tea contrasted beautifully with the rust-red hue of the sandstone walls.

Clouds moved in overnight, bringing a decided coolness to the morning air. I suggested exploring Texas Canyon, although some of the crew expected it to be mundane. Several lads discovered swimming holes nearby in Butts Canyon, but it was too cool for a morning dip. Surprisingly, we accidentally found a swimming hole in Texas Canyon.

After hiking an hour into Texas Canyon, a small waterfall blocked our way, pouring itself into a tiny plunge pool. A large, weathered log angling slightly upward provided an access route across the pool, and then a short scramble on a rock wall would allow us to skirt the falls. Agile Andy Green proceeded smartly across the wet log and then moved with ease up the rocks. Kermit was next. He didn't have a day pack, so he carried his backpack stocked only with the day's supplies. Kermit treaded more cautiously on the dampened log, inching his way across. Suddenly, his arms flung out in one direction and his legs in the other. *Splash!* Kermit lay sputtering, face up in the cold, wet pool—his eyes bulging and mouth wide-open in hopes of recapturing his stolen breath.

In my entire career with Troop 117, I cannot recall seeing so many people spring into action so quickly. In seconds, adults and Scouts rushed to Kermit and pulled him from the frigid water. Without instructions, kids scattered to find dry firewood. Paper appeared from nowhere and kids stuffed it into a tiny wooden tipi frame; soon flames started dancing. Kids gathered more wood and piled it onto the fire while someone detached Kermit's wet clothing and boots from his body. Blood dripped slowly from a cut on his lower right leg, and our first-aid wizards immediately treated the wound. Others constructed wooden frames around the fire to dry his soaked clothing. This is a big part of what Scouting is all about: knowing how to respond in an emergency, having the ability to do it, and doing it with speed and agility. I almost thanked Kermit for providing Troop 117 with this opportunity, but I didn't feel he was in the mood for gratitude at that moment.

In honor of the event, we promptly named that geographic feature in Texas Canyon, "Kermit Falls." We presented a proper memento at the Fall Court of Honor.

The junction of Arch with Texas and Butts canyons was an

ideal campsite—large, shaded, and providing easy access into these branch canyons. Plus, we could camp for several days without hoisting packs. This also gave the old Scoutmaster time to sit down individually with kids and practice Tenderfoot knots, map and compass reading skills, or whatever they needed to advance to the next Scouting rank. The cooking was exceptional. I recall freckle-faced Ron House and grinning Darren Brinker proudly displaying a pan of freshly baked rolls. Of course, another Eagle in the making, Plug Zentner, was always ready to devour food from anybody, anytime, anywhere.

The weather heated up the next day, and into Butts we headed with swimsuits and towels. In one or two instances, sans swimsuits, *butts* had a far more natural connotation. Water in Butts cascaded down a series of sandstone terraces, providing cool showers, but limited swimming. It was a time to lollygag and lay in the warm, desert sun.

We set up camp halfway back on the route out and explored a small side canyon for ruins but with no success. The success of this trip was already established: a host of new, young Scouts led by a new breed of junior leaders proved they could backpack in the desert, and they could react like true Scouts—with quick-acting and quick-thinking first-aid skills—when needed.

Soaked at Weston Pass

That summer, a pair of Bobs—Tharp and Finnell—headed up our 10-day summer camp at Peaceful Valley Scout Ranch with a total of 133 completed merit badges. As usual, Troop 117 won every camp-wide event and the coveted Ranch Award. It was getting to be a habit. One evening, Tharp and I cut loose with a rendition of *Slewfoot Sue*, a song we both sang with gusto as Scouts and that probably wouldn't make it in today's more sanitized Scouting environment. But the kids loved it. In early August we ran another of our infamous wilderness survival camps in East Lost Park; participants spent approximately 20 hours alone on the woods with nothing but what they carried in a day pack. The summer camp merit-badge program, which featured a group camping with a pound of hamburger, just didn't suit the level of preparedness we sought for our kids. We scheduled a unique Eagle Court of Honor for Joel Slaten (the kid who never wanted to be a Scout) at the Littleton Museum, complete with a command performance of the Wasechies, who danced especially for Joel.

The final pack trip of the summer turned out spongy. We headed toward Weston Pass near Fairplay, Colorado, and chose a 12-mile loop trail. This was an inaugural trip for our fancy new patrol tarps that we could set up in a variety of configurations. The trail was steep enough to have both Roy Kannady and me puffing, and not on our pipes! A gentle pitter-patter began that evening, and by midnight it evolved into a massive downpour. The tarps kept us dry, but stepping outside come morning became a poncho parade. Stuffing wet gear into your wet pack on a wet morning is even more dreary than the apparent forecast. We slogged off, slipping and sliding on a muddy trail and by mid-afternoon we hadn't found a camping location that didn't resemble the Dismal Swamp. A cursory glance at the waterlogged stoics didn't reveal one smiling face. Well, mine wasn't glowing either, and Roy couldn't even keep his pipe lit. Common sense prevailed. We put the pedal to the metal tromping with resolve through the remainder of the 12-mile loop, snuggled into cars with heaters blazing, and hustled home to the warmth and snugness of our own beds.

"Into every life a little rain must fall." The wilderness can be tough in good weather; continuous rain can make it miserable. Had I said, "We're staying," the guys would have grumbled, but they would have survived. I knew that, and they knew that. Coupled with the fact that no one was having fun, a "strategic withdrawal" was viewed as judicious rather than cowardly. This backpacking retreat was a Troop 117 first.

Tragedy Strikes

For decades, monthly Thursday evening troop committee meetings were a part of my life. We helped the kids develop the troop
program, and we identified problems and opportunities. The
committee, consisting of a devoted group of parents, reviewed
our plans and their feasibility from all aspects—from manpower
to economics—then did their best to make these plans happen.
A well-functioning committee is a godsend to a Scoutmaster. I
was meeting with our supportive committee on the evening of
January 15, 1987.

A knock sounded at the door of the small out-building
we used for our gatherings. Son David stuck his head in and
motioned me outside. He was choked but spoke without hesitation. "Jim Colburn was killed." I stood there in the cold winter
evening in disbelief.

"How?" I asked.

"I don't know. Barb called and just said that he was killed in
an accident at work."

I felt as though the blood rushed from my head. I walked
back into the meeting and told the committee that Jim had died
and that I had to leave. I headed immediately to his home to be
with his wife, Barb, and their kids.

Jim, the red-haired, red-bearded, Scot-blooded geologist
had purchased, with a partner, a preformed concrete company
after the petroleum industry took a nose dive in the mid-1980s.
Meeting Jim was one of the great things that happened to me in
Colorado. His warmth, humor, friendliness, generosity, and his
little-boy grin, combined with our neatly meshing compatibili-
ties, quickly drew us into a friendship so tightly bound it was
nearly hermetically sealed. During Scout campouts we would
wander a hundred yards or so into the woods, find a log, and
chat for hours with that special element of friendship and security that lets you unleash your innermost thoughts and feelings.
There are very few men with whom I could do that in comfort.
We'd argue, sometimes about politics, but it was never bitter; we

were both seeking solutions to problems. My heart went out to Barb and the kids, and for me, too. Jim's vanishing act would leave an abysmal void.

Hundreds of kids knew him as a mentor and friend. Although he could be firm, his gentle manner made him approachable. He was a team player, yet maintained his individuality. In ten years as an Assistant Scoutmaster, he never once wore a uniform. He didn't like uniforms and thought they were unnecessary. Jim felt that knowing how to help the injured; how to be a good friend and companion; how to safely hike, backpack, run a river, and camp in the wilderness; and how to be a part of the wilderness were important.

Barb asked if I would speak at his memorial service. Although Jim was a spiritual man, he would not have wanted a religious service. We began to put together some ideas. I asked Bob Clark, the pastor at the church where the troop met, if we could use the church. He asked who would conduct the service. Embarrassed, I told him it looked like I would conduct it. This must have shocked him; it certainly shocked me.

The church had never witnessed such a crowd. It overflowed into the entryway. A guitarist opened the service. After a few words, I introduced Jim's twin sister who revealed that he was even a gentleman at birth, allowing her to exit first. Scouts such as Jim Mahoney laughingly retold how they tricked Jim on his own compass course. And other tales reflected the kind of man he was—a man who was comfortable with who he was. Others told about Jim the geologist, a man skilled in his profession. Another related how Jim's home, often filled with people from around the world, was a virtual United Nations. How he and Barb never let race, religion, or ethnic background stand in the way of establishing human relationships.

I explained that we, as a group, were brought together in a common bond, and the work we had to do was to overcome our shock and grief and then gradually let Jim go.

Knowing his love of Native cultures, I read a short poem I

had jotted, called "The Release."

> He stood alone, shrouded in clouds,
> watching in silence
> as those who loved him most
> circled and released him.

> As the long, labored drone of the drum ceased
> he felt a thrust of energy
> and a newly born sense of freedom.

> He smiled then turned north
> and began his trek
> through the forests and the mountains of the heavens
> in search of the camp of everlasting peace.

As Jim knew, all our activities—camping, backpacking, running wild rivers, and Indian dancing—were gimmicks, devices to help a young man develop into a "whole being," a person who is stable, who likes himself, likes others, and is sensitive to others' individuality and their needs. He worked to help the boys and young men of Troop 117 develop physically without having to be "jocks." And he helped them discover the advantages of being mentally sharp and morally cognizant.

Jim helped kids discover that the world can be a pretty neat place, but they have to expect to pay the admission fee, and perhaps face a little pain every day. But instead of running from life or trying to hide, they must face their problems, solve them, and become better people for having done so.

The February issue of the troop newsletter summed up our feelings:

> In mid-January, the troop suffered a major loss with the untimely death of Jim Colburn. For nearly 11 years, Jim faithfully served this troop as Assistant Scoutmaster, but more important, as a friend to kids and adult leaders alike. It is difficult to sum up in a few words what kind of man Jim was and what he meant to each of us. He was a

man of principle, a man who cared, and a man who liked kids. It showed in the hours he spent, not only at troop meetings and outings, but in the vast amount of time he gave boys at classes he held, whether at his home or on the Platte River in canoes.

We will all miss that little grin hidden behind a bushy red beard and the generous heart that was enclosed in that small frame of his. He never asked for any recognition, in fact, he never wanted it. He chose not to wear any badge of office but was only interested in being there for kids.

In Jim's memory and in his honor, let's make certain we live this dream he had for all of us: appreciating nature, being comfortable in the great outdoors, treating it and people with respect, and growing up to be contributing members of our community.

With the aid of several dads, we constructed a small equipment shed behind the church. An attached bronze plaque read, "James A. Colburn Memorial Outhouse." Man, he would have loved that.

Now, with a record number of boys registered that month, we would have to move on—but without our best friend.

21

THE END OF A LONG TRAIL

The Weekend of the Smoking Tipi

With 40 kids sporting number 117 on their Scout shirts, we found little time to mourn Jim, although losing him sapped away a slice of my spirit. Big Bob Finnell, my new right-hand man, was backed by seven other Assistant Scoutmasters answering to the names of Ken Conway, Walt Kixmiller, John Stolp, and Bob Zatorski, plus three troop grads: Andy Green, Dave Sholes, and Ian Zahn. The committee was filled, while Doug and Christy Ayers continued to oversee the dancers. Scouts Ken Calwell and Jeff Rallo published the troop's newsletter, *Smoke Signals,* and with all this youthful computer savvy, the newsletter evolved into artsy as well as newsy.

The annual Arapaho District Klondoree was looming on the winter horizon. A Klondoree was a humongous organizing task, and in 1987 our troop volunteered to host it. Klondorees are meant to be winter events, yet the fickle Colorado weather often compelled kids to push Klondike sleds through dry leaves and pine needles as they darted from event to event. Not this year. The troop chose a site high on 10,000-foot Kenosha Pass. Keeping with the 117's Indian tradition, we named it the *Medicine Wheel Klondoree* and designed a beautiful leather attendance patch in a medicine-wheel motif. While others may shiver in their tiny tents, Troop 117 would "rough" the two cold, high-altitude nights in the comfort of five tipis complete with stoves and stovepipes. With age creeping into my bones, admittedly, I too enjoyed "comfy camping" more and more.

Late Friday evening, about 100 cars and pickups zoomed up to the pullout at the top of the pass, loaded with kids and enough gear for everyone to live comfortably beyond the spring equinox. Scouts toted tents, sleeping bags, food boxes, and backpacks filled with warm clothing through the snowy, dark woods to respective troop areas on a wild variety of sledges resembling Mormon push carts on skis. Our committee and troop staff, bundled like Inuits, darted from pillar to post directing vehicular and sledge traffic, answering a gazillion questions, and rescuing lost kids who wandered away from their troop site, all while preparing a dozen contest events.

For most, sleeping on a dark, cold, wintry night meant snuggling early into a (hopefully) warm sleeping bag. Emerging at dawn from a bag in the winter at high altitude is as appealing as chewing frozen oatmeal. But the sun came up, the sky was Colorado blue, and the snow on the mountain slopes towering over our meadows glistened like thousands of tiny sparklers. With breakfast fires lit throughout the camp, Scouts huddled as close to the flames as possible, hats over their ears and stomping their feet to encourage circulation while warming both their hands and their stomachs with cups of hot cocoa. Well, nearly everyone had protective hats. Cotton-pickin' Robert Hill strutted arrogantly in his Dallas Cowboys baseball cap, letting his ears transform to ice cubes, just to agitate his Scoutmaster, a dyed-in-the-wool Bronco fan. Plug Zentner, so named for his fire-hydrant physique, resembled an overgrown version of *Bambi's* Friend Owl hiding behind his ski goggles and huge, woolen hat. In retrospect, the camp must have looked like a convention of bank robbers—everyone was incognito in either ski masks or mufflers rolled around three quarters of their faces. But the Medicine Wheel Klondoree wasn't billed as a fashion show; it was time to let the fun begin.

After a brief group meeting to cover rules and assign contest rotations, the Arapaho District version of the Winter Olympics got underway. Near the parking area, the wild *paisano* Joe Conti nearly bit through his lip while concentrating on sailing his axe into a huge, log target. In the meadow, the quantity of flying arrows was reminiscent of a John Wayne western. Snowshoe and cross-country ski racers wisely maintained a respectable distance. Others stood, deeply pondering first-aid problems or orienteering calculations. In the pioneering area, ropes were flying with knots, hitches, and lashings, everyone straining to help their patrol win a championship banner. But the classic event was the centipede ski race: five guys with their feet attached to two boards attempting to move in tandem over a 25-yard course. This event required teamwork, balance, speed, and agility. When all that failed, teams disintegrated into a combination of belly-aching and belly-laughter as they lay in the snow, struggling to rise to the occasion.

The fun day in the snow-mantled mountains ended with sizzling pots of beef stew, chili, and other belly-warming concoctions. The evening concluded with a big campfire with songs and skits and, of course, presentations of the coveted ribbons to the winning patrols.

Troops who left Saturday night missed the Sunday morning excitement. A hot stovepipe kissed the top of one of 117's tipis, brightening the morning sky with dancing flames. An expedient drop into the snow doused the fire, but the damage was extensive. Now who was so mentally numb that they burned down their home away from home? Who stood red faced before the troop in shameful embarrassment? The Leadership Corps? Ouch!

The Man and a Gulch Keep Calling

During the next two springs, we marched the newer lads through our two favorite Utah haunts: the canyons of All American Man and Grand Gulch. When you uncover something so exceptional, a four-year rotation to these magical hideouts makes sense. Younger Scouts finally get to plant their boots on the same trails they've heard older boys rave about for years.

Describing these trips would prove redundant, but one event on the "Man" journey deserves reflection. Committeeman Herb Banister, who led this Salt Creek expedition, sat quietly near Four Face Ruin absorbing the sunset along with long-time Scout and now Assistant Scoutmaster Jeff Andrus. Peace prevailed as the kids, far off in a distant meadow, dashed about in their usual high-decibel mode. Jeff, a die-hard Coca-Cola fan, obviously hot and dry, muttered, "Gee, what I wouldn't pay for an ice-cold can of carbonation." Herbie contemplated that remark for several moments and replied in his dry, matter-of-fact demeanor, "Well, Jeffrey, just how much *would* you pay for an ice-cold can of carbonation?"

Without changing his expression, Jeff responded, "Right now, I'd pay twenty bucks." Herb nodded. They sat and chatted a bit longer. Finally, Herb pushed himself up and slowly wandered down toward the creek. In a few moments Jeffrey watched as he sauntered back to their perch, carrying two ice-cold cans.

"There's four more where they came from, Jeffrey. So where's your twenty?" Jeff stared in disbelief. He couldn't have been more jolted had Herb waltzed back with a bikini-clad blond. Herb stood over him with his hand extended. "Come on, man, show me your cash." Shaking his head, Jeff eased out his wallet and painfully extracted two, crisp ten-dollar bills.

As he handed them begrudgingly to Herb, Jeff muttered, "I can't believe that you—who prides yourself on packing so darn light—carried six cans eight miles into the desert."

Herb rubbed his chin and popped his can. Letting an ever-so-subtle smile creep onto his lips, he responded, "Well Jeffrey," he paused for a second, "*I* didn't!"

It took a moment for Herb's response to sink in for Jeffrey. When it did, the weight of his pack suddenly made more sense.

A Muddy Brown River Named Green

In 1988 we set foot in Utah twice. We backpacked into a canyon in March, and then in June it was time to explore a new Western river. High in the Wind River Range of northwestern Wyoming, the trickle of snow melt transforms into one the West's major flowages: the Green River. In 1869 Major John Wesley Powell and the nine men he recruited commenced their hazardous exploration of the Green and Colorado Rivers at Green River, Wyoming, in four specially constructed boats. They had no idea what they were about to encounter. We, in turn, commenced our adventure in Green River, Utah, with eight jam-packed canoes filled with five adults and 11 Scouts. We knew exactly where we were heading and thought we knew what we would encounter, planning a calm, strategic exit out of the Green River at Mineral Bottoms. As Major Powell discovered, the action explodes once you make a right turn to enter the Colorado River and nose into the frothing waters of Cataract Canyon.

Just before reaching Green River, Utah, my Jeep station wagon suffered major engine-stopping trauma. Herb towed me into town where we left the debilitated chariot at a garage and decided to worry about it later. After moving cars to our take-out location, the kids set up camp within spitting distance of the high-running, muddy-brown Green River. Canoes and gear stood ready near the bank, awaiting the anticipated early-morning departure. The June runoff was exceptional, so even with the mild one-foot-a-mile drop, the volume of this fast-moving water was hinting at an exciting ride.

The night was clear and peaceful, except for the hourly clickity-clacking of freight trains rumbling over the Rio Grande Railroad bridge immediately downstream. That bridge would be our first real obstacle, since running close to the abutments in high water could dump a canoe. Two guys who capsized there a week earlier reportedly had the pleasure of swimming for seven miles as they tried to catch up with their run-away canoe. In the morning, with life jackets firmly attached and lucid instructions to shoot right down the middle, we weighed anchor on our five-day jaunt. In minutes we were at the bridge. Like paddling pros, the kids steered their vessels well away from the concrete bow-bangers and scooted safely through.

The terrain along this section of the Green leaves everything to be desired. It's probably the most boring stretch of river through which I've ever pushed a paddle. A thick wall of Asian tamarisk guards both banks, stealing water from native plants, even crushing the seedlings of the tall shade-producing cottonwoods. Water fights broke out to combat the monotony as well as the heat of the late-morning sun. Often three or four canoes clustered together into a large raft to enhance chit-chat and trade junk-food morsels. Meandering through flat, ranch country we finally arrived at Crystal Geyser. Reportedly it spurts sulfur-tainted mineral water at irregular intervals, sometimes as high as 50 feet, from an old, abandoned, test well. Even it failed to perform that day, and the sun was beating hotter.

After a lunch stop with cool drinks, the canoes—again in raft formation—floated lazily toward McCarthy Bottom. *Bottoms* are river terraces that develop on bends where silt and sand accumulate. Perhaps the most adored one on the Green, due to its name, was June's Bottom, awaiting us farther down the river.

By mid-afternoon on a somewhat dull day, the guys sought excitement. Sure enough, it waited just around the bend. We beached on the right side of the river where a wide sandbar drifted out into the chocolate-tainted stream. This seemed like an inviting place for a break and a cool drink. A few guys waded aimlessly around in the water. But Kyle, one of the younger boys on the trip, took wading to a deeper level.

Adorned in high-top sneakers, Kyle amused himself by twisting his feet from side to side, allowing them to penetrate a bit deeper into sand that was covered with about a foot of river water. This sand, saturated with water, frequently goes by the name of *quicksand*. Slowly Kyle began sinking deeper before announcing with a hint of alarm, that he couldn't raise his feet. "Well, pull your feet out of your shoes," someone suggested. The lower portion of his sneakers were tied tight, but the high-top uppers weren't—they flared out and made extraction about as expedient as removing a fishhook from your finger! Initially his predicament was humorous; guys tossed out jokes about needing to simply leave him behind with food and drink. Three hours later, it was no longer a laughing matter.

Initially no one was too alarmed. Several boys pulled off their canoeing shoes, brought buckets from the canoes and started digging. Trying to scoop sand out from underneath someone's foot—while he's standing in a foot of water—proved futile. When you scoop one full bucket of sand, adjoining sand immediately sloshes back into the cavity. The project was suddenly taking on greater proportions.

What were we going to do, dam the river? That's exactly what we had to do: dam the river! Canoe crews hustled to remove contents from their boats and then quickly positioned them into a horseshoe-shaped barrier around Kyle. Kids tightly packed mud between the canoes to prevent leaks, and the long task of emptying the area of water began. Kids used everything from bailing buckets to hats. Trevor Banister, Dan Conway, Brett Finnell, the Kixmiller boys, Eric Zink... everyone tossed muddy water across the canoe dike and back into the river. Scott Kannady and Plug Zentner kept repairing leaks and occasionally Gentleman Joe Conti would walk over with words of encouragement to Kyle, who needed those words more and more as the clock ticked on.

Every so often big Andy Green would position himself behind Kyle, grab him under the arms, and lift. But instead of an upward movement of Kyle, there was a downward movement of Andy. Over an hour and a half passed and inches of water still remained in Kyle's "pool." Kyle tried to smile, but he was now one concerned kid. He wasn't alone. Herb, Ken Conway, and I feared that our victim was becoming a little "shocky," and progress was sluggish. The bailing continued nonstop. Thank goodness, our dam was holding.

We were two-and-a-half hours into the exercise when vigorous digging and pulling finally freed the first foot. Ken Conway proudly held the shoe high with the glint of an Olympic victory. Our cheer must have been heard all the way back to town. We couldn't let the freed foot return to the sandy prison, so kids supported Kyle from behind while digging continued on foot number two.

Finally, just shy of three hours, Kyle again joined the free world. I was proud of Kyle and of his host of rescuers. Again, they showed their mettle and their ingenuity in an emergency situation. "Let's get the heck out of this place," someone yelled. I don't recall any naysayers. We converted our dam back into canoes and piled in gear and people.

A good camping site appeared a short distance down the river, and soon cooking stoves hummed and hungry river rats devoured a quick meal. After that unscheduled debacle, no one that evening, especially Kyle, needed to be reminded to shut the eyelids.

We woke up looking forward to a short day on the river. This gave us more shore time to hunt for ruins and rock art or simply bobble aimlessly down the center of the river in our life preservers.

Before noon, we passed Anvil Butte, the first geologic feature worthy of a picture. But the horizon, now alive with an endless array of towering buttes and mesas, became an exciting preview of things to come. When we arrived at the mouth of the San Rafael River across from Ruby Ranch, we decided to pull in, explore, swim, and make camp. We didn't realize that the little black cloud that had hung over Kyle had surreptitiously drifted over the head of Joe Conti.

The kids found a rope suspended from a tall cottonwood near the bank, apparently used by other river rats to swing out from the bank and drop into the river.

"Wait, let's check this out," adults admonished.

We sent swimmers into the river to determine the water's depth and detect any possible submerged objects. Once swimmers declared the area was safe, the fun began. Starting on a platform, kids launched and swung to the full pendulum length of the rope, then let fly. Splash! This was a great find and great fun—until it was Joe's turn. Failing to release at the apogee, Joe drifted back nearly to shore before he released. Immediately below his departure point rested a huge, submerged boulder. Splash! Crash! We had a casualty. Lacking x-ray vision, I proffered an uncertain diagnosis based on the bruise and his localized pain: a foot fracture. We were still two days from our takeout point. We bound Joe's foot and ankle, iced it to reduce swelling, and kept him off his foot the remainder of the evening. We would decide in the morning how quickly to hustle him down the river.

When the sun peeked over the canyon wall, Joe wanted to continue as planned, which is a natural feeling but not always prudent. His pain was minimal and the foot was well secured and cooled. Should we move it and cut the trip short or take the two days as planned? We decided to play it by ear. Joe seemed comfortable in the bow of the canoe, his foot resting on the gunnel, a red bandana firmly attached to his head, Navajo style, and his subtle smile painted on his face. He was young and gutsy. At each stop, Joe was aided by his buddies and by a rustic crutch they created from a tree branch. They would get him comfortably seated, and then wait on him royally.

The scenery that day was spectacular, especially through Labyrinth Canyon and Trin-Alcove Bend. We were back in red-rock country. Soon, we were eyeball to eyeball with June's Bottom. Exciting!

Our river guidebook listed petroglyphs upstream from Ten Mile Canyon, but from the river, rock art is difficult to spot. I knew there were ancient sites along here, because I'd discovered a chipping station 50 yards back from the river's bank years ago. Using a time-honored method, I sat at the location of most of the debitage, or flakes. Knowing that even the best flintknappers would blunder now and then, I picked up a stone of arrow-point size and—using an appropriate expletive—threw it. This would be the search parameter. Sure enough, I found a bifacial point with a broken tip. I guess this proves that tempers haven't changed much over a millennium.

The Green's famous river register near mile marker 78 hides on a curve near an eddy and is enclosed in a rocky cove on the east side of the river. Here, for more than a century, river runners have left their marks on the red-sandstone walls: signatures, sophisticated artwork depicting people and animals, dates, and eccentric scribbles. Herb used his trenching tool to sculpt a size-able "T-117" and elegantly leave our mark on history.

After a few more turns and steep-walled canyons we arrived at the famous Bowknot Bend. The river takes seven miles to tour around this bend, yet if you scramble up a 750-foot canyon wall, you see that the end of the river's bend is only a few hundred yards away as the crow flies. While a few hard-core scramblers clambered up and over, the rest of us paddled the seven miles and met them after they descended the canyon wall. As with our early trips on the San Juan, the Green River was nearly void of people. Unfortunately, today it practically requires traffic lights!

We relished our final night of camping, good food, and chatter before paddling into the Mineral Bottoms landing the next morning. Joe hobbled to a "soft" rock seat while we unloaded canoes and crammed gear and people into cars. The steep, dusty, switchback road winding up and out of the canyon ranked as one of the most exciting segments of the trip. I was several switchbacks behind watching Andy's yellow Jeep chug up the narrow shelf road, pulling a four-canoe trailer. As we gained elevation, I could see the remains of rusty vehicles whose owners steered them intentionally (or perhaps unintentionally) over the side of this precipitous, rocky cliff.

While most returned to the town of Green River, Herb and I drove Joe to a doctor in Moab who verified my fractured-foot diagnosis and applied the appropriate cast. The fix wasn't as simple for my fractured Jeep. Unfortunately, its surgical requirements were far beyond the capabilities of local "medics."

This trip was accented with turmoil and trauma, yet the challenges on the Green River elevated the stature of all these kids. In my eyes, they all looked a little bit taller. They lived by their wits for five days on the river, paddled with ease on fast water, and competently handled a real-life rescue and first-aid emergency. Kyle was now smiling; Joe was on the mend. The Jeep, with a new oversized piston, survived surgery, although for only another year and a half.

My Boots Were Wearing Out

The evening Mark Trevithick, a Scout in my early days with Troop 117, showed up to enlist his son felt as though someone was holding up a mirror to my aging face. Am I really ready for the next generation of Scouts? My hearing was shot, thanks in part to that six-foot thunder drum; my hair was snow white; my eyes needed trifocals; and my backpacking legs became stiffer with every trip.

I looked around me. Here was a troop that employed drive-in camps as a last resort. Instead, we tossed packs on our backs, clambered up mountains, cruised down wild rivers, and explored the vast wilderness areas of the West—a beautiful land we were fortunate to be near. We sought the spirit, teamwork, and friendship that could only develop in close harmony with Mother Earth as we mingled with the beauty of a wooded forest, withstood the rugged demands of the desert, or faced harsh winds on a towering mountain peak.

In many cultures, boys experience a rite of passage into manhood. In our culture, this amounts to obtaining a driver's license. I've always felt that boys in this culture were being neglected and short-suited, that they deserve a greater challenge.

A strong Scouting program can provide greater challenges. Accomplishing this level of programming demands a Scoutmaster who encourages kids and wisely uses outdoor activities to challenge boys and help them mature as they develop into men. Preferably, a Scoutmaster *leads* them: arrives at the summit of 14,000-foot peaks with the kids; is the first one down a 60-foot rappel; or tests the waters by pointing his canoe into unknown rapids. That's the style of adult leadership that works, the style that kids at Troop 117 were used to, and the style I believed they continued to deserve.

But it happens with all of us—time takes its toll.

In addition, my business demanded a greater commitment and more time, which left less time for Scouting. Thankfully a covey of dads were filling most of the gaps. However, some seemed eager to move the troop into a more militant posture than I was comfortable with, approaching problems and solutions from a completely different ideological perspective. Granted, kids lack the maturity and the experience of adults so their planning and programs lack polish, but it behooves the adults to let boys make some mistakes and learn from their mistakes—as long as we don't mitigate their safety or break the bank. Adults who constantly step in, dictate, and dominate do the troop and individual boys a disservice.

I wanted to ensure that as I phased out of the troop some these philosophies would continue to hold. I started updating troop documents such as the First Class Test, Junior Leadership Responsibilities, and the operations of the Wasechie Indian dance group. Hopefully these documents would provide the next Scoutmaster with helpful guidelines. I presided at the fall Court of Honor on September 19, 1988, and three days later turned in my resignation, effective the first of the year.

Four factors eventually greased the skids to my retirement from Scouting:

1. The church hired a new pastor who opposed using the multi-purpose sanctuary for Scout meetings, and the troop needed a new sponsor.

2. An edict from BSA was en route stating that adult Scouters could no longer sit alone and talk with a boy; they could no longer hug or embrace a kid. How many kids had I encountered who needed a close, unmonitored relationship with an adult male? How many boys had I worked with who seldom, if ever, received a hug at home or were made to feel wanted and cared for? Were we killing the patient to make him safe? My *modus operandi* would be seriously compromised.

3. After decades, I was leaving Littleton and moving 35 miles south. I would need to make a 70-mile-round-trip commute to attend every meeting.

4. Assistant Scoutmaster Ken Conway, for whom I had much respect, consented to take the troop reins.

Perhaps the final months of disharmony proved to be a blessing in disguise. The conflicting factors camouflaged my intense pain of leaving a program and the people who had composed such a significant slice of my life for so many years.

I didn't know it at the time, but a bit more of that joy and adventure waited just 35 miles down the road.

22

A TEN-YEAR EXTENSION WITH VENTURE POST 757

It's Hard to Say No to Girls

The move to Perry Park, situated halfway between Denver and Colorado Springs, proved to be better than expected. Perry Park is nestled in the midst of a dense ponderosa forest, infiltrated by massive, 300-million-year-old, red-sandstone outcroppings. The nearest town is 12 miles away, and it's 30 miles to the nearest mall. That's what brought Karen, a mother of two teenage girls, Corinne and Vanessa, to my door one evening.

"The kids out here," she explained, "have nothing to do. I'd like to start some kind of a hiking and backpacking club."

That sounded like a great idea, but I cautioned that she had one major problem. "I don't want to rain on your parade, Karen, but when you take a group of kids into the backcountry, you leave yourself wide open to personal litigation if someone gets injured."

"Whoops! I hadn't thought of that. What do you think I should do?"

The answer was simple: Start a coed, high-adventure Explorer Post. Then the leaders and the kids have the backing and protection of the Boy Scout organization.

That suggestion got me in trouble. "Great idea!" Now she

was smiling. "Hey, I heard you were a Scoutmaster—would you help?"

At this stage of my life, all I needed was another Scout unit! But how do you say no to pretty, pleading eyes?

I admit that I missed backcountry jaunts with kids, and now that I was retired from my business, I had the time again. The big question: Do I really want to take on another Scouting group?

I agreed to host a meeting with interested parents and kids, and a genuinely excited crowd showed up. One new resident to the Park, a teacher named Pati, bounded in. Her enthusiasm was contagious. She had two girls, Jeni and Kallie, and exclaimed that it would be no problem enlisting a dozen or more kids. With some trepidation, I committed to help start the group, but I truly didn't want to lead it. Within weeks, a Perry Park civic organization agreed to be our sponsor and Explorer Post 757 was officially born.

These neighboring kids, nearly all girls, were impressive. They wanted to hike, backpack, and explore the wilderness. With the fire bell dinging, it's hard to keep even an old fire horse subdued. The long and short of it? For the next decade, I was putty in their hands. I became the male advisor and returned to working with kids, exploring the wilderness with aging feet and legs.

Shifting from a Scout troop to a high-adventure Explorer unit took adjustment. Troops have uniforms, an advancement program, weekly meetings, monthly campouts, patrol leaders, patrol dads, courts of honor... none of those activities would fly with this group. These high schoolers were busy with school and extracurricular activities, many worked, and all they wanted was an occasional adventure. I suspected that, with their mid-teen "let's boogie, let's leave today" attitude, they didn't think they needed outdoor training before exploding into the mountains and the deserts. Karen and Pati agreed with me—training was mandatory. That winter we taught basic skills, cooking, camping, map and compass reading, first-aid, and survival. They enjoyed it, and so did I. All winter we hiked and cross-country skied, so by spring this group of ten kids was chomping at the bit for high adventure.

Exploring the Gulch with a New Gender

With spring break rapidly approaching, backpacking was their chief desire. But where should we go? With a congregation of backcountry unknowns on my hands, I suggested we choose a location that I knew well: Grand Gulch, Utah. They seemed game for a 25-mile backpack trip, and after a long winter, the desert sounded especially appealing. Plus the intrigue of ancient Anasazi ruins sparked curiosity and excitement. Grand Gulch certainly piqued my interest, even through I had ventured into there several times before, yet I was somewhat reluctant not knowing the backpacking capabilities of this new group. I was especially reticent when a local exchange student coordinator whose daughter was in our Post asked if we had extra space on the trip to include three international students. Now we add-ed Patrick, from Germany; Alex, from Russia: and Leyla, from Azerbaijan. I learned that Leyla had never spent a night camp-ing, much less backpacking, and I wasn't sure about the boys' outdoor experiences. And we were going to spend five days on a 25-mile desert backcountry trek!

Several weeks later, with Patrick and Alex, seven young gals, and our two other leaders (Karen and Pati), I hesitating-ly dropped back into the depths of Bullet Canyon. Karen and Pati had organized the logistics of meals and eating groups— the tough stuff. I was simply Grandfather Guide and "Anasazi expert." We entered Bullet in the afternoon, and we made camp a short distance into the canyon next to a small stream. My eat-ing group choked down my spicy Cajun shrimp dinner. Soon Leyla, sore and tired, limped up, pouting, "Oh Tom, I vish dat I vood never come." I gave her a hug thinking, "I might be of the same persuasion, my dear."

Breakfast scored no higher on their epicurean hit parade. I concocted *huevos revueltos*—scrambled eggs injected with leftover Cajun spices. I think they thought *huevos revueltos* meant *revolting eggs*! During breakfast, it became obvious that Jeni wasn't a morning person. I learned later that, years before, her mother had dubbed her *Morning Thundercloud*. I wondered if potential husbands ever learned any of this stuff. Her sister Kallie was sunny and smiley. Not yet 14 and the youngest on the trip, Kallie was nothing but happy, and a pure delight. Genetics is a puzzle!

Leyla showed signs of temperamental moments, too. I decided to tip-toe into early morning conversations with Leyla. I would ask, "On a happiness scale of one to ten, Leyla, where are you?"

"Two!" she responded the first time, somewhat abruptly.

"Well, let me know when you get up to five, and then we might talk." Her mood did improve immensely with time.

Early morning grumbles dissipated once we hiked into Perfect Kiva Ruin and Jail House Ruin. Eyes popped and spirits soared. They liked what they saw. They were up and down the ladder into the kiva, then into the ruin. When some kids appeared on the roof, it was time to say, "Hey gang, there are things we don't do around these ancient ruins such as climb on them, touch rock art, or pocket artifacts. Wouldn't it be nice to bring your grandkids down here someday and have everything still standing, the way you saw it?" They got the message. Questions about these ancient people were thicker than the spring flies. How could a kid not be intrigued by such a discovery? And a lot more Anasazi hangouts waited for us in the miles ahead.

Post 757, Perry Park, CO explore Grand Gulch, UT

Our first unplanned game of hide and seek happened where Bullet Canyon meets Grand Gulch. The junction isn't readily evident to the uninitiated. Patrick, our speedy German whiz, vent da wrong vay! He turned left and headed straight for the San Juan River. Pati, with several girls, innocently Pied Pipered behind him. Send a Russian runner! The wayward folks looked drawn and quartered from the backtracking after Alex rounded up the strays and herded them back. Their sullen, grimaced faces brightened when they saw our green, grassy, restful campsite in a large alcove high above the Gulch. Following a hot dinner, Leyla and I wandered accidentally into a great, circular ruin. It looked like a short tower or a surface kiva, plus a gallery of intriguing Anasazi rock art adored an adjoining wall. As darkness approached, several tents popped up, but most of the Explorers snuggled into their bags under a moonless sky dancing with an endless array of twinkling stars. On the third day, shoulders and feet ached en route to Split Level Ruin. Rambo to the rescue. We called Kim "Rambo" for good reason. This daughter of a Denver Broncos linebacker had the strength of an Indian elephant and would carry anything for anyone. Although Kallie and Leyla, the blister sisters, were hurting, they never complained; they just limped on. When I finally pulled them over to assess their foot problems, the bubble on Kallie's foot was the largest I had ever encountered. Repair time. We punctured and bandaged, and soon, like a parade of battered warriors they staggered into Split Level Ruin where the real fun would begin.

Much like the trip with the Boy Scouts, the charm of Split Level Ruin lifted their sagging spirits and sent them buzzing about with excitement. While I was at the ruin explaining waddle-and-daub construction, Explorer leader Karen plopped her weary bottom directly onto a sharp, pointy, prickly, needle-nosed member of the cacti clan. Ouch! A social get-together with a cactus is like an oatmeal breakfast—it sticks with you. So who would get *derriere* duty? Not me! No, good-old Tom can treat blisters, pull slivers, immobilize broken feet, bind sprained ankles, fix cuts, and treat scorpion bites. For this surgery, Pati got the call. I was glad to have both Pati and Karen on this trip, particularly when those two gals saved me later that evening.

The female leaders erected their tent on the lower terrace next to Leyla and Kallie. Everyone else planned to star gaze and didn't put up tents. I popped up my three-man shelter one terrace higher, but the stars were so brilliant I, too, chose to snooze directly beneath those sparklers. I knew if bad weather blew in, my tent was up. I'd be prepared, right? About an hour later, I felt a few moist tap-taps hitting my head, but before I could adjust, the "Den Mothers" were up and carefully covered me with a tarp. Never before was I lavished with such tender, loving care on a backpack trip. However, soon the drips evolved into a deluge. I waited it out for a few minutes but could see myself swept off the upper terrace, into the Gulch, and eventually into the San Juan River without a paddle. Time to dash for the tent.

The downpour pounded my bare back as I hurriedly unzipped the flap—there sat six shivering kids huddled together in my three-man tent! "Sorry, Sholzie, there's no room."

"But… but it's *my* tent!" I wasn't as prepared as I had thought.

Barefoot, grasping my sleeping bag, and without glasses and flashlight—in lightning, thunder, and pouring rain—I darted through land mines of cacti expecting to be skewered while yelling "Who has some room in their tent? And be forewarned, I'm wet, and I'm in my underwear." That information was more than Kallie and Leyla could handle.

Finally I heard a response. "We'll take you as you are," and the flap opened on the leaders' tent.

"Thank God."

I was wet, and I was cold. While the ladies chuckled, I, in my damp undies, quickly snuggled into my reasonably dry sleeping bag. Unfortunately, it was only reasonably dry for about 15 minutes. The tent suffered a leak or two, and where was I? In the valley.

It was heartwarming to eventually see the sunrise. Plus, Leyla got some just deserts that day: she slipped and fell into a huge puddle and required a full change of clothing. The Azerbaijani maiden may have wished she had never ventured into these canyons, but a day later, chugging upward, she was the first one to emerge out of the canyons. I suspect she was proud of her accomplishment.

In one aspect, the old Boy Scouts and the new Explorers were in perfect harmony: Immediately after escaping the clutches of the canyon, hunger pangs began dancing. It was time to introduce this crew to Hogie's chow house in Monticello, Utah. The girls chose burgers and fries, while the Kraut and Ruski devoured a virtual mountain of mashed potatoes and gravy. Would you believe it? No one ordered Cajun shrimp.

A month later at a celebration party we bestowed appropriate awards to everyone including a Rambo doll to Kim and a Tasmanian Devil to Jeni, whose morning demeanor somewhat resembled that creature. Everyone jotted memories on each others' green "I Survived Grand Gulch" t-shirts while the tired old

Scoutmaster sat back smiling, knowing he was in for another great ride.

Don't We Tire of This Place?

Over the next decade, Explorer Post 757 chugged three more times into the clay and sand of infamous Grand Gulch. They loved it; I loved it. It was always the same, yet always different. For me, the lure of the Gulch seemed to overwhelm the copious wealth of lush mountain trails and hidden nooks and crannies in the West, pulling me back like a mystic magnet. Maybe it was the comfort and familiarity of the place, but I'd guess it was the joy and fun of introducing this bastion of natural beauty and ancient history to kids who never before had experienced something this memorable, this unique.

The next year's trip contained a new element that would keep me on my toes: a new member of the Explorer Post named Louise. I can't say I hadn't been forewarned. Pati had informed me, "I've finally found someone to meet your match."

Louise stood about as tall as a Navajo yucca and had a tongue nearly as sharp. Her eyes screamed mischief, and her broad grin disarmed you in seconds. And she was witty. Yes, I *had* met my match. Louise and I had a running gun battle for the next four years. If I said something was red, she'd say it was green. If I'd say difficult, she'd insist it was easy. But it was the morning near Junction Ruin she'd never let me forget.

"Bathroom" privacy in the wilderness is rarely a problem with a coed group. Everyone simply drifts off with their TP and trowel to find a private spot. On that morning, I thought the whole gang was down at the creek filtering water, so in a bit of a rush, I took a short jaunt off a side trail. In the middle of this endeavor—when no one wants to be disturbed—I was jarred by a bellowing screech, "Oh my God!" There stood Louise, hands in the air, shaking her head. She turned and stormed toward the creek waking the neighboring county as she expounded her embellished disdain. Louise ensured this disturbing sighting would be the talk of the camp for the rest of the trip. Even years later at a group graduation party, she and Kallie proudly presented me with a "memorial copy" of Kathleen Meyer's classic, *How to S--- in the Woods*. Sweet.

As charming little Louise added a handful of years, she also added adornment. I guess I wasn't enough torture for the poor girl; she pierced her ears, eyebrow, nose, and finally her tongue. I hoped the weight dangling on her oral appendage would slow it down but instead seemed to give it momentum.

On the other end of the spectrum was one of Louise's best friends, "Mormon Mary." This was quite a dichotomy. Mary was the first LDS kid I ever had in Scouts. Boy Scouting is a major youth activity for Mormons, and boys tend to be tethered to their Wards' troops. Being a "fountain" of Mormon history in southeastern Utah, I enjoyed introducing Mary to the lore of the region we were exploring, pointing out the Mormon trail that cuts across Cedar Mesa, and pondering how those early pioneers must've felt when they faced the Great Wall of Utah: Comb Ridge, towering 700 feet high, located east of Comb Wash and stretching nearly 100 miles in length. In every way this happy, smiling, tall, lanky basketball player was an active participant of the Explorer Post. Well, nearly every way. One evening while wallowing in the comfort of a Durango inn, the crew checked out a movie titled *Bad Girls*, a Western featuring spunky Mary Stuart Masterson, which was the primary reason I watched it. I guess the title scared Mary away. At breakfast, I told her the title was misleading; the movie wouldn't have corrupted her morals. But, on the other hand, it would have done little to enhance her intellectual enlightenment. Mary was a joy to have in the group. We were loaded with joys.

I wondered how long it would take before guys learned about this backpacking covey of females. Sure enough, guys began joining the Explorer Post, but surprisingly many didn't stay. Blame it on the girls. Their speed, strength, and backcountry savvy simply embarrassed the daylights out of those poor studs. I loved it. Nothing like seeing macho males plopped into the rumble seat by the so-called "weaker" sex.

Ice, Snow, and Quicksand

One spring, my daughter-in-law Teresa and 15 year-old grand-daughter Melissa hitched along to Grand Gulch. Plus our old Eagle Scout, long, tall Andy Green joined us. Our total number exceeded the group maximum, so we split into two groups. My contingent kicked off through Bullet Canyon while Pati's group hit the trail downstream at Collins Spring. The plan: meet half-way, camp together one night, exchange keys, then join up several days later at the Kane Gulch ranger station.

It was cold in the canyon, and the narrows with the water-fall in Bullet looked glaciated—the waterfall was completely iced over. Between Andy's size, Kallie's ingenuity, and a slow, cautious pace, we slid and skidded everyone safely down. We hustled to set up camp and prepare chow across from Jail House Ruin. The night was chilly and windy, but morning was worse. We woke to nearly a foot of fresh snow. Later we learned that the white stuff had collapsed tents in the other group. Call it character building. Bundle up, and move on.

This was Teresa's trip to sink or swim. Jumping across a nar-row section of the gulch that morning, she landed shy of the bank and looked surprised (and somewhat silly) standing thigh-deep in ice-cold water. Afterward, I looked equally silly with her soggy, lace-bottomed long johns adorning my pack and flowing behind me, drying in the wind. Teresa's adventures didn't end there. The next day, she hopped, skipped, and jumped across the creek—right into quicksand. She couldn't budge. Big Andy charged in. With a bear hug around her waist and his feet on a sturdy rock, he huffed and puffed and promptly popped her out of the muck.

When we met Pati's group at the halfway point, we detailed

our slow, challenging descent down the icy waterfall. Pati considered the alternatives. She and her group decided to shove it in reverse and head back to Collins Spring with us. This portion of Grand Gulch was new territory for me: beautiful jumps with waterfalls and new ruins. And we spotted the famous Big Man rock art panel high on a bordering wall. On our last day, Pati turned, looked around, and asked, "Where's Matt?" Her 12-year-old, first-time backpacking son had vanished. We knew he'd been behind us and no one had seen him pass. Losing a kid in the wilderness is not fun. For a mother, it's instant panic. Was he hurt? Did he make a wrong turn into a side canyon? We all blew whistles, and everyone shouted, but no Matt. Earlier, Andy and several older guys had dashed ahead to drive back and retrieve cars at the Bullet trailhead and bring them to the Collins Spring trailhead. Within hours we learned, with immense relief, that Matt had joined them. Losing kids—whether perceived or actual—creates tortuously long minutes, long hours.

After five days of enduring desert heat and sometimes snow, a hot shower felt like a therapeutic massage. Girls preferred going home clean. (Boys generally didn't care.) So identifying the next night's lodging sometimes prompted debate. On an earlier Utah jaunt we camped one last night among the stunning monoliths of Arches National Park, a nature lover's Mecca. Here the gang could run, climb, and hike amid scores of red-sandstone arches, fins, and spires and explore miles of foot trails unencumbered by heavy packs. But the campground offered no showers. Motel locations were limited: Blanding or Monticello, Utah, or driving farther to Durango. Moab is a fun place, but during spring break this small town usually hosts a bike fest, Jeep fest, float fest, or running fest. *Fest* in Moab was a euphemism for *no rooms*. Some of the romantically inclined preferred Durango, a college town, and we stopped there after two Grand Gulch trips. Eventually Pati arranged a price deal at a Monticello hotel with a pool and hot tub, which became the immediate destination—following a shower, of course.

One time we waltzed into a nice eating establishment before any of us shook hands with a shower. The fragrant bouquet of a dozen sweaty backpackers intermingling with Caesar salads and meatloaf dinners could curb, if not obliterate, customers' appetites. In one instance, a nearby elderly couple actually requested moving to another location in the dining area.

A waitress would innocently ask, "What would you care to drink?"

"Water!" everyone would shout. Cool, clear water. This dehydrated army instantly swallowed so much water waitresses would finally ease their stress and deliver the cool, wet stuff by the pitcher. And after five days of backpacking cuisine, the food consumption was nearly embarrassing... like we hadn't fed them. It was always nice to take the kids home and get rid of them, but two days later I would be missing their smiling faces and snide comments.

The Green Looked Mean

After three years of exploring Grand Gulch and its various side canyons, it was time for another mode of adventure. How about a river? I hesitated to test this group's lack of paddling prowess on something as zippy as the lower San Juan River, plus who wanted to wait a lifetime for a permit? Let's explore the placid Green River. Gathering enough canoes was a true scavenger hunt. We finally borrowed four from a Scout troop in north Denver and added them to the two our Explorers owned. I invited Joe Conti to join us, since his last venture on the Green was something of a fractured event.

We planned to hit the water at Green River, Utah, in early June when the runoff is at its peak. Well, the runoff was at its peak! When we arrived, the Green hovered just shy of flood stage—complete with floating logs, bloated cows, and other exciting debris. Pati stood by the shore watching the swirling, muddy mass, and I could read her mind. Her mothering instinct was kicking in.

"We can't put the kids on this water," she said.

Yet we headed out to drop vehicles at Mineral Bottoms. As we turned off onto the dirt road leading to the Bottoms her tears kicked in. We stopped and turned around. What should we do for Plan B? We huddled, discussed options, took a vote, and immediately put Plan B into action. We found safe lodging for our trailer of borrowed canoes in Moab and continued with two canoes to Recapture Reservoir north of Blanding, Utah. Here was a peaceful place to camp, paddle in safety, and set up a centrally located base for excursions into the archaeological haven of Cedar Mesa. Daily we'd head south through Blanding and west to the mesa country for a day of seat-of-the pants exploring. On one hike up to the Mule Canyon Ruins we met the notorious desert gnats, the "no see 'ems." While the kids dashed over sandstone ridges seeking access to well-protected ruins, those surreptitious little gnats presented us with scores of bites. Some of my bites blossomed to the size of silver dollars. At Blanding's Edge of the Cedars State Park Museum, the kids hustled through the adjoining ruins and paused to peruse the Anasazi pottery on display—one of the finest collections in Utah.

Post 757 Breaks for Lunch near Mule Canyon Ruins, UT

But our highlight was the descent into a steep, lonely canyon to find the phenomenal Moon House Ruin. Due to the steepness, access is tricky, but reaching the goal was well worth it. An 85-foot wall of Anasazi masonry encloses an alcove with a single entrance. Two high windows illuminate a patio area leading into several large rooms, all decorated with a series of small, round, white "moons" painted on the upper walls. Bob Lister, a highly respected Southwestern archaeologist and educator, died in the ruin several years before when he led a group of friends here; a noble way for an old digger to go. This was the finest backcountry ruin these kids had ever seen.

Canoeing in Recapture Reservoir, hiking, and exploring proved fun, but certainly wasn't as exciting as running the Green. Unfortunately, when the excitement did occur on that trip, I slept through it! Joe was sharing my tent when Pati came and woke him, asking him to be alert to any possible trouble. (With my hearing aids out, I could sleep through World War III.) Pati had awoken to some yelling below us and toward the lake. She proceeded down there to give our kids a solid tongue lashing. But, whoops, they weren't our kids. She discovered an out-and-out war between a group of Latino youth and a group of Navajos. Her concern: would they turn their attention toward a bunch of Colorado gringos, especially a covey of cute girls? Apparently her distant scolding ended the battle and scared off both groups. She might have sounded tough at the time, but she was jelly-legged once she realized the potential threat to our kids.

Wet Drawers on the Gila

Looking for a new and different place to explore, I suggested the Gila Primitive Area in south-central New Mexico. I truly wanted to experience this raw wilderness terrain, plus it would be an exciting challenge for the Explorers. As it turned out, I couldn't make the trip, and with over 60 river crossings, it may have been more of a challenge than anyone wanted.

As Pati relayed the story to me, the four-day adventure into the Gila Wilderness was exactly as its name implies, a "monster." The guidebook tagged the trip as strenuous. No one disagreed. A vigorous spring runoff from the nearby Mogollon Range turned the Gila River into a raging torrent. That made it impressive, especially wading across it 67 times! Add to this challenge, an altitude-gaining exit route from this frothy turbulence via a 1,100-foot ascent over Plane Crash Mountain. The result was a trip to remember.

"With so many first-time backpackers," Pati told me, "I was wary to begin with. Then I saw my New York niece, Christina, our guest backpacker, depart her plane in a miniskirt, leather jacket, and newly manicured nails and dripping with jewelry. I had visions of disaster."

It's a long day's drive to New Mexico's Gila Wilderness, and it turned out to be a long night thanks to a marauding skunk invading backpacks. At least it didn't leave a calling card. In the morning the wet-boot brigade marched off. Soon, it wasn't wet boots that worried Pati, it was wet arm pits! The first brave, young lady was only steps into the river crossing when the force of the water eroded her footing. *Splash!* Fortunately her gear, pushed by the force of the river and bobbing downstream, was rescued by the arms of fallen branches stretching from both banks. The next entry met a similar fate. It was time for a strategy session. They solved the problem by entering the river gingerly in twos and threes, each helping to stabilize the others.

Day two uncovered a welcome contrast to the freezing water of the Gila River. For hours they lathered in the luxury of a natural hot spring where the soothing, warm waters did wonders for their frosty, tired feet and aching muscles. Pati nearly had to use cattle prods to force them onto the trail again.

And quite the trail it was: more icy river crossings before finally switchbacking up and up over 1,100 feet over Plane Crash Mountain. The heat on this ascent gave the coolness of the river a new perspective, with beads of sweat now dripping off foreheads and slipping down to sting eyeballs. "Ain't there no happy medium out here!"

Gila proved to be an exceptional challenge, and the greater the challenge, the greater the sense of pride that both kids and adults feel. Everyone knows they accomplished something they never dreamed they could.

"Adventures like this change your outlook on life," Pati told me. "You start to appreciate simple things, like turning on the faucet to get a glass of clean water."

And Christina? Well, it wasn't Rochester, New York, out there, but like our Azerbaijani gal, she too proved to be adaptable, tough, and durable.

Illegal in Escalante

In 1776, Spanish friar Francisco Atanasio Dominguez led a small expedition into the eastern Great Basin and the Colorado Plateau seeking a route from Santa Fe to Monterey, California. Today, you don't hear much about Dominguez, but you do hear about his scribe, Fray Silvestre Velez de Escalante, who chronicled this remarkable trip and apparently overemphasized his role. It's Escalante whose name denotes geographic sites all over the map in the Four Corner states, proving the advantage of being the expedition chronicler rather than the leader. For example, the Escalante River flows through the Escalante Wilderness, which is on the edge of Escalante, Utah. And we're not talking about a little Escalante Wilderness here, but over 150-million acres of virtually unspoiled wilderness. However, the term *unspoiled wilderness* draws developers like flies to a manure pile, so in 1996, to the rumble of distraught mining and gas companies, President Bill Clinton gave enduring protection to this magnificent area by creating the Grand Staircase-Escalante National Monument.

I first set foot into the Escalante in the mid-1970s with my son Scott and his buddy Fergie as we explored Dry Coyote Wash and Hurricane Wash all the way to the Escalante River and back. I knew these canyons would be an adventure that the Explorers group, now titled *Venturers* by the BSA, would relish. New regulations for the national monument limited the number in a party to ten. And ten is exactly what we had until one lad, who had a difficult family situation, decided at the last minute he could go. That made our number 11. Yes, we would be breaking the rules, but Pati and I decided he should go.

We camped one night at Capitol Reef National Park in Utah, and then stopped to pick up our permit (for a maximum group of ten), before driving down Hole in the Rock road to the Hurricane Wash trailhead. The trail into the canyon doesn't have the feel of a canyon. It's sandy and tough walking, and it remains dry for nearly four miles. As we entered a narrow maze leading into the national monument, green vegetation accompanied us to Coyote Wash. This looked like an excellent place to camp for the night. Everyone scattered to find tent sites when a backcountry ranger from Upper Coyote Gulch appeared.

"Howdy, campin' here tonight?" he asked. "Good spot. Got yer permit? How many have ya got with ya?"

He was already counting heads, so I 'fessed up. "We have one more than we're supposed to have."

"Well, 'fraid I'm gonna have ta ticket ya. It'll cost ya fifty bucks."

I motioned the gentleman to walk with me away from the kids, and using my best disarming charm (for example, injecting "sir" into every sentence), I explained the situation with the last-minute boy. Hoping the ranger was a family-minded dad, just maybe he would appreciate the rationale behind our transgression.

"Well, tell ya what I'll do... " he drawled. He proposed to tear up our permit for ten people and write one permit for five people and one for six. However, the groups would have to camp at least a mile apart. There went togetherness, but to save 50 bucks and a possible rapid exit, we agreed. Pati and her gang quickly dispersed farther into Hurricane Wash.

The ranger had barely left and in marched a bunch of college kids hoping to camp in that same spot. I explained the limitation and they understood and agreed to move on. We conversed a moment, and I asked where they were from. They said the University of Wisconsin at La Crosse. My old alma mater! Of course, I couldn't miss an opportunity to tease them. "La Crosse," I said, "that's on the Mississippi, right?" They nodded. I added: "There's a bluff, Granddad Bluff." They were intrigued. "And a road comes down the bluff onto Main Street and goes past Doerflingers and the State Bank Building all the way to Levy Park." Their mouths dropped—how could I have guessed these details? Finally, laughing, I cleared up the ruse, and we became instant friends.

My group was up and at it early. We met Pati's gang and forged ahead to set up a base camp farther in with plans to assault the Escalante River the next day. The route was lush due to water seeping from walls along the way. Soon we spotted Jacob Hamblin Arch and passed under Coyote Natural Bridge, standing like a huge gateway into the beauty of this narrow, red-rock canyon. I knew we were near a seep pond where I had camped years before, a pond filled with sweet water. High above the trail, we found a well-hidden campsite where both groups could illegally spend the night together.

Pati, along with one of the kid's moms, consented to lead the kids to the river while I combed the area to search for ruins. The kids had a fun day seeing the narrow Escalante River, the last river discovered in the United States and, across the river, the massive Stevens Arch. Someone reportedly flew a small plane through that large but narrow arch. The trail to the river is not without challenges. In fact, you must shimmy up a log ladder in one spot to access a terrace route. Meanwhile, as the gang was winding down to the river and splashing in, I was climbing higher. The terrain opened into a flat, green meadow. Just above the meadow, snuggled into a rock wall, I discovered a well-preserved Anasazi dwelling. It was small with only a few tiny rooms, yet finding it and being completely alone with it was exciting. A sizable undisturbed midden flowed from the site and was scattered with surface artifacts. Later, I met the La Crosse gang, some of whom were in the University's archaeology program. They had never seen an Anasazi ruin. They went home having visited one.

That evening proved special: a beautiful sunset, great food, and exchanging exciting stories outlining a fun day of exploration. The next morning we faced a long, hot hike on a sandy trail bordered by jagged, red-sandstone walls. As we neared high noon, the water in our containers was rapidly depleting, with no further springs or pools in sight. But we knew the road and the cars were near. I could nearly taste the cool liquid refreshment waiting just down the dusty road that led into the tiny village of Escalante.

A short while later, hydrated and with the taste of ice cream on our lips, we headed the cars back across the Escalante River and back through that wonderland of red-rock spires and outcroppings, with far-off Denver as our destination. The kids were quiet, simply looking out the windows, soaking in all the color. I knew some of these kids were feeling my anguish. As always, it hurt to leave behind the peace and beauty of the red-rock country. And it would get worse as I drove through Grand Junction, passed the ever-expanding clutter of Vail, and neared the explosion that was Denver and the front range of the Rockies. Yet we all came home as better-prepared outdoors people carrying with us lasting memories of having tread gently through a remote locale enveloped in raw, natural beauty.

Unscheduled Survival

The original gang of 14- and 15-year-olds was well into college when I made my final trip with the Venturers. We chose to investigate the Mule Canyons on Cedar Mesa. On this trip we gave our high-achieving, high-school-age guys and gals nearly total decision-making responsibility, including finding our way into South Mule, finding water and a good campsite, and then using the topo maps and my new GPS unit to determine the best way up and out of South Mule and down into paralleling North Mule canyon.

South Mule Canyon is a well-traveled route due to its easy access and miles of ancient archaeology. To reach the head of the canyon only requires a six-mile hike, garnished with an abundance of well-preserved Anasazi ruins. However, water can be scarce, so the goal was to trek as far into South Mule Canyon as possible, find a remote campsite with water, and spend the first night there. The series of dwellings, nestled in the walls along the way, became the focal point of interest, especially for the newer kids who had never experienced this ancient culture. One ruin located near our chosen campsite had touchy access but offered a unique entry wall and a dark, spooky interior. The gang was in magpie mode that evening, continuously cackling with laughter and exclamations, a key indicator of group happiness.

The mystery day arrived: how do we work our way up and out of South Mule and drop into North Mule Canyon? I was hoping Mystery Day wouldn't disintegrate into Misery Day. Michael Kelsey's hiking guide of the Colorado Plateau assumed a route out of South Mule and into North Mule Canyon, which was identified on a map. This exit looked to be roughly a mile and a half farther in from our campsite. Three small box canyons cut to the right, and his assumed exit route appeared to skirt along the edge of the third canyon. I caught up with the kids waiting by the mouth of one side canyon with a faint trail paralleling it.

"This is it!" they yelled with the air of juvenile certainty.

I had my doubts; several sets of footprints on the trail moved farther into the canyon, plus from my count, this was only the second side canyon. I suggested they Scout this side canyon, and I would head farther up and try to locate a third side canyon. Within a half mile, I found the third canyon. But when I returned to side canyon number two, all but one of the merry madmen had left; he assured me they had found the correct exit route. With pangs of uncertainty, I followed him in and when we finally caught up to the stragglers, we faced a steep, precipitous, and unappealing wall at the end of a box canyon. Where were my compatriots? They were scrambling with full packs up this virtually impassible route. Now I was certain this had become Misery Day.

To a 17-year-old kid, everything (other than cleaning the garage) is a snap. To a guy pushing 70 and carrying a 60-pound pack, this climb looked suicidal! I estimated that this talus slope was at least 500 feet straight up. I decided to go, thinking, "My hair can't get any whiter."

Pati is a tough backpacker, but she was struggling. In spots it was like climbing a sand pile, one step up while sliding two steps back. The boys were making progress and finding a route, such as it was. Handholds were at a premium, and long ago I had learned not to grab onto vegetation thinking the roots would provide support. After an eternity, I spotted Matt winding back down and, like a true gentleman, grabbed his mother's pack. From my perspective, the route still looked like the Great Wall of China. I placed one foot ahead of the other and tried not to slip and orchestrate a rapid descent. About the time I decided to die and be buried there, along came another stud who purloined my pack and disappeared in an upward direction. "Bless you my son. May Saint Peter have a gallon of ice-cold water waiting for you when you eventually arrive at the Pearly Gates." With the weight off, the remaining climb was borderline tolerable. But what I should've been wishing for was five gallons of water when we finally reached the top.

We now stood on flat land high between the two canyons. The terrain, dotted with some juniper and pinyon, mostly hosted scrubby shrubs. Pottery shards, mostly black on white and corrugated, were scattered across terrain that hadn't seen a footprint for ages. This was agricultural land for the ancients, probably planted with corn, squash, and beans a millennium ago. What was missing? In addition to any other footprints, water! At this late hour we had a beefsteak's chance in a kennel of finding our way down to sip the cool liquid flowing in North Mule Canyon. All right, how much water do we have?

At best, everyone had about a pint left, barely enough for the night and the five-mile hike out the following morning—if we didn't cook. The evening menu suddenly took on a taste-tempting aura... *cote de granola, sans eau*! And breakfast would prove even lighter, unless you relished dry oatmeal. Let's call it on-the-job, desert-survival training.

Watching the sun set below the flats was a relief; less heat equals less thirst. The sky was clear. We built a small fire and laid out sleeping bags, yet no one seemed tired. I found a cozy spot about 50 yards off, spread out my pad and sleeping bag, and hung my pack in a tree. I returned for the light-evening fare and some fireside chit-chat. But soon my muscles became infiltrated with the effects of the steep climb. The crew was in good spirits and no tongues were dangling in thirst, so I wished everyone good night and went off in the direction of my bag. However, like a court jester I returned to the fire a short time later announcing I couldn't find my bed. Wiseacre Matt led me right to it and suggested I get a GPS reading on it.

Come morning, one topic dominated our collective minds: water. Without a clue to an entry point into North Mule, the crew combined all remaining food and water, divided them equally, and with a due-east compass bearing to the road, we headed out across the rapidly heating desert.

But in a short time individuals were inadvertently spreading out. With the clusters of scrub oak and other foliage, it became difficult to see one another, so whistles were tooting. Everyone shared the water they had left. Matt found a sack of lemon drops and dropped a couple into each hand to activate dry mouths and curb thirst. I hung back to spot anyone who might fall behind. Tucker, a high-school guy with proven sensitivity and an obvious gift of leadership, finally called the group together, knowing this was no place to become separated with such little water. He recommended we all had to keep tabs on each other; should a person move out of sight, either ahead or behind, toot a whistle—at which time everyone would halt. I relished that kind of concern and leadership. This is what I was hoping to see with them.

In country like this, it's nearly impossible to see a dirt road unless you spot a vehicle or a cloud of dust. We estimated the distance at five miles, but after several hours, some became concerned that we had missed the road. But that wouldn't happen as long as we continued due east. Short distances seem much farther when your dry tongue is dangling in the dust. The temperature kept climbing, and beads of perspiration rolled down our foreheads. Then, out of nowhere, there was a road—*the* road. The last drops of liquid trickled down thankful throats while several huskies briskly hiked to the cars, parked less than a mile away, and delivered the cars, water, and rescue to the thirsty, weary, group.

I doubt if any of the Venturers realized the true lesson of that adventure unless they took time later to ponder it. My guess is they ignored the fact that they didn't take time to study the map and, consequently, they missed the correct route. After all, the climb and the subsequent survival proved to be the real adventure. Fear and panic are the evil antagonists in survival situations. Thankfully, we saw neither.

The road back to Blanding seemed far too long knowing that our favorite restaurant would soon supply an endless fountain of ice-cold water. We found the right roads that day, and we found mature behavior in a difficult desert situation. Good show, gang.

The Explorer Era Fades

High-school graduation loomed less than two months away for most of these adventurous Venturers. Soon they would scatter in many directions, off to jobs or college, and face full lives to be lived. For us adults, a good chunk of our lives were now memories, many of which the kids had helped to provide. Neither Pati nor I could muster the zest needed to head back to the starting gate again. Yet I happily wallowed in the memories of an extended decade of trudging up hills and down into desert canyons with lively bunches of teenagers who were full of fun, full of spunk. Karen and Pati had unleashed an outlet for their passions and talents. In that decade, the kids gained a tremendous amount of insight about the world around them and about themselves. That alone gave value to our time and our efforts.

Admittedly, kids tend to age you in one sense, yet, over the years, they were major players in helping to keep my mind and body young in both prowess and spirit. In the process I also learned, surreptitiously, much more from them than I probably ever taught.

Scouting. Rocks or no rocks, I'm glad I tried it. I liked it.

APPENDIX: LIST OF SCOUTS AND TROOP/POST LEADERS

TROOP 186 EAGLE SCOUTS 1959-1963	
Jimmy Nixon	Steve Dahlgren
Dexter Dose	

TROOP 117 EAGLE SCOUTS 1964-1990	
Don Lowe	Joel Slaten
Jim Miller	Jim Mahoney
Ross Kershaw	Mark Zentner
Paul Hendricks*	Brian Kannady
Don Fitzsimmons	Jeff Rallo
Dale Marshall	Trevor Banister
Steve Weir	Robert Hill
Bill Shorthill	Steve Keckler*
Greg Schroer	Greg Zentner
Rick Theis	Scott Kannady
Brian LaGrone	Doug Kixmiller
Jerry Moore	Ron Clark
Brian Parsons	Joe Conti
Alan Parsons	Robert Lewis*
Grant Johnson	Darren Brinker
Lane Slaten	Darren Kixmiller
Steve Richardson	Kyle Marquand*
David Sholes	Mark Baker
Andy Green	Mike Thompson
Paul Carnell	Paul Adams*
Paul Conway	Todd Zentner
Grady Holder	Curtis Weibel
*Awarded by a different troop	

ADULT ASSISTANCE			
DURING TOM SHOLES'S TENURE AS SCOUTMASTER			
YEAR	ASM	TCC	IR
TROOP 186			
1959	Fred Nixon	Ralph Underhill	John Anthony
1960	Fred Nixon Chas. Farr	Ralph Underhill	John Anthony
1961	Fred Nixon Chas. Farr	John Rysgaard	R. Underhill
1962	Fred Nixon	John Rysgaard	Bill Bachman
1963	Dick Cone George Wright	Keith Lackey	John Anthony
TROOP 117			
1964	Irv Johhson Ed Knight	Leon Kershaw	Bill Dolin
1965	Irv Johnson Ed Knight	Leon Kershaw	Bill Dolin
1966	Ed Knight Harry Weir	Leon Kershaw	Bill Dolin
1967	Art Trevithick Brad Kershaw	Hank Bennett	Bill Dolin
1968	Brad Kershaw Jack Dillman Art Trevithick	Leon Kershaw	Bill Dolin
1969	Brad Kershaw Jack Dillman Ed Fitzsimmons Skip Oliver	Bob Scheller	Maurice Worley
1970	Brad Kershaw Skip Oliver Ed Fitzsimmons George Schneider	Cliff Marshall	Irv Johnson
1971	Brad Kershaw Ross Kershaw Ed Fitzsimmons	Cliff Marshall	Irv Johnson
1972	Brad Kershaw Ross Kershaw Ed Fitzsimmons George Barger	Dick Theis	Irv Johnson
1973	Brad Kershaw Ross Kershaw Bob Parsons	Dick Theis	Irv Johnson
1974	Ross Kershaw Bob Parsons	Dick Theis	Irv Johnson
1975	Ross Kershaw Bob Parsons	Dick Theis	Irv Johnson
1976	Ross Kershaw Bob Parsons	Duane Newell	Irv Johnson

1977	Jim Colburn Norm Tuccy	Duane Newell	T. Terwilliger
1978	Jim Colburn H. Atchinson	Duane Newell	T. Terwilliger
1979	Jim Colburn	Duane Newell	T. Terwilliger
1980	Jim Colburn Leroy Moberly	Jay Williams	T. Terwilliger
1981	Jim Colburn	Jim Haines	T. Terwilliger
1982	Jim Colburn	Duane Zentner	T. Terwilliger
1983	Jim Colburn Jeff Andrus	Duane Zentner	T. Terwilliger
1984	Jim Colburn	Duane Zentner	T. Terwilliger
1985	Jim Colburn Bob Zatorski Jeff Andrus David Sholes Lane Slaten Andy Green	Duane Zentner	T. Terwilliger
1986	Bob Zatorski Bob Finnell Andy Green Ian Zahn Mark Zentner	Duane Zentner	T. Terwilliger
1987	Bob Finnell John Stolp David Sholes Ian Zahn Andy Green Walt Kixmiller Ken Conway Bob Zatorski	Bob Tharp	John Zink
1988	Bob Finnell Bob Blackburn Ian Zahn John Stolp Walt Kixmiller Ken Conway Bob Zatorski Jeff Andrus	Bob Tharp	John Zink
1989	Bob Finnell Dave Lester Andy Green Walt Kixmiller Bob Blackburn Ken Conway	Lou Conti	John Zink

MEMBERS OF TROOP 186 1959-1963 (by year entered)
Scouts in the unit or entered in 1959
Gary Hiner, Bob Ramsey, Don Johnson, Lloyd Underhill, Don Johnson, Ron Johnson, George Gardner, Dwight Butler, John Isakson, Calvin Boomer, Harvey Boomer, Jerry Duke, Dale Tilden, Bob Weinbolger, Roger Eicher, Tom Goserud, Tom Vorpohl, Bill Powers, Paul Metters, Bob Worra, Pete Moulds, Duane Duke, Jeff Poehler, Perry Neil, Gary Thomas, Tom Huras, Jack Hockeneyer, Steve Dahlgren, Larry Peterson, Roger Neuman, Rick Levin, Jim Marchand, Jack Marchand, Ed Calph, Jim Skjelstad, Mark Claesgens, Mark Erickson, Glen Larson, Howie Myers, Jim Nixon, Rich Spengler, Dave Nelson, Bruce Johnson, Lynn Donohue, Ollie Frederick, Greg Flint, Tom Rysgaard, Tim Nelson, Dave Gooden, Dave Butler, Paul Rolvaag, Les Lagerstrom, Mike McFarland, Doug Sparks, Mark Johnson, Ron Christenson, Mark Stevens, Dick Sowers, Craig Buetow, Tom Levin, Doug Kruse, Tom Carlson, Dennis Wilson, Todd Rassmuson, Paul Johnson, Dexter Dose
1960
Denny Judson, Terry Cone, Robert Newell, Bruce Tinklenberg, Mike Donohue, Steve Crawford, Roger Lange, Bill Jwanouskos, Frank Cadwell, Bill Parry, Reese Peterson, Jim Axtell, Dave Thompson, Rich Simpson, Robert Simpson
1961
John Bachman, Jim Mann, Glen Dove, Rick Swanker, Dave Johnson, Orin Hultin, Roy Gray, Tom Nelson, Darrel Kruse, Dennis Sparks, Rich Hiner, Bart Beutow, Brad Buetow
1962
Gary Newell, Pat Donohue, Keith Lacky, Steve Anthony, Craig Schultz, Jeff Bell, Tim Hedlund, Mike Clark, Tom Cone, Ken Hakel, Ed Lange, John Lappegaard, Lyle Weegman, Harold Sneide, Greg Dose, Lee Ramsey, Eric Anderson
1963
Chuck Amdahl, Lee Hackel

MEMBERS OF TROOP 117
1964-1988
(by year entered)
Scouts in the unit or entered in 1964-1965
Don Lowe, Dave Holt, Jim Miller, Chas. Hatfield, Brad Kershaw, Rick Barton, Dave Holt, Bruce Lemke, Rick Worley, Don Hatfield, Kim Purcell, Rick Lemmons, Chas. Frost, Ross Kershaw, Mark Bayci, Danny Seese, John Miller, Bob Bechtel, Kent Wimmer, Steve Munger, Dave Hinds, Bret Bayci, Paul Worley, Mike Barbera, James Morse, Steve Light, Rod Knight, Doug Knight, Rick Trujillo, John Trujillo
1965
Bob Brill, Terry Collins, Denny Peterson, Reed Wimmer, David Irey, Gordy Hemple, Neil Mortenson, Mike Trantow, Jim Sullivan, Paul Hendricks, Dale Marshall, Mike Copeland, Dave Wright, John Dawson, Jim Nelson, Steve Weir, Lloyd Douglas, Mark Trevithick, Paul Trevithick
1966
Greg Neary, Rich Luedke, Dennis Kirby, Richard Munger, Chas. Roberts, Greg Munger
1967
Jon Brighton, Bruce Gard, Jon Chenault, John Koontz, Steve Scott, Robert Burns, Harry Nuce, Carl Koontz, Doug Otten, Don Fitzsimmons, Steve Yates, Fred Hoffower, Ken Dysart, Mike Dillman, Greg Eldridge, Jerry Ondler, Louis Eisley, John Dillman, Mark Kenning, Tom Cory, Ray Weeks, Tim Trevithick, Bill Farley, Dave Coddington
1968
Blane Clark, Larry Starkloff, David Carter, Robert Paine, Tom Moore, Walter Board, Eric Jones, Casey Veenendaal, Paul Beck, Mark Scheller, Denny Daugherty, Ron Skoty, Kevin Mihalik, Doug Cummings, Ron Collins, Joe Green, Kevin Amen, Doug Milliken, Todd Smith, Greg Marshall, Paul Parker, Greg Oliver, Matt Wilson
1969
Mike Hayward, Kevin Thomas, Bill Shorthill, Rocky Williams, James Pullen, Andy O'Neill, Mike Betzer, Mark Paulakovich, Ed Kerin, Steve Thornhill, Kevin Phillips, D. Zeihm, Mike Johnson, Tom Mullis, Kevin Lillrose
1970
Bob Armstrong, Jerry Kelton, Don Prentice, John Glassa, George Jimas, Rick Theis, Bryan Johnson, George Schneider, Doug Barger, Greg Schroer, Bill Mills, Gene Fitzsimmons, Chris Redio, Brian Parsons, Robert Aldrich, Scott Ferguson, Dave Aldrich, Robby Carolus, Ken Moore, Jerry Moore, David Hale, Mark McMilian, John Revesz, Chris Barger, Greg Jones

1971

John Revesz, David Rebesne, Bob Grabau, Bruce Marshall, Scott Sholes, Paul Farley, Karl Theis, Bryan Ferguson, John Lee, Dave Lanford, Mike Johnson, Kirk Parsons, Mike Bergen, Chris Bergen, John Shorthill

1972

Steve Nelson, Steve Kelton, Allen Parsons, Bryan McLendon, Paul Arrigo

1973

Eric McKinley, Jeff Murphy, Mark Newell, Andy Thomas, Brian LaGrone, David Hart, John Weber, Scott Christianson, Jeff Andrus, Chuck Stephens, Grant Johnson, Steve Malincar

1974

Doug Williams, Kevin Kristpeit, John Brells, Mitch Brells, Matt Brown, David Ott, Andy Thomas, David LaGrone, Mark Johnson, Mike Tanner, Kirt Browning

1975

Ron Tanner, Jay Tuccy, Mike Newell, Mark Kielwitz, Dave Buckley, Jeff Williams, Jeff Tuccy, Jim Mitchell, Marty Tanner, Alex Colburn, Andy Haines

1976

Karl Nyquist, John Hershey, Chad Wynne, Paul Shugard

1977

Dave Wathen, Gary Atchinson, Matt Marrion, Jay Williams, Lane Slaten, TJ Steinkonig, Steve Richardson, Kevin Ransom

1978

David Sholes, Ricky Mitchell, Jay Stogsdill, Andy Green, Matt Borger, John Tuccy, Chris Theis, Brian Moberly, Lee Onsager, Art Gillson, Jeff Gillson

1979

Paul Carnell, Paul Conway, Jeff Gilson, Ian Calkins, Court Hughes, Tim VanVleet, Grady Holder, Billy Rich, Andy Gillson, Joel Slaten, Jim Mahoney, Jeff Zink, Steve Keckler, AC Stutson, Mark Zentner

1980

Duane Crandall, Scott Kealiher, Bryan Kannady, Jack VanVleet, John Speed

1981

Ted Colburn, Jason Ayres, Andy Borger, Troy Terwilliger, Jeff Rallo, Eric Zink, Robert Powers, Kevin Bundy, Wayne Faber, Jeff Jurgenson

1982

Marc Behm, Nathan Lamos, Trevor Banister, Doak Mahlik, Mike Nigg, David Rich

1983
Todd Kenyon, Chris Hanson, Robert Hill, Mark Stubbert, Greg Zentner, Scott Kannady, Ken Caldwell, Lance Caffrey, Doug Kixmiller, Mark Hanson, Ron Clark, Karl Franklin, Matt Robinson
1984
Davin Zink, Bobby Kline, Ryan Randolf, Adam Bowles, Paul Adams, Sean Bundy, Derek Christy, Joe Conti, Dan Conway, John Bowman, CJ Miller, Robert Lewis, Brett Finnell, Matt Zatorski
1985
Jeremy Reed, Darren Brinker, Curt House, Darren Kixmiller, Kyle Marquand, Carl Singleton, Mark Cusick, Joe Currant, Mike Kline, Mark Baker, Mike Thompson
1986
Jason Crist, Brady Fox, Tom Hearty, Seth Shugart, Mike Stolp, Rick Thompson, Jason Hall, Tom Kenyon
1987
Sean Radford, John Adams, Chris Markwell, Wm Currant, Todd Zentner, Brian Broxson, Curtis Waibel, Marc Aiello, Chris Lawhead
1988
Doug Blackburn, Ryan Fox, Chris Plummer, Frank Allen, Stephan Lester, Gavin Schwan, Kent Bozlinski, Brian Winterhalter, Brian Richard, Beau Courtage, Mark Stolp, Josh Trevithick

ADULT ASSISTANCE DURING TOM SHOLES AND PATI PALUMBO'S TEN-YEAR TENURE AS JOINT ADVISORS OF POST/CREW 757	
Karen Ballestrassi	Mike Palumbo
Rick Ballestrassi	Andy Green
Celene Santiago	Joe Conti
Teresa Sholes	Frank Martorano

MEMBERS OF ADVENTURE POST 757
1994-2003
(by year entered)

1994

Corinne Ballestrazzi, Vanessa Ballestrazzi, Alex Kozyrev, Patrick Muller, Jeni Palumbo, Kallie Palumbo, Leyla Saifutdinova, Angie Scherible, Kim Yancher

1995

Nathan Scherible, Kelly Schmidt, Julie Thomas

1996

Mary Buckwalter, Louise Martarono

1997

Dylan Buffington, Justin Merritt, Anna Santiago, Dom Santiago

1998

Ryan Baldwin, Russell Cook, Corey Galindo, Matt Palumbo

1999

Brye Abbott, Tara Van Howt, Brett Neinberg, Clint Packo, Mark Packo, Carolyn Pearcy, Kyle Smith, Jon Sullivan, Justin Weatherly

2000

Perry Abbott

2001

Christina Magri, Brian Weatherly

2002

Kelly Waldman

2003

Moriaha Bain, Kevin Lichtenstein, Tucker Waldman, Alex Wellman

ABOUT THE AUTHOR

In his four decades as a Scout leader, Tom Sholes built a wide-ranging reputation as a "Scoutmaster's Scoutmaster." During his leadership tenure, Tom inspired over 500 Boy Scouts and Explorers; nearly 50 of whom achieved the rank of Eagle Scout. This leader combined his deep commitment to help Scouts grow into responsible adults with his enduring love of the wilderness. Scouts and leaders tested their mettle high on snowy mountain peaks, paddled canoes through whitewater rivers, and survived dry desert canyons rich with Native American ruins and rock art.

Awarded the rank of Eagle Scout in La Crosse, Wisconsin, in the 1940s, Tom kept his love of Scouting alive for another 30 years, serving as Scoutmaster first in Roseville, Minnesota, and later in Littleton, Colorado. His leadership and devotion to Scouts earned him such honors as the District Award of Merit and the coveted Silver Beaver. Tom spent an additional ten years as an advisor to a high-adventure Explorer Post near his home in Larkspur, Colorado.

Tom is a contributing writer to *Scouting* magazine, has developed an accreditation program for home healthcare agencies, and is a student of Southwestern archaeology and native cultures. Tom and his wife Charlotte have four children and eight grandchildren. Tom's sense of adventure continues in his backcountry explorations and in his travels, having wandered through more than 60 countries.

ISBN 978-1-60530-331-4

9 781605 303314

90000>